Irish Writing London: Volume 1

Bloomsbury Studies in the City

The history of literature is tied to the city. From Aeschylus to Addison, Baudelaire to Balzac, Conrad to Coetzee and Dickens to Dostoevsky, writers make sense of the city and shape modern understandings through their reflections and depictions. The urban is a fundamental aspect of a substantial part of the literary canon that is frequently not considered in and of itself because it is so prevalent.

Bloomsbury Studies in the City captures the best contemporary criticism on urban literature. Reading literature, drama and poetry in their historical and social context and alongside urban and spatial theory, this series explores the impact of the city on writers and their work.

Titles in the Series:

The Contemporary New York Novel
Mark Brown

Irish Writing London: Volumes 1 and 2
Edited by Tom Herron

London in Contemporary British Literature
Edited by Nick Hubble, Philip Tew and Lynn Wells

Salman Rushdie's Cities
Vassilena Parashkevova

Irish Writing London: Volume 1

Revival to the Second World War

Edited by

Tom Herron

BLOOMSBURY

LONDON · NEW DELHI · NEW YORK · SYDNEY

Bloomsbury Academic

An imprint of Bloomsbury Publishing Plc

50 Bedford Square
London
WC1B 3DP
UK

175 Fifth Avenue
New York
NY 10010
USA

www.bloomsbury.com

First published 2013

British Library Cataloguing-in-Publication Data
A catalogue record for this book is available from the British Library.

ISBN: HB: 978-1-4411-6805-4

Library of Congress Cataloging-in-Publication Data
A catalog record for this book is available from the Library of Congress.

Typeset by Fakenham Prepress Solutions, Fakenham, Norfolk NR21 8NN
Printed and bound by CPI Group (UK) Ltd, Croydon, CR0 4YY

Contents

Notes on Contributors

Allan Hepburn is Professor in the Department of English at McGill University, Montreal. He has edited three volumes of Elizabeth Bowen's writings: *The Bazaar and Other Stories, People, Places, Things: Essays by Elizabeth Bowen*, and *Listening In: Broadcasts, Speeches, and Interviews by Elizabeth Bowen*. He is author of *Intrigue: Espionage and Culture* (2005) and *Enchanted Objects: Visual Art in Contemporary Fiction* (2010). In addition to writing a book about faith in mid-century British culture, he is currently working on a monograph on Bowen's fiction.

Eleni Loukopoulou completed her doctorate at the University of Kent, Canterbury on the topic of James Joyce and London. She has published essays, review articles and conference reports in the *Literary London Journal*, *James Joyce Quarterly* and the *James Joyce Literary Supplement*, and has contributed to *ABES* (Routledge). Her essay, 'Joyce Exhibits at Cambridge's Literary Laboratories', on the publication background of an extract of Joyce's work in the magazine *Experiment* appeared in the *Journal of Modern Periodical Studies* in Autumn 2011. Further work drawing on her PhD research is due to appear in the *James Joyce Quarterly*, and the forthcoming edited collections *The London Reader 1* and *James Joyce and D. H. Lawrence*. Currently she is working on a project that examines the pamphlets published in T. S. Eliot's *Criterion Miscellany* series (1929–36).

Deaglán Ó Donghaile is Senior Lecturer in Literature and Cultural History at Liverpool John Moores University. He holds a PhD from Trinity College, Dublin, and was Government of Ireland Postdoctoral Research Fellow at the Department of English, the National University of Ireland, Maynooth from 2007–9. In 2009 he was a Visiting Research Fellow at the William Andrews Clark Memorial Library at the University of California, Los Angeles, where he began work on his next monograph, *Oscar Wilde and the Radical Politics of the Fin de Siècle*. His work has also been published in *Journal of Postcolonial Writing* and he is currently editing a special edition of *Literature and History*, focusing on literary representations of anti-imperial violence. In 2009 he was named Young Conrad Scholar of the Year by the Joseph Conrad Society of America in recognition of his essay, 'Conrad, the Stevensons and the Imagination of Urban Chaos'. His research interests are in late-Victorian and modernist political fiction, popular literature, radical journalism and anti-imperial writing of the late nineteenth and early twentieth centuries.

Adrian Paterson is Lecturer in English at the National University of Ireland, Galway. A graduate of Worcester College, Oxford and Trinity College, Dublin, he has published widely on nineteenth and twentieth century literature with a particular interest in the artistic collisions of Yeats, Joyce, and Ezra Pound (http://thebicyclops.wordpress.com). He is completing an IRCHSS funded history of poetry and music in Ireland entitled *Perfect Pitch: Music in Irish Poetry from Moore to Muldoon*; his monograph *Words for Music Perhaps: W. B. Yeats and Musical Sense* is in press.

Michelle Paull has worked as the Curator of Modern Literary Manuscripts at the British Library, as a researcher for the PeoplePlay project for the Theatre Museum in London, and as an Archivist on the Leyhausen-Spiess Collection at the Archive of Performances of Greek and Roman Drama at Oxford. She now lectures in Drama at St. Mary's University College Strawberry Hill, Twickenham where her special interests include Irish drama – especially Sean O'Casey, Bernard Shaw and Oscar Wilde; Daphne Du Maurier; contemporary writing for theatre and adaptation studies. Michelle is currently working on a book entitled *Sean O'Casey: The Critic and the Canon*. She works on three online journals – *Drummings*, devoted to Sean O'Casey (of which she is the editor), *UpStage* on *fin de siècle* theatre, and *The Oscholars*, dedicated to Oscar Wilde.

Pádraigín Riggs is Statutory Lecturer in the Department of Modern Irish, University College, Cork. Specializing mainly in post-Revival literature in Irish, on fiction and poetry in Irish, and Ireland's cultural history, she is the author of *Donncha Ó Céileachair* (1978) and *Pádraic Ó Conaire: Deoraí* (1994). She has also edited *Dáibhí Ó Bruadair: his historical and literary context* (Irish Texts Society, 2001), *Dinneen and the Dictionary: 1904–2004* (Irish Texts Society) 2005, *Tadhg Dall Ó hUiginn: his historical and literary context* (Irish Texts Society) 2010, and Pádraig Ó Conaire's *An Chéad Chloch*, (Mercier, Cork) 1999.

Whitney Standlee completed her doctorate on Irish women's writing 1890–1916 at the University of Liverpool. She has published articles on the politics of Irish women's writing of the *fin de siècle* and novels written by Irish women living in Britain. Her essay on George Egerton, James Joyce and the Irish *künstlerroman*, which appeared in *Irish Studies Review*, was awarded the British Association of Irish Studies postgraduate essay prize for 2010. She currently lectures at the University of Worcester and is acting as co-editor of a volume of essays entitled *Advancing the Cause of Liberty: Irish Women's Writing 1880–1922*.

Tara Stubbs is a University Lecturer in English Literature and Creative Writing at Oxford University's Department of Continuing Education. Her monograph, *American Literature and Irish Culture, 1910–1955*, will be published by Manchester University Press in early 2013. The book focuses on the Irish interests of a range of modernist American writers, including F. Scott Fitzgerald, Marianne Moore, Eugene O'Neill, John Steinbeck and Wallace Stevens. Since completing her PhD on Moore and Irish writers in 2007, she has published articles in *Peer English*, the *Irish Journal of American Studies*, and *SHAW* (the Annual of Bernard Shaw Studies), and has a chapter on Moore and Maria Edgeworth in *Romantic Ireland from Tone to Gonne* (Peter Lang, 2013). She is also writing a chapter on the Irish poet Thomas MacGreevy and American modernists for a new critical collection on MacGreevy (Continuum, 2012). She recently edited a special issue of *Comparative American Studies* (June 2011) on 'The idea of influence in American literature'. Her interests include Irish and American modernist poetry and fiction, transatlantic studies, and W. B. Yeats.

Simon Workman was educated at Trinity College Dublin where he recently completed a doctoral thesis on the poetry and radio drama of Louis MacNeice. He has published on twentieth-century Irish poetry, and has a particular interest in Irish writers working at the BBC. He is a lecturer in English at St. Patrick's College Carlow.

Timeline

Volume 1

	historical / political	literary / cultural
1748		Laetitia Pilkington's *Memoirs* (vols 1 and 2)
1750		(July) Laetitia Pilkington dies in Dublin
1754		Laetitia Pilkington's *Memoirs* (vol. 3)
1779		(May) Tom Moore born – Dublin
1798 (May)	Rebellion of the United Irishmen begins in Wexford	
1798 (Dec)	Death of Wolfe Tone	
1800 (July/Aug)	Acts of Union create the United Kingdom of Great Britain and Ireland	
1801	Census – population of London is 1,096,784	
1801 (Jan)	Acts of Union become law, abolishing Dublin Parliament	
1803 (July)	Rising led by Robert Emmett	
1803 (Sept)	Execution of Robert Emmett	
1811	Census – population of London is 1,303,564	
1815	End of Napoleonic Wars	
1815 (Mar)	First steam packet service from Dublin to London	
1817	Near-famine conditions in parts of Ireland	
1820		(Oct) Dion Boucicault born in Dublin
1821	Census – population of London is 1,573,210	
1823	The Catholic Association formed by Daniel O'Connell	
1829 (April)	Catholic Emancipation Act allows Catholics to enter Westminster	
1829	Metropolitan Police Force established	
1831	Census – population of London is 1,878,229	

1832	National Schools system begins
1841	Reform Act
	Census – population of London is 2,207,653
	Census – population of Ireland is 8,175,124
1842 (Oct)	*London Assurance* (Boucicault) premieres at Theatre Royal, Covent Garden
	The Nation newspaper founded by Charles Gavan Duffy, Thomas Osborne Davis and John Blake Dillon
1843 (Aug)	O'Connell's 'monster meeting' at Tara
1845 (Sept)	Potato blight first noted
1845–52	The Great Famine
1847	Death of O'Connell
1847 (Nov)	Bram Stoker born in Clontarf
1848 (Aug)	Irish Mail train from Euston to Holyhead introduced
1851	Census – population of London is 2,651,939
	Census – population of Ireland is 6,552,385
1852 (Feb)	Tom Moore dies at Sloperton, Wiltshire
1852 (Oct)	George Moore born – Carra, Co. Sligo
1854 (Oct)	Oscar Wilde born – Dublin
1856 (July)	George Shaw born – Dublin
1858	The 'Great Stink' leads to Bazalgette's London sewerage project
1858	Formation by James Stephens of the Irish Republican Brotherhood
1861 (Jan)	Katharine Tynan born – Clondalkin, Co. Dublin
1861	Census – population of London is 3,188,485
	Census – population of Ireland is 5,798,096
1861 (Feb)	Fenian disturbances in England
1863	First underground line (Paddington to Farringdon Road) is completed
1865 (June)	William Butler Yeats born – Sandymount, Co. Dublin

Year	Historical events	Literary/cultural events
1867		Yeats moves to London with his family
1867 (Feb)	Attempted attack by Fenians on Chester Castle	
1867 (Nov)	Execution of Fenians – The Manchester Martyrs	
1867 (Dec)	Fenian explosion at Clerkenwell Gaol	
1871	Census – population of London is 3,840,595	
	Census – population of Ireland is 5,412,377	
1873	Issac Butt initiates Home Rule League	
1876		Shaw moves to London
1877 (Aug)	Parnell becomes President of Home Rule Confederation of Great Britain	
1879 (Oct)	Irish Land League founded by Michael Davitt	
1880		(Mar) Seán O'Casey born – Dublin
1880 (May)	Parnell elected Chairman of Irish Parliamentary Party	
1881	Census – population of London is 4,713,441	
	Census – population of Ireland is 5,174,836	
1881 (Oct)	Parnell arrested	(Feb) James Joyce born – Rathgar, Dublin
1882		(Feb) Pádraic Ó Conaire born – Galway
1882	The Phoenix Park Murders	
1882	Southwark Irish Literary Club founded	
1883 (Jan)	Foundation of the Gaelic Athletic Association	
1884 (Nov)		
1885	The First Home Rule Bill defeated in the Commons	*Louise de la Vallière and Other Poems* (Tynan)
1886	Irish National Land League founded by Michael Davitt and Parnell	
1887	Bloody Sunday in London	
1887 (Nov)	The Irish Exhibition at Olympia, West Kensington	
1888 (June-Oct)		*Poems and Ballads of Young Ireland* (O'Leary, Tynan and Yeats)
1889		*The Wanderings of Oisin and Other Poems* (Yeats)

Year	Events	Literary / Cultural
1890		Yeats and Ernest Rhys found The Rhymers' Club
		The Picture of Dorian Gray (Wilde)
1891	Census – population of London is 5,571,968	
	Census – population of Ireland is 4,704,750	*John Sherman and Dhoya* (Yeats)
1891 (Oct)	Parnell dies at Brighton	
1892	Second Home Rule Bill passed by Commons but defeated by Lords	
1892	Irish Literary Society founded in London by T. W. Rolleston, Charles Gavin Duffy and W. B. Yeats	
1893 (July)	Gaelic League founded by Douglas Hyde and Eoin McNeill	
1893		
1895		*Mrs Warren's Profession* (Shaw)
		The Celtic Twilight (Yeats)
		Esther Waters (Moore)
	(April)	Wilde vs Queensberry libel trial
		Crown vs Wilde trial
		The Importance of Being Earnest (Wilde)
1896	London GAA established	
1897	London Gaelic League founded	*Dracula* (Stoker)
1899 (May)	First production of Irish Literary Theatre	
1898	London Irish Rugby Football Club founded	
1898		
1899		*The Ballad of Reading Gaol* (C.3.3. / Wilde)
	(June)	Elizabeth Bowen born – Dublin
		Heart of Darkness (Conrad)
		The Dear Irish Girl (Tynan)
1899	Irish Literary Theatre established in Dublin by W. B. Yeats, Augusta Gregory, George Moore and Edward Martyn	
1900		
1901	Census – population of London is 6,506,889	
	Census – population of Ireland is 4,458,775	
	(Nov)	Oscar Wilde dies in Paris

Date	Events	Literature / Publications
1902 (April)	Premiere of *Cathleen ni Houlihan* (Gregory and Yeats) at St. Teresa's Hall, Dublin by the Irish National Dramatic Company	
1903		*The Cabinet of Irish Literature*, 4 vols (Tynan, ed.)
1903	The Land Purchase Act	
1904 (Dec)	Abbey Theatre opens in Dublin with three one-act plays: *On Baile's Strand* (Yeats), *Cathleen Ni Houlihan* (Gregory and Yeats), and *Spreading the News* (Gregory)	
1904 (Dec)	Abbey Theatre opens	*John Bull's Other Island* (Shaw)
1905 (Mar)	Ulster Unionist Council formed	
1905 (Nov)	Sinn Féin founded by Arthur Griffith	
1906	Suffragettes demonstrate in Trafalgar Square	
1907	(Jan)	*The Adventures of Alicia* (Tynan)
	(Sept)	*The Playboy of the Western World* (Synge)
		The Playboy Riots, Abbey Theatre
		Louis MacNeice born – Belfast
1907		Bowen moves to London
1907		*The Secret Agent* (Conrad)
		The House of the Crickets (Tynan)
		Nóra Mharcais Bhig agus Scéalta Eile (Ó Conaire)
1908	Patrick Pearse founds St. Enda's School / Scoil Éanna, Rathfarnham	
1909		*Deoraíocht* (Ó Conaire)
1910 (Nov)	'Manet and the Post-Impressionists' exhibition at the Grafton Galleries, London	
1910		
1911	Census – population of London is 7,160,441	
	Census – population of Ireland is 4,381,951	
1911	Third Home Rule Bill is passed in the Commons	
1911 (Aug)	Formation of Irish Women's Suffrage Federation	(April) Bram Stoker dies in London
1912	Ulster Covenant	

Date	Event	Literary works
1912 (April)	Sinking of the RMS *Titanic* south of the Grand Banks of Newfoundland	
1912 (April)	Larne gun-smuggling episode	
1912 (Sept)	Solemn League and Covenant signed in Ulster	
1912	Ulster Volunteer Force founded	
1913	Irish Volunteers founded	*Sons and Lovers* (Lawrence)
1913	Irish Citizen Army founded	
1914 (July)	The Curragh Mutiny	
1914 (Aug)	UK and Germany at war	
1914		*Dubliners* (Joyce)
1914		*Children of the Dead End* (MacGill)
1914 (Sept)	Home Rule Bill suspended	
1914–15		*A Portrait of the Artist as a Young Man* (Joyce) published in The Egoist London
1915	The funeral in Dublin of Jeremiah O'Donovan Rossa	
1915 (May)	First zeppelin bombing raid on London	
1915 (May)	RMS *Lusitania* sunk by German submarine off west coast of Ireland	
1916 (April)	Easter Rising and the Proclamation of the Republic	
1916 (May)	Execution of revolutionary leaders	
1916 (July)	Battle of the Somme begins	
1916 (Aug)	Roger Casement hanged at Pentonville Prison	
1917 (Jan)	Silvertown Explosion	*Prufrock and Other Observations* (Eliot)
1918 (Feb)	Representation of the People Act extends franchise to women over 30 years of age	
1918 (Dec)	Irish General Election – Sinn Féin win 73 (of 105) seats	
1918 (Dec)	Constance Markiewicz elected to Westminster as Sinn Féin member	
1919 (April)	First meeting of Dáil Éireann	
1919 (Sept)	Dáil Éireann declared illegal	
1919–21	War of Independence	
1920 (Jan)	Recruitment of Black and Tans begins	

Year	Event	Cultural/Literary
1920	Government of Ireland Act	
1920 (Oct)	Terence McSwiney dies on hunger strike	
1920 (Dec)	Bloody Sunday in Dublin	
1921	Census – population of London is 7,386,755	
1921	George V opens the new Northern Ireland Parliament	Michael Robartes and the Dancer (Yeats)
1921 (June)	Burning of Cork City centre by British Army	
1921 (Dec)	Anglo-Irish Treaty, signed in Downing Street	
1921 (Dec)		
1922		Ulysses (Joyce) published in Paris
1922 (June)	Irish Civil War begins	The Waste Land (Eliot)
1922	Royal Ulster Constabulary officially established	The Wandering Years (Tynan)
1922 (Dec)	Foundation of the Irish Free State/Saorstát Éireann	
1922 (April)	Special Powers Act introduced in Northern Ireland	
1922 (Nov)	BBC begin radio broadcasting	
1923	Censorship of Films Act (Free State)	(April) The Shadow of a Gunman (O'Casey) premieres at the Abbey Theatre
		(Feb) Brendan Behan born – Dublin
1923	Irish Free State joins League of Nations	Yeats wins Nobel Prize for Literature
1923		
1924		(Mar) Juno and the Paycock (O'Casey) premieres at the Abbey Theatre
1925		Shaw wins Nobel Prize for Literature
		Mrs Dalloway (Woolf)
1926 (Jan)	2RN (later Radio Éireann) begins broadcasting	(Feb) The Plough and the Stars (O'Casey) premieres at the Abbey Theatre
1926		
1926 (May)	The General Strike begins	Donall MacAmhlaigh born – Bearna, Co. Galway
1926		

1928	(May)	William Trevor born – Mitchelstown, Co. Cork
1928	(Oct)	Pádraic Ó Conaire dies in Dublin
1929		
1929 (Sept)		*The Last September* (Bowen)
1929 (Oct)		
1930		*Collected Poems* (Tynan)
1931	(April)	Katharine Tynan dies in Wimbledon, London
1931	(April)	Joyce and Nora Barnacle move to London
1932		
(Sept/Oct)	(Jan)	George Moore dies in London
1933 (Jan)	(Nov)	John McGahern born – Knockanroe, Co. Leitrim
1934		Elizabeth Bowen moves to London
		The House in Paris (Bowen)
1935		*Ulysses* published in London by The Bodley Head
1936		
1936 (May)		*The Death of the Heart* (Bowen)
1936 (Jul)		*Murphy* (Beckett)
1936 (Oct)		
1936 (Oct)		
1937		
1938 (June)		
1938		
1939 (Jan)		
1939		

Censorship of Publications Act
BBC begins television broadcasting
Wall Street Crash
Census – population of London is 8,110,358

Great Hunger March culminates in Hyde Park, London
Hitler becomes chancellor of Germany

Inaugural Aer Lingus flight (*Iolar*) from Dublin to Bristol
Spanish Civil War starts
The Jarrow March
Battle of Cable Street
Bunreacht na hÉireann/the Irish Constitution approved
Douglas Hyde inaugurated as first Uachtarán na hÉireann / President of Ireland
Yeats dies in Menton, France
Census – population of London is 8,615,050

1939	(Jan)	Yeats dies – Menton
1939		*Finnegans Wake* published by Faber
		The Collected Poems of W. B. Yeats (Yeats)
1939 (Sept)		Second World War begins
1939 (Sept)		The Emergency declared in the Free State
1939		IRA declares war on Britain with bombing campaign in English cities
1939		*Autumn Journal* (MacNeice)
1940 (Sept)		Beginning of the London Blitz
1940 (Sept)		Battle of Britain begins
1941	(Jan)	James Joyce dies in Zurich
1941		*Between the Acts* (Woolf)
1942		*The Great Hunger* (Kavanagh)
1942		*Bowen's Court and Seven Winters* (Bowen)
1944 (June)		First V1 flying bombs hit London
1944	(Sept)	Eavan Boland born – Dublin
1944 (Aug)		Education (Butler) Act
1945 (July)		Labour Government comes to power
		Ivy Gripped the Steps and Other Stories (Bowen)
1945 (May)		Victory in Europe Day
1945		*Animal Farm* (Orwell)

Introduction: London – The Other Capital

Tom Herron

With an audacious historical sweep and an almost giddy sense of optimism, this is how London's great 'biographer' characterizes the city's allure for those migrants from all corners of the earth who, in search of a better life for themselves and their families (and no matter how 'foreign' they and the city may at first appear each to the other), soon assume their part in a collective performance of civic identity that overlays any national, or racial, or cultural identity they had hitherto possessed:

> it was the city itself which seemed to summon them, as if only in the experience of the city could their lives have meaning. Its population has been likened to the eighteenth-century drink 'All Nations', made up of the remains at the bottoms of various bottles of spirits; but this is to do less than justice to the energy and enterprise of the various immigrant populations who arrived in the city. They were not the dregs or leftovers; in fact the animation and enterprise of London often seemed to invade them and, with one or two exceptions, these various groups rose and prospered. It is the continuing and never-ending story. It has often been remarked that, in other cities, many years must pass before a foreigner is accepted; in London, it takes as many months. It is true, too, that you can only be happy in London if you begin to consider yourself as a Londoner. It is the secret of successful assimilation. (Ackroyd, 2000: 701)

Set against all the stories, all the records and all the studies that remind us that life for so many migrants in London was marked by discrimination, hostility and poverty; and by a general harshness of existence allied to a yearning for a lost homeland that very often had betrayed their needs and aspirations, Ackroyd's account might seem at worst, insensitive, or at best, naïvely heroic. It is an account that is unswervingly assimilationist in its sense that, within a remarkably brief timespan, every immigrant group ('with one or two exceptions') becomes enmeshed into the city's fabric thereby creating, for its individual members, a new subject position: Londoner.

Although such a sanguine vision is belied in the work, and in the lives, of a fair number of the writers considered in *Irish Writing London* (especially in the second volume), it may come as a surprise that, in the majority of cases we examine, London is negotiated rather deftly, rather successfully: even, now and then, rather pleasurably by the Irish writers who have made the city their subject matter or their home. When we remember that London is, in effect, little more than the accumulated traces of waves and trickles of migrants; that, since its pre-Roman origins, it is migration into, through, and sometimes out of the city that has been its defining feature *par excellence*; that, in the long run, it has remained the fiefdom of no one hegemonic group; and that among the hundreds of immigrant groups who have shaped the city's cultural fabric, it is the Irish who, for almost two centuries now, have constituted 'the largest ethnic minority ... in London's workforce' (Hickman and Walter, 1997: 7), living and working in almost every part of the city, then Ackroyd's longer view becomes more palatable. Whilst acknowledging the natives' frequent but by no means universal suspicions and hatreds of incomers as well as the appalling destitution of many of those trying to make a go of it in the city, Ackroyd possesses a deep faith in London's capacity to harbour, absorb, and then transform immigrant groups in new configurations of citizenship.

And, for the Irish at least, we have finally arrived at a moment when their incalculable individual and collective contributions to the life of the city, and to the nation of which it is at the centre, is at long last beginning to be recognized in some of its complexity. No longer is it adequate to reduce the rich multiplicity of Irish life in the city to, as one sociologist memorably if reductively put it, 'nothing but the same old story' of victimhood, in which the 'London-Irish' were endlessly subject, on the grounds of racial, religious, national or cultural differences, to discrimination in employment, housing and access to services; that they were habitually addicted to nostalgia for the homeland; that they carried, albatross-like around their necks, a sense of irredeemable cultural and linguistic loss. Indeed, no longer does it seem tenable to regard the migrant experience of the 'London-Irish' as constituting entirely or unproblematically a 'diaspora' as such, especially if that term is understood in its classic sense of expulsion, of enforced migration (Safran, 1991) with no way back to the homeland. For many, such as those who in the catastrophic circumstances of the Famine (1845–52) faced the choice of starvation at home or exile abroad, the term is entirely appropriate. But, among the many people who left Ireland to live in London and other British cities and towns (many of them moving back and forth between Ireland, Scotland and England as seasonal or itinerant labourers), a different understanding is required.

This is especially the case with the majority of writers discussed in these volumes, for whom a to-ing and fro-ing between London and Ireland seems to be the dominant pattern of living (and, in many cases, of thinking). In one or two instances – Dónall Mac Amhlaigh comes immediately to mind – there is little social or economic difference between their experiences as itinerant workers and the collective experience of those hundreds of thousands of workers who from the mid-nineteenth century, when developments in transport meant relatively quick and cheap journeys, regularly followed the work in Ireland and Britain. But for the most part, what emerges in these volumes is a sense of the relatively privileged status of those Irish writers who chose to make London their home, and this is particularly the case for those living and working in the city before the Second World War. They – and we are thinking most obviously of those whom Declan Kiberd terms the 'London Exiles': Wilde, Shaw and Yeats – were privileged not simply in the sense that, due largely to class or professional status, they could exercise considerable choice in the matter of where to best position themselves in order to further their sparkling careers; and not simply in the sense that they were able to articulate *via* literary production something of their various travails in London (though we need to guard against the temptations of transforming fiction into autobiography); but also because many of them belonged to those groups of people supposedly in danger, according to Roy Foster, of being 'forgotten or excluded from mainstream history' (Foster, 2005: 12) not for any reason of anonymity or subalternity, but for their very success at the heart of London literary life. The Conquering England exhibition at the National Portrait Gallery in 2005 demonstrated that, alongside the London Exiles, a whole range of Irish artists, journalists, politicians, and theatre entrepreneurs (foremost among them, Daniel Maclise, Charles Stewart Parnell, T. P. O'Connor, Dion Boucicault and Bram Stoker) rose to prominence in Victorian London that throughout the nineteenth and into the early twentieth century was a 'magnet for generations of middle-class Irish *arrivistes* determined to make their mark' (Foster, 2005: 14). This first volume of *Irish Writing London* extends the range of London-Irish success beyond the Victorian era and its predominantly male cabals to encompass figures such as Katharine Tynan, Elizabeth Bowen, Louis MacNeice, and James Joyce, all of whom articulate in particularly self-conscious ways their (and their literary characters') experiences of living in 'the Other Capital'; of being Irish in London; of imaginatively occupying two places at the same time; and of being professional writers taking full advantage of all the networking and publishing opportunities that London provided.

Several factors need to borne in mind when we are considering Irish writers in late-nineteenth century and early-twentieth century London. Since the creation, under the terms of the 1800 Acts of Union, of the United Kingdom of Great Britain and Ireland, the Irish 'were strictly speaking, internal migrants rather than immigrants *per se* (though they were often perceived as such)' (Swift: 2002: 8). It is debatable to what degree such constitutional arrangements featured in the lived experience of Irish workers travelling to and settling in Britain (one suspects that for many it was entirely irrelevant). But the incorporation of Ireland within the United Kingdom in tandem with developments in transport, such as the steam-packet services from Ireland to England and the burgeoning railway system, meant that Britain was increasingly an option for Irish workers – many of them itinerant, but decent numbers of them skilled and professional. And it was as a small part of the latter group – made up of ambitious, articulate, and canny Irish people in London – that most of the writers discussed in this first volume belonged.

So, by our starting point in the 1880s and early 1890s – Katharine Tynan's first volume of poetry *Louise de la Vallière and Other Poems* was published in 1885; the first expression of the Irish Literary Revival, *Poems and Ballads of Young Ireland*, edited by John O'Leary, Yeats and Tynan appeared in 1888, and Wilde's *The Picture of Dorian Gray* was published in 1890 – the Irish were no longer an exotic presence in London and many other British cities. While British politics remained inflected by Irish issues and tensions – notably the interminable progress and regress of the various Irish Home Rule bills that floundered at Westminster, the impact of Parnell and his fall from grace, the increasing pressure of Irish farmer tenants to reduce rents and gain rights on the land they tended – thousands of Irish-born, and second- and third-generation Irish now lived in London and cities such as Manchester, Liverpool,

Glasgow and Bristol. In London they were not restricted to Little Irelands – such as St. Giles in the Fields and Whitechapel, and St. Olave, Southwark – but they were to be found in every part of the city (Lees, 1979: 20). Indeed, the nineteenth-century influx of Irish migrants – that by the 1880s had waned significantly in comparison to the levels of the 1840s and 1950s – was only the latest in a discontinuous history of Irish settlement in the city that stretches back to at least as early as the eleventh century.

For much of the period prior to that covered in these volumes, the story – fragmentary as it is – appears to be much the same. When Irish people in London were considered they were considered, more often than not, as a nuisance, as a contamination, as a criminal or at least a 'suspect community' (Hillyard, 1993). Although not limited to the Irish in London, J. P. Kay's 1832 critique of the Manchester-Irish ('Debased alike by ignorance and pauperism, they have discovered, with the savage, what is the minimum of the means of life, upon which existence may be prolonged'), Thomas Carlyle's negative view of the Irish in Britain (in his 1839 pamphlet, 'Chartism'), and Thomas Beames' account of life in *The Rookeries of London* (1852) seem somewhat remote when viewed from the 1880s, and should perhaps be best considered as the tail-end of that litany of English opprobria levelled at the native Irish by a long line of apologists of a putative Englishness that to a large degree defined itself against Ireland and the Irish (Ellis, 1985). Inaugurated by the *Laudabiliter* itself and continued by Giraldus Cambrensis ('this is a truly barbarous people. They depend for their livelihood on animals and they live like animals … This is a filthy people, wallowing in vice') and comprising later adherents such as Sidney, Tremayne, Spenser, Kingsley, Froude and many others, this is a tradition that, to put it at its most delicately, was wedded to a certain view, a certain set of assumptions and prescriptions relating to the native Irish. But as for the Irish living in London, even those regarded as most base – and it was indeed the inhabitants of the Rookeries in the St. Giles area (London's 'heart of darkness') who occupied this most lowly status – were rarely considered as *uniquely* in need of moral improvement or legal restriction.

Even the racial caricaturing of the Irish (Fenians, in particular) in *Punch* cartoons of the 1840s and 1850s – during which period the Irish in Britain were subject to a fair amount of abusive attention in cartoons and opinion pieces (Foster, 1993: 184) – seems to belong to a different era to that of the 1880s when the immigrant Irish, had become, according to David Fitzgerald, 'less important as a component of the total migratory population of Britain … their notoriety as undesirable guests was probably exceeded by that of the Jewish "immigrant aliens" from Russia and Eastern Europe. By which time even the most blinkered observer could no longer claim that the Irish were confined to ghettoes and Irishtowns within major cities' (Fitzgerald, 1989: 14).

Literary writers constituted a minuscule proportion of the hundreds of thousands of people who left Ireland in search of better lives in London and elsewhere in Britain, and so it would be foolish to claim that in their representations of London and London life can be found some articulation of a collective migrant experience. Even the material brought together by Liam Harte in his ground-breaking collection of autobiographical writing by Irish people living and working in Britain reveals the extent of the sheer lack of evidence left by people whose priorities were to survive and thrive in often difficult circumstances rather than record their experiences in memoir or, perhaps even more challenging, to reshape those experiences into 'literary' form.[1] In general, and with the sole exception of Pádraic Ó Conaire whose novel, *Deoraíocht* (1910), is intimately concerned with the often grotesque fate of migrant labourers in the capital, the literary production of Irish writers in London from the Revival period through to the outbreak of the Second World War is somewhat removed from the working-class or subaltern groups who constituted the greatest numbers of Irish migrants in London. There is little sense that those writers regarded themselves as spokespeople for some larger constituency of 'London-Irish' people: inevitably, however, they were part of that constituency.

So, what picture of London does emerge in these writers' work? In the first chapter of this volume Deaglán Ó Donghaile examines the ways in which Oscar Wilde's Dorian Gray experiences the dark pleasures of London's underside. Reflecting, according to Ó Donghaile, Wilde's own sense of his incomplete assimilation into London literary and social culture, Dorian's exploration of sexual and social freedom on the capital's streets, represents a critique of British metropolitan and imperial culture that initially seems to be undertaken from within the metropolitan mind set, but that – and bearing in mind Wilde's republicanism and socialism – is in fact undertaken from a revolutionary perspective.

Two chapters are devoted to the importance of London – especially its literary, publishing, political and esoteric coteries – within the work of W. B. Yeats. By considering the poet's participation in the London Ghost Club, Tara Stubbs reveals intriguing connections between Yeats's spiritual investigations and his poetic method. Analysis of archival material reveals that experiments Yeats carried out while a member of the Club find fruition in major works such as 'The Second Coming' and *A Vision*. A similar London strand within Yeats's poetry and fiction is considered by Adrian Paterson who, in his discussion of the poet's best-known work 'The Lake Isle of Innisfree', brings together the poem's urban 'origins' with a hitherto little-discussed suburban aspect, to establish the poem as a more complicatedly London text than is normally imagined.

Like Yeats, George Shaw made his name in London. But it was not simply as a playwright that he was best known in the capital. Before he began his career in theatre, Shaw was deeply involved in local and national politics, and in her discussion of *Mrs. Warren's Profession* Michelle Paull shows the ways in which Shaw's Fabianism and feminism (developed largely during his time as an activist and local government councillor in London) are fundamental to the play's dramatic and rhetorical strategies.

Whitney Standlee considers the ways in which, once she had arrived in London, Katharine Tynan's literary path would veer widely from the cultural/political project that she, Yeats and other revivalists had developed with a view to the rejuvenation of Ireland's cultural life: so crucial was she to the initial project that George Russell (A. E.) asserted that 'Katharine Tynan was the earliest singer in that awakening of our imagination which has been spoken of as the Irish Renaissance'. Charting her movement from the radical circles in Dublin to the rather safe literary coteries in London, Standlee's reading of Tynan's London-based work is sympathetic to Yeats's sense that 'literature "for Ireland's use" was not likely to be produced from a space of expatriation' and at the same time appreciative of Tynan's abilities to forge for herself a successful career as a novelist in the metropolis.

Pádraigín Riggs examines the relatively under-appreciated role of Pádraic Ó Conaire in the development not only of modern literature produced in the Irish language, but within the incredibly vibrant revivalist movement in London. Although not a native speaker, the fact that Ó Conaire produced his best work, all of it in Irish, during the 15 years in which he lived in London is, as Riggs suggests, something of a paradox. So too, is the purpose to which that language is put to use. An instance of early Irish literary modernism, *Deoraíocht*'s vision of London is as a 'City of Darkness' (Ó Conaire, 1994: 23). Set up as the binary opposite to Galway, the city is imagined as neither a place of opportunity nor of hope, but rather as a realm of nightmare in which the traumas visited upon the colonized are replayed time and again in all their grotesque horror.

Eleni Loukopoulou addresses a persistent silence in Joycean studies: the important place of London within Joyce's career. Although he is normally associated with Dublin and the three locations with which he signs off *Ulysses* ('Trieste-Zurich-Paris'), Loukopoulou shows how Joyce undertook his 'fifth hegira' among London's publishing houses in order to push for publication of his major works. The centrality of London appears in the coded portmanteau word 'Londub' that features in *Finnegans Wake*, and Loukopoulou carries out a detailed reading of the multiple meanings produced by it – not least the word's gesturing towards a reconfigured relationship between the capital cities of Britain and Ireland.

As well as living on London's Regent's Park between 1935 and 1952, Elizabeth Bowen continued to own and keep on Bowen's Court, a Georgian country house in County Cork from 1930 until 1959. For Allan Hepburn, this balancing of city and country, of London and Ireland provides for Bowen much of the tension evident in her representations of London life. Concentrating on those aspects of her writing that are concerned with houses, architecture and post-war urban planning, Hepburn reveals how Bowen's writing of the city invokes the national and colonial legacies that persist between England and Ireland. Profoundly sceptical of the ability of human beings to thrive in the metropolis, Bowen advocates the precedence of the neighbourhood over the metropolis. It is through a type of rural city and its architecture that a sense of urban belonging can take place.

Finally in this volume, Simon Workman explores the ways in which the changing atmosphere of London and the increasing tensions of Londoners are captured and reimagined in Louis MacNeice's monumental poem, *Autumn Journal* (1939). London is, as Workman argues, 'at the heart of the poem and seems almost to gain a voice in the narrative character'. As well as writing of the city, MacNeice as a BBC writer and producer, wrote *to* it, and as part of his analysis of London within the poet's wider output, Workman includes a consideration of the remarkably interesting wartime propaganda broadcasts that MacNeice produced, and also considers the later poems in which post-war London is rendered as a kind of dystopia, shorn of its war-time energy, and lost in faceless and surreal re-development.

Autumn Journal brings us to the threshold of a war from which the Irish State exempted itself on the grounds that, as Joe Walshe, the Secretary for External Affairs, put it, small nations like Ireland do not and cannot assume a role as defenders of just causes except [their] own ... Existence of our own people comes before all other considerations ... no government has the right to court certain destruction for its people; they have to take the only chance of survival and stay out. (Quoted in Collins, 1993: 371)

Notwithstanding the State's policy of neutrality, thousands of Irish men and women would contribute – as soldiers, as merchant seamen, as munitions factory workers – to Britain's and its allies' struggle against the Axis powers. The participation of Irish people in the war underlines the degree of inter-connectedness between Ireland and Britain that is a recurring feature within the work of each of the writers considered in this volume. The relationship is not always pacific, and it is certainly characterized by the inequities of power fostered by the fundamentally colonial relationship between the two. But each of these writers contributes in their own way towards a nuancing of the colonial or post-colonial story. Admittedly at some remove from the great majority of Irish migrants who settled in London and elsewhere in Britain, their writing of the capital constitutes a diverse but thoroughly intra-national literature in which the cultures and politics, the people and places of both countries are brought together in new imaginative configurations.

Note

1 Liam Harte (ed.) (2009) *The Literature of the Irish in Britain: Autobiography and Memoir, 1725–2001*. London, Palgrave Macmillan.

1

Oscar Wilde's Other London

Deaglán Ó Donghaile

At the very beginning of *The Picture of Dorian Gray* (1890), Basil Hallward discusses the subject of his latest painting, Dorian Gray, with his louche, aristocratic friend, Lord Henry Wotton. The conversation takes place in the artist's suburban studio where the finishing touches are being put to the portrait, while distant but encroaching sounds can be heard emanating from the city. Fascinated by the content of the piece and engrossed by their discussion about abstract notions of beauty, the pair ignore the more immediate and urban conditions that have influenced the portrait's production and within which Dorian Gray is thoroughly embedded. Art may be produced in this surreal and sealed atmosphere where light glimmers with a decadent, Paterian 'flame-like' luxury, but it also has distinctly material origins, a point that Wilde stresses by taking care to convey to the reader how lifeless the synthetic and 'momentary' environment in Hallward's studio actually is. Populated with fixed and 'immobile' images that, for Wotton, are reminiscent of Japanese art, the studio and the things that it contains are sealed off from their more vital urban surroundings: 'The sullen murmur of the bees shouldering their way through the long unmown grass, or circling with monotonous insistence round the dusty gilt horns of the straggling woodbine, seemed to make the stillness more oppressive' (Wilde, 2000: 5)[1]. From Hallward's studio the 'dim roar of London' can be heard, sounding like the 'bourdon note of a distant organ' (Wilde, 2000: 5). The painting, then, is composed in an atmosphere that contains the influence of two contrasting environments, as the still, orientalist tableau of this bourgeois space exists at the edge of an uncontained, over-spilling city that threatens to penetrate the hermetic splendour of Hallward's workplace. Yet he and Wotton appear oblivious to this, despite Wilde's insistent privileging of perception. The studio, despite its luxuriousness, is a stifling, even 'oppressive' space (Wilde, 2000: 5) and Wilde represents the sprawling metropolis of London, which is just within earshot of the garden, as a far more adventurous and unpredictable place.

Late nineteenth and early twentieth century Irish literature, including the work of exiles like Wilde, William Butler Yeats, George Bernard Shaw, Bram Stoker and James Joyce, engaged with the crises that were generated by British imperialism. As a result of the direct experience of empire, these authors were preoccupied by the theme of subjective immobility which has, for the colonized, as Seamus Deane has noted, 'all the characteristic features of underdevelopment, of being removed from history' (Deane, 1997: 167). Wilde located his novel in the heart of the metropolis because the tension between bourgeois and imperial 'immobilism' and the liberating possibilities of the darker pleasures to be found on the streets of the underside of the metropolis, which I will term the Other London, sustained, in his imagination, a subversive sense of imaginative, political and erotic possibility. Dorian's interest in, and enjoyment of, the alien spaces and subjects of this alternative city reflects Wilde's own experience of his incomplete assimilation into metropolitan culture. As an Irish republican and socialist, Wilde deliberately disguised his Irishness so as to criticize imperial and metropolitan culture from within, a practice that invested his writing with its deeply antithetic character. Dorian's view that England is 'the native land of the hypocrite' (Wilde, 2000: 145) is echoed in other works by Wilde, including his 1888 story, 'The Young King', which, although a work of fantasy, criticizes British imperialism both in Ireland and in its farther-flung colonies, and 'Lord Arthur Saville's Crime' (1891), which portrays the sponsorship of terrorism by bourgeois society, while his anti-British sentiments were publicly expressed on a number of occasions during his 1882 tour of the United States.[2]

However, Wilde's most sustained focus on 'native' English hypocrisy, which is consistently treated as a symptom of bourgeois and imperial decadence in his work, is expressed through the discussion of class and city in *The Picture of Dorian Gray*. The novel's capacity to shock contemporary readers lay in its fusion of the opposed spheres of bourgeois and working-class experience (whether sailors, thieves, prostitutes or drug dealers, the urban poor are professionals of one type or another). One reader famously reacted to the novel by describing it as the effort of 'a literary dung-fly', while a review of the Lippincott's serialized edition, published in *The Christian Leader*, praised the novel's fusion of 'culture and corruption'. 'We can only hope', the critic went on, 'that it will be read and pondered by those classes of British society whose corruption it delineates with such thrilling power'. The tale's class dialectic was also recognized by none other than Walter Pater, who pointed to Wilde's 'wholesome dislike of the common-place' that was 'rightly or wrongly identified by him with the bourgeois, with our middle-class – its habits and tastes' and that, in turn, lead him to 'protest emphatically against so-called "realism" in art'. However, as Pater suggested, this did not necessarily make *The Picture of Dorian Gray* comfortable reading for the well-to-do, as it offered 'anything but a homely philosophy of life for the middle-class'. Pater enjoyed the novel's relevance and 'pleasant accessory detail' that, he believed, was inspired by contemporary tastes and 'taken straight from the culture, the intellectual and social interests, the conventionalities, of the moment'. For Pater, Dorian's slide into corruption mirrored that of the late Victorian middle classes as a whole, and the novel's appeal, he reckoned, would lie in its characteristically modern treatment of its subject matter.[3]

The urban underclass and imperial excess

Throughout the novel, we find the urban poor and their environment facilitating Dorian's pursuit of certain types of freedom. The exact nature of these freedoms (or transgressions) remain unclear but they appear consistently attractive because they require the crossing of the spatial and class boundaries that protect Hallward's studio from the encroaching 'noise' and confusion of the metropolis on which his middle-class neighbourhood borders. Dorian immerses himself in this community until it instils the 'hideous sympathy' (Wilde, 2000: 102) that he feels for his other double, the portrait. But while the image on Hallward's canvas ages, Dorian, like the Irish colonial subject identified by Deane, remains static and undeveloped. Going abroad in the Other London is the only remedy for this condition, and in experiencing its dangers as well as its pleasures, Dorian encounters its underclass of prostitutes, sailors and opium addicts within the liminal and uncertain urban space of the docks and East End. These districts are entirely at odds with the 'lovely surroundings' of bourgeois London that Wilde regarded as being at odds with the purposes of art. The subaltern cultures of the metropolis threaten, on occasion, to spill across the supposedly stable borders that fix and divide the city's urban terrains, and their potential to invade the spaces and even consciousness associated with the bourgeois self, underlines the porous quality of the borders designed to separate London's multiple communities. The failure to prevent these territories and subjectivities from becoming mixed and confused is taken advantage of by the aptly named Dorian Gray, whose very identity reflects the sexual, national and political ambivalences that characterized British experience in the British capital at the *fin de siècle*.[4]

Wilde explores the appeal of the urban textures of the city when Wotton recalls walking past a fanatical preacher at Marble Arch. Remarking that 'London is very rich in curious effects of that kind' (Wilde, 2000: 205), he suggests that such encounters matter because they are evocative of 'suggestion' rather than certainty. These phenomena are, he maintains, the city's most valuable experiences because the 'things one feels certainly about are never true', as they underline, for him, much of 'the fatality of Faith, and the lesson of Romance' (Wilde, 2000: 205). Wilde uses such self-consciously reflexive moments in the novel to interrogate the quality of unorthodox experiences in late Victorian London but, apart from Dorian, his characters manage to resist the urge to immerse themselves completely in the alternative pleasures offered by the Other Capital. Through Dorian Gray, Wilde draws the reader's attention to a number of anxieties generated by late Victorian modernity, including concerns over doubling which, in turn, highlighted issues such as selfhood, class and empire. The novel is also preoccupied with the doubling that is inherent in its geographical setting of London – a theme that, as an Irish writer, Wilde was particularly drawn towards. As an Anglo-Irish subject, Wilde's own identity was culturally and politically bifurcated, and his consciousness of this phenomenon is amplified in London. As the centre of the British Empire, London afforded Irish writers like Wilde an opportunity to become assimilated into the literary and cultural heart, if not of darkness, then at least of moral and political greyness, or ambivalence.[5]

Dorian accepts that his 'mad hungers' (Wilde, 2000: 124) can only be satisfied within the confines of this 'imperial Neronian' metropolis (Wilde, 2000: 125), and pursues pleasure among its Gothic urban spaces, where 'unreal shadows' cast doubt over the ability of Paterian stillness to sustain the interest of his adventurous and modern subjectivity. The city's underside contrasts with the mundanity of everyday experience, or 'the real life' that he has known before his initiation into this sphere, where the world is 'refashioned anew in the darkness for ... pleasure'. Dorian's consciousness of this new, if decadent, world of 'fresh shapes and colours' is one within which, he finds, 'the past would have little or no place, or survive, at any rate, in no conscious form of obligation or regret, the remembrance even of joy having its bitterness, and the memories of pleasure their pain' (Wilde, 2000: 127). While Hallward's garden is a much smaller and more contained affair, the Other London is an enormous temporal and moral void, the enormity and nearness of which many of the novel's bourgeois characters would rather not contemplate. The metropolitan imagination is marked by 'such worlds as these' and by their 'strangeness' (Wilde, 2000: 127) as this alternative urban dominion, like the dangerous pleasures that Dorian so enjoys, exerts 'subtle influences' over the modern subject (Wilde, 2000: 127). It is the richness of its phenomena that draws Dorian towards the city's poorer districts, where he falls under the spell of experiences that exert as much control over his imagination as does Basil Hallward's self-indulgent doctrine on art and excess. This landscape has a capacity to gratify Dorian's desire for sensation, which increases after his rejection of Sibyl Vane, when a direct encounter with a harsh scene of poverty, neglect and violence contradicts his artist friend's ideal of material and aesthetic perfection.

Dorian's gravest transgression is that he allows the subaltern universe of the docks and East End to seep into the private sphere of wealth and privilege.[6] After informing Sibyl of his disappointment in her, his walk through a series of badly-lit streets brings him 'past gaunt black-shadowed archways and evil-looking houses' and culminates with a spectacle of urban horror:

> Women with hoarse voices and harsh laughter had called after him. Drunkards had reeled by cursing, and chattering to themselves like monstrous apes. He had seen grotesque children huddled upon doorsteps, and heard shrieks and oaths from gloomy courts. (Wilde, 2000: 86)

But, on passing this atavistic scene of poverty, deprivation and degeneration, Dorian safely reaches the more familiar territory of a 'polished, empty street' near Covent Garden, where, at the break of dawn, he watches workers preparing for the day's trade. Here he is struck by a carter who, on offering him some cherries, refuses payment for them, and Dorian is confused by the possibility of free pleasure, as this kind of enjoyment cannot be processed by the bourgeois imagination.

Experienced during the moment prior to the spectacle of consumption that is the Covent Garden market, he has stumbled upon another site of alterity (and this time it is political) where, at least until the market opens, the flow of capital is resisted by workers. But, like Dorian, the fruit is rather cold and the scene presents us with a paradox, because, unlike the workers, he is incapable of kindness, having just sacrificed his innocence by rejecting Sibyl. As the figure in the portrait begins from this point to assume an increasingly cruel appearance, it conveys with growing intensity Dorian's hostility and antagonism towards the lower classes, whose ability to appreciate and share pleasure seems, to him, quite pointless. In failing to appreciate the true value of the cherries, Dorian misses the very point of gratification: in a novel that situates indulgence so squarely within the sphere of the material, it is the solidarity and innocence represented by the carter's kind but entirely misunderstood gesture that, for Wilde, contains something much finer than the world of bourgeois value. The ideology that leads to this moment – underwritten by Dorian's class values and his 'feeling for luxury' – causes the portrait to change, but he cannot comprehend the meaning behind the transformation of its image because, as a bourgeois, he is incapable of comprehending his own guilt (Wilde, 2000: 87). Just as Hallward is indifferent to the noises encroaching on his studio, Dorian also fails to understand the significance of the carter's gift and it is his failure to do so, as much as his destructive rejection of Sibyl Vane, that leads to the immediate change in the painting.

As John G. Peters has argued, *The Picture of Dorian Gray* is predicated on Wilde's ability to convey sensory perception, a tactic that he uses in order to distance its characters from possible moral judgements of their actions. Peters suggests that the novel's 'lyric' rather than realistic scenes are designed to remind the reader of the pre-eminence of art over the actual, an effect that is repeatedly achieved by shifting its emphasis away from events and towards an 'intrusive' and self-consciously stylistic form of description. In this manner, Dorian's swapping of appearances with the portrait underlines the novel's overall concern and principal manner of style – the fusion of form with content. As Peters points out, Wilde uses this strategy to construct a world – deliberately conceived as a bourgeois environment – in which any consciousness of impending crisis is averted for the benefit of privileged imperial-metropolitan types like Hallward and Wotton. This spillage of one world into the other is ultimately contained with Dorian's death, but it is what underlines his sinfulness, as he embodies the transference of the 'loathsome' values and realities of the Other London (Wilde, 2000: 213) onto a blissfully ignorant bourgeois city.[7]

The painting's mirror-function manifests more than the physical transformations that Dorian's body is spared as it also registers the withering effects of the sexual, class and social transgressions that he commits by traversing the metropolis and exploiting its working class, impoverished and addicted inhabitants. As Simon Joyce argues, Wilde did not attempt to engage in self-justification in writing *The Picture of Dorian Gray* but, instead, sought to present his readers with an image of bourgeois complicity in maintaining the structures of social inequality. Therefore, Dorian's self-indulgent 'slumming' and his attendant abuse of the urban poor contains a subtle political commentary that draws attention to the novel's key paradox by offering a critique of aesthetic hedonism along with its 'ideological underpinnings of disinterestedness', its 'overinvestment in pleasure and beauty', and its persistent denial of consequences.[8] Like the geography of London, the surface of the portrait contains moral blind spots, or 'secret places', that promise to afford Dorian the freedom to perform as another self or selves, but this is achieved at an enormous moral cost. On leaving his original, more innocent self behind the screen covering the canvas, his other selves appear to move much more freely across the metropolis, and across the boundaries that separate and protect the bourgeois world of Basil Hallward and Harry Wotton from the desperate subjects of the Other London. Hallward is eventually murdered for drawing attention to this problem, and for criticizing Dorian's inclusion of young aristocratic men and women in his process of urban thrill-seeking. The artist insists that this activity violates the class norms and boundaries that must be maintained by the privileged because, as Wotton also warns at the beginning of the novel, the threat of revolution, or the 'rage of … English democracy' is never far from the city's surface (Wilde, 2000: 12).

Dorian is boycotted by his friends among the metropolitan élite for transgressing the boundaries that separate and protect them from the lower orders of society when it becomes known that he is frequenting the East End:

> For, while he fascinated many, there were not a few who distrusted him. He was very nearly blackballed at a West End club of which his birth and social position fully entitled him to become a member, and it was said that on one occasion, when he was brought by a friend into the smoking-room of the Churchill, the Duke of Berwick and another gentleman got up in a marked manner and went out. Curious stories became current about him after he had passed his twenty-fifth year. It was rumoured that he had been brawling with foreign sailors in a low den in the distant parts of Whitechapel, and that he consorted with thieves and coiners and knew the mysteries of their trade. His extraordinary absences became notorious, and, when he used his to reappear again in society, men would whisper to each other in corners, or pass him with a sneer, or look at him with cold searching eyes, as though they were determined to discover his secret. (Wilde, 2000: 136)

Dorian's shocking and even violent encounters with the urban poor underline the paradox that is inherent in Wotton's statement that 'the true mystery of the world is the visible, not the invisible' (Wilde, 2000: 24). Wilde explores the apparent, if unacknowledged, role of the metropolitan poor in bourgeois experience and, in doing so, engages with urban, bourgeois and imperial guilt. Wotton tries to limit his own consciousness of this reality with his near-insane denial of age and celebration of youth. In refusing age, or, as he regards it, straightforward 'degeneration' – a term applied freely in relation to urban populations such as immigrants, addicts and workers at the *fin de siècle* – (Wilde, 2000: 25), he expresses a desire to disengage from the material conditions of urban modernity, and it is no coincidence that the view that experience rots is voiced by an aristocrat: his crudely elitist version of aestheticism denies the possibility of change, transmission and growth because his ideal world is one of stasis. Associating with thieves, counterfeiters and sailors, Dorian's increasingly liminal position also reflects what Curtis Marez has termed the deepening contradictions and 'fissures in colonial subjectivity' along with the 'sutures that join the colonized to the colonial power'. At large in the opium dens and docks, where imperial culture and subjectivity are invaded on the most intimate bases, Dorian's perceived recklessness also conveys some of Wilde's own Anglo-Irish sensibility. Like the racially and culturally impure Malays with whom Dorian associates, Wilde was himself an embodiment of the inherent contradictions that underline late Victorian imperial ideology: having origins in a marginal culture that was itself a direct product of colonial contact, Wilde reveals in this passage how imperialism tries to stay the 'ideological traffic' that is the result of empire.[9]

The underside of the city and its 'dreadful places' filled with 'secret pleasure' (Wilde, 2000: 135) connect Dorian to an enlivening and sensuous existence that fills the void created by his over-indulgence in commodities. The portrait, like his former self, remains sealed in his locked room, allowing him to move around the capital:

> Upon the walls of the lonely locked room where he had spent so much of his boyhood, he had hung with his own hands the terrible portrait whose changing features showed him the real degradation of his life, and in front of it had draped the purple-and-gold pall as a curtain. For weeks he would not go there, would forget the hideous painted thing, and get back his light heart, his wonderful joyousness, his passionate absorption in mere existence. Then, suddenly, some night he would creep out of the house, go down to dreadful places near Blue Gate Fields, and stay there, day after day, until he was driven away. On his return he would sit in front of the picture, sometimes loathing it and himself, but filled, at other times, with that pride of individualism that is half the fascination of sin, and smiling, with secret pleasure, at the misshapen shadow that had to bear the burden that should have been his own. (Wilde, 2000: 135)

Here we find the conscious doubling of the portrait's duality with that of London. The erasure of Dorian's guilt and the fulfilment of his desire can only take place if he has free access to the city's underside around Whitechapel while, on his return, the moral cost of his activities is projected back onto the painting. The relationship between Dorian, the city and the portrait captures the essential ambivalence of the novel, and of its characteristic aesthetic of inversion. He experiences freedom and individualism within the poorest districts of the city, as Wilde also reveals that Wotton's objective – to 'cure the soul by means of the senses, and the senses by means of the soul' (Wilde, 2000: 176) – can only be achieved in the more 'sordid' quarters of the capital. The rainfall that creates an indistinct atmosphere lit by 'blurred street-lamps' provides a suitably ambivalent setting for Dorian's exposure as the notorious Prince Charming. Seeking escape in an opium den, where he intends to obliterate the memory of recent transgressions by indulging in an even greater 'madness', he descends into a gothic urban setting that is 'clogged with a grey-flannel mist' and where the moon appears to manifest his guilt, hanging 'low in the sky like a yellow skull' (Wilde, 2000: 176). Seeking to erase the memory of Hallward's murder, Dorian enters the confusing and 'interminable' streets like the black web of some sprawling spider'. Suggestive of the Other London's lure, this image indicates that Dorian has been trapped within the East End, where the atmosphere congeals as mist thickens. Driven past brickfields and over badly paved roads, he observes the alien environment that is inhabited by the working poor:

> Most of the windows were dark, but now and then fantastic shadows were silhou-etted against some lamp-lit blind. He watched them curiously. They moved like monstrous marionettes, and made gestures like live things. He hated them. A dull

rage was in his heart. As they turned a corner a woman yelled something at them from an open door, and two men ran after the hansom for about a hundred yards. The driver beat at them with his whip. (Wilde, 2000: 177)

Rendered from a bourgeois perspective, the encounter between Dorian and these representatives of the Other London is unsettling because his contempt for the poor is reflected back at him in gestures of resistance, with the woman yelling at the cab and its pursuit by a pair of robbers. However, Wilde highlights what Dorian perceives as the threatening quality of the Other London by drawing the reader's attention to his hostile perspective on his surroundings, and its inhabitants, whom he regards as being as lifeless as the role that they have been assigned ...according to bourgeois ideology. Believing that, like puppets, they lack agency, he expects them to behave passively, and their perceived monstrosity lies in their refusal to be manipulated or contained. While Gothic literature has always been predicated on uncertainty, the unpredictability of the urban poor in this passage serves to highlight the new and consciously modern application of terror at the *fin de siècle*. Acting 'like live things', and moving of their own volition, these unruly urban subjects defy the roles that have been assigned to them by Dorian's class, which expects that they will fulfil its own 'terrible' ends and pleasures. Much like the carter who refuses payment at Covent Garden, they deny their assigned role as indifferent and obedient figures in the bourgeois economy, but they do so here in an entirely aggressive manner.[10]

This shock ultimately whets Dorian's appetite for sensation, and its quickening in 'each trembling nerve and fibre' underlines the decadent appeal of coming so close to such misery and danger: 'Ugliness that had once been hateful to him because it made things real, became dear to him now for that very reason' (Wilde, 2000: 177). The thrill is amplified because, while driving through this part of the city, he comes to realize that its lack of beauty is the only condition, or 'one reality' (Wilde, 2000: 178), that his imagination can tolerate. Dorian's unusually high tolerance for danger and cruelty is the end product of his urban conditioning and of the friction between the classes. The visible result of this is manifested in the outward and aesthetic register of the ever-changing painting which, like the urban environment that influences it, refuses to remain steady or fixed. Having transferred his inner self onto Hallward's canvas, Dorian has, paradoxically, become a simulacrum, or copy of the bland and unimaginative urban surfaces of bourgeois London. Like the subjects that fascinate him, his real identity, which is concealed behind a screen, is more authentic than his new self that, on the surface at least, appears to dissolve the link that binds his urban surroundings to the bourgeois construction of identity. Truth, however, is to be found in the Other London, where life is violent, chaotic and strangely beautiful: 'The coarse brawl, the loathsome den, the crude violence of disordered life, the very vileness of thief and outcast, were more vivid in their intense actuality of impression, than all the gracious shapes of Art, the dreamy shadows of Song. They were what he needed for forgetfulness' (Wilde, 2000: 178). Combined with Dorian's keenly Paterian sense of the immediacy of the moment, the sights, events, subjects and sensations that he encounters in these frightening parts of London allow him to experience genuine sensual immersion in the metropolis.

The opium den serves as a microcosm of this forbidden environment, as its dangerous pleasures involve descending, with the aid of narcotics, to alternative and rather fluid realities that are at once the 'strange heavens' and 'dull hells' that, like the underside of the city, Dorian enjoys exploring (Wilde, 2000: 179). Addicted to opium because it induces a liberating state of consciousness, whereby he can find release from being 'prisoned in thought' (Wilde, 2000: 179), he proceeds towards the docks, traversing an environment that is at once fractured and uncertain, and where light is 'splintered' and shaken by its reflection in puddles. Dorian's refusal to acknowledge boundaries of class and urban geography, along with his 'fatal' (Wilde, 2000: 144) sexual preferences disturbs the finely calibrated balances that are carefully maintained by bourgeois society and housed in the élite clubs and homes from which he is barred. His unacceptable presence in the East End mirrors his absence from these places but it is the 'unreality' and 'shallow psychology' of this world that is challenged by his sexual, drug-fuelled experiments among the poor: Dorian's objection to London society stems from its refusal to acknowledge that, like the city, modern man is a 'complex multiform creature' whose personality contains 'myriad lives and myriad sensations' (Wilde, 2000: 137). His movements across London and his regular disappearances underline this uncertainty, as does his denial of the necessity to maintain the 'good name' that, as Hallward insists, is vital to his status as a gentleman and his only protection from emerging 'vile and degraded' (Wilde, 2000: 143). This erosion of political propriety also assumes a more personal manifestation as Dorian's double identity is also marked, increasingly, by his sexual ambivalence, which is noted by both Hallward and Lord Staveley, who discuss his corruption of 'pure-minded' girls and his 'fatal' friendships with young men, in whom he has instilled an incurable 'madness for pleasure' (Wilde, 2000: 144–5). Despite his charm, youth and charisma, the threat posed by Dorian's liminal experiences is felt by the society ladies whom he has involved in these encounters, and this is noticed by his detractors: 'some of those who had been most intimate with him appeared, after a time, to shun him. Women who had wildly adored him, and for his sake had braved all social censure and set convention at defiance, were seen to grow pallid with shame or horror if Dorian Gray entered the room' (136). For Dorian the appeal of liminality also applies to Sibyl Vane, the working-class actress to whom he is attracted after he watches her perform in a male role.

The city as art

Wilde offered his views on the condition of London during a lecture that he delivered at the Royal Academy in June 1883, at a moment when the city was undergoing an exponential burst of growth and development.[11] Stressing the artist's relation to stimuli offered by the 'external' and urban world, Wilde warned his audience that the cost of such unprecedented transformation would be the rapid loss of the city's more beautiful, if entirely unco-ordinated and eclectic surroundings. Claiming that the issue of urban renewal was 'one of the most important questions on modern art', he attacked the increasingly mundane appearance of modern London that he regarded as an inelegant fusion of bad and imitative styles. In doing so, Wilde drew attention to what he considered to be the most worrying aspect of the city's recent architectural shifts, while, at the same time, informing his listeners that that aestheticism was particularly concerned with questions of urban taste:

> perhaps you will tell me that the external beauty of the world has almost entirely passed away from us, that the artist dwells no longer in the midst of the lovely surroundings which, in ages past, were the natural inheritance of every one, and that art is very difficult in this unlovely town of ours, where, as you go to your work in the morning, or return from it at eventide, you have to pass through street after street of the most foolish and stupid architecture that the world has ever seen; architecture, where every lovely Greek form is desecrated and defiled, and every lovely Gothic form defiled and desecrated, reducing three-fourths of the London houses to being, merely, like square boxes of the vilest proportions, as gaunt as they are grimy, and as poor as they are pretentious – the hall door always of the wrong colour, and the windows of the wrong size, and where, even wearied of the houses you turn to contemplate, the street itself, you have nothing to look at but chimney-pot hats, men with sandwich boards, vermilion letter-boxes, and do that even at the risk of being run over by an emerald-green omnibus.[12]

Clearly, Wilde despised the kind of architecture being designed for the requirements of the expanding middle classes. Its replacement of the city's more interesting traditional urban environment amounted, he believed, to a form of cultural hollowing and his lecture attacked what he perceived to be the increasingly coarse and boring appearance of the city's bourgeois environment. Looking, at once, anti-Hellenic and anti-Gothic, the new visual texture of London was, he feared, assuming an un-artistic, even anti-cultural role, while the inhabitants of this new and 'unlovely town' were assimilating the worst characteristics of their purpose-built background. In criticizing bourgeois style, with its elevation of practicality over appearance and its rather bland and imitative architecture, Wilde pointed to what he regarded as the relatively sudden emergence of an increasingly functional urban environment. With its dull buildings and even duller inhabitants, modern London appeared to him to be far less interesting than the more authentic and alternative world to which Dorian Gray is drawn. The lecture highlighted Wilde's antagonism toward the metropolitan middle classes and his dislike for the values expressed in their surroundings, and it is this unoriginal and utilitarian aspect of bourgeois London that is countered by the urban Gothic of *The Picture of Dorian Gray*.

For Wilde, middle-class London, along with its streets and inhabitants, served as a lesson in urban failure and decay and was, at once, insincere, inorganic and aesthetically impoverished. Although Dorian represents the Hellenic ideal of which, he complained, the capital was being evacuated, his rather false and unchanging existence, which mirrors middle-class experience by being 'simple, permanent, reliable' (Wilde, 2000: 137) – much like the still moment described in the novel's opening scene – is far less intriguing than the Gothic qualities of the Other London, where one might encounter anyone and experience anything. In a novel filled with paradoxes, one of its most insistent inversions is its simultaneous insistence on Paterian stillness, beauty and perfection and the expression of the uniqueness of a much more complex consciousness of urban Gothic. This is manifested in Wilde's representation of the Other London, where we find the most complete accounts of the sins that provide, in Lord Henry's words, 'the only real colour-element left in modern life' (Wilde, 2000: 30). It is Dorian's contact with this place and his experience of it that comes to ravage Hallward's impossibly perfect portrait; his behaviour, along with his movement between two socially and politically distinct Londons, underlines Wotton's complaint that 'the costume of the nineteenth century is detestable' (Wilde, 2000: 30). In attempting to free himself from bourgeois and imperial hypocrisy, Dorian meets with encounters and experiences that can only occur in the metropolis, where uncertainty charms and 'mist makes things wonderful' (Wilde, 2000: 196). These delights are what he also understands to be the city's most wonderful effects because, as Wilde insists, 'The things one feels absolutely certain about are never true' (Wilde, 2000: 205). Dorian's crimes are many and unpleasant and his engagement with the labyrinthine late Victorian metropolis results in his crossing of the moral, political and geographical boundaries that distinguish bourgeois London from its other, alien and working-class environments. Having traversed both territories, and having been seen to do so, his life, according to this world's standards, can only end in destruction.

Notes

1 Quotations are from Oscar Wilde (2000) *The Picture of Dorian Gray*. Harmondsworth: Penguin. Citations are provided in the body of the essay throughout.
2 For a discussion of late nineteenth century Irish literature's engagement with colonial crises, see Seamus Deane (1998) *Strange Country: Modernity and Nationhood in Irish Writing Since 1790*; especially 89–94. Declan Kiberd has discussed the writer's deliberate suppression of his Irishness as a subversive literary and political strategy: see Kiberd (1991) 'The London Exiles: Wilde and Shaw', *The Field Day Anthology of Irish Writing*: 372–6. See also Kiberd's 'Oscar Wilde – The Artist as Irishman' in his *Inventing Ireland: The Literature of the Modern Nation*: 33–50. In 'The Young King' Wilde refers to colonialism in Ireland via the story's discussion of conquest, destruction and famine, while in 'Lord Arthur Saville's Crime' Fenian violence is processed as anarchist subversion. See *The Complete Works of Oscar Wilde*: 213–22 and 160–84. For a discussion of the deliberate confusion of Fenianism with anarchism in late Victorian fiction, see chapters 1–3 of my *Blasted Literature: Victorian Political Fiction and the Shock of Modernism*. Wilde's critical views on the British occupation of Ireland were aired in public lectures given in St. Paul, Minnesota and in San Francisco during his tour of the United States. See Lloyd Lewis and Henry Justin Smith's 'Oscar Wilde Discovers America: 1882' and Wilde's 'Irish Poets and Poetry of the Nineteenth Century'. Closer to home, Wilde also attacked British imperialism in his review of J. A. Froude's historical novel of 1889, *The Two Chiefs of Dunboy*, as shameful and cruel: see Wilde's 'Mr. Froude's Blue Book' in *The Pall Mall Gazette*, Saturday 13 April 1889: 3.
3 See T. E. Brown's 'To the Editor of *The Scots Observer*' (undated) reprinted in Stuart Mason's *Oscar Wilde: Art and Morality*: 103–9 and 104. The review from *The Christian*

Leader, 3 July 1890, is reprinted in Mason: 138. Walter Pater's 'A Novel by Oscar Wilde', originally published in *The Bookman*, October 1891, is also reprinted in Mason: 189 and 191.

4 As Joseph McLaughlin has pointed out, *fin de siècle* urban fiction often projected London as 'an imaginative domain that calls forth heroic action' including 'exploring, conquering, enlightening, purifying, besting'. However Dorian seems increasingly content with co-existing with, rather than subduing, his urban others. See McLaughlin (2000) *Writing the Urban Jungle: Reading Empire in London from Doyle to Eliot*. Charlottesville and London, University of Virginia Press: 3.

5 London appears as the locus of Irish success and mobility in James Joyce's short story 'A Little Cloud' which appeared in his 1914 collection *Dubliners*, but the city's Gothic potential was famously exploited by Bram Stoker in his 1897 novel *Dracula*. Stoker's late-Victorian Gothic romance amplifies London's parallel identity: presented as being at once modern and anachronistic, the city becomes the site upon which anxieties over Irish colonial experience are enacted. These fears are also present in Sheridan Le Fanu's vampire story of 1872, 'Carmilla', in which such anxieties are displaced, at an even further remove, to a ruined rural Austro-Hungarian borderland. 'Carmilla' exercised a clear influence over Stoker's more urban tale of horror, in which nineteenth-century Irish political problems are transplanted directly into the British metropolis. For an account of Stoker's interest in Le Fanu's fiction, see Paul Murray (2005) *From the Shadow of Dracula: A Life of Bram Stoker*. London, Pimlico.

6 Christopher Craft has suggested that the processes of mirroring and reflecting, that are key elements of the novel's Gothic doubling, 'compound its estrangements' and 'alienate its alienations', since Dorian functions as a copy of the portrait as much as it reproduces his own image to spectators like Wotton and Hallward. As Craft argues, this intense process allows Wilde to 'map the saturated, irreal space that intervenes between a self-apprehending subject and the mimetic apparatus that returns the subject to himself'. Craft insists that this dialectic of doubling and alienation, or 'mirror-work', are so 'self-directed' as to be 'abyssal', functioning within an essentially interiorized process that leads to Dorian's adoption of the guise of 'objectal or phantasmal other'. However, I would suggest that, rather than driving Dorian towards a destructive cycle of withdrawal, his increasingly alienated consciousness draws him toward the alternative social and cultural sphere of the Other London, where he experiences freedoms and pleasures that cannot be encountered in the official landscape of the bourgeois metropolis. This underground sphere offers Dorian the freedom to realize his desires among the poor and marginalized and, in doing so, serves as another mirror, this time reflecting a more interesting reality that is, for him, far more alluring than the rather sterile environment he is accustomed to. See Craft (2005) 'Come See About Me: Enchantment of the Double in *The Picture of Dorian Gray*', *Representations*. 91: 109–36. Quotations are from pages 109 and 114–16.

7 See John G. Peters (1999) 'Style and Art in Wilde's *The Picture of Dorian Gray*: Form as Content', *Victorian Review*. 25 (1): 1–13. Quotations are from 6 and 8–10.

8 See Simon Joyce (2002) 'Sexual Politics and the Aesthetics of Crime: Oscar Wilde in the Nineties', *ELH*. 69: 510.

9 For discussions of contemporary degeneration theory and its assimilation of imperial and class anxieties in *fin de siècle* literature and culture, see Stephen Arata (1996) *Fictions of Loss in the Victorian Fin de Siècle: Identity and Empire*. Cambridge: Cambridge University Press; William Greenslade (1994) *Degeneration, Culture and the Novel 1880–1940*. Cambridge, Cambridge University Press; and Daniel Pick

(1989) *Faces of Degeneration: A European Disorder, c.1848-c.1918.* Cambridge, Cambridge University Press. Curtis Marez points out that, given the appropriation of imperial ideologies by hyphenated colonial communities like the Anglo-Irish, who also transmitted nationalist ideas among their colonizers, the notion of imperial unity was an abstract concept. Laura Otis has also pointed to the late nineteenth-century preoccupation with 'contagionism', that led to attempts within the British, American, German and French empires to limit the inherent and inevitable potential for cultural, sexual, biological and political exchange between occupiers and the occupied. See Marez (1997) 'The Other Addict: Reflections on Colonialism and Oscar Wilde's Opium Smoke Screen', *ELH.* 64 (1): 257–8. See also Otis (1999) *Membranes: Metaphors of Invasion in Nineteenth-Century Literature, Science and Politics.* Baltimore, The Johns Hopkins University Press.

10 As Jean-Paul Riquelme has suggested, the novel's Gothic preoccupation with the strangeness and subjective estrangement that are instilled by modern experience are reflected in the text's non-linear form, which anticipates the stylistic preoccupations of literary modernism. See Riquelme (2000) 'Oscar Wilde's Aesthetic Gothic: Walter Pater, Dark Enlightenment, and *The Picture of Dorian Gray*', *Modern Fiction Studies.* 46 (3): 609–31.

11 As Jerry White has noted, the city spread largely eastward at the end of the nineteenth century where, between 1881 and 1901, growth averaged at an unparalleled 185 per cent. See White (2008) *London in the Nineteenth Century: A Human Awful Wonder of God.* London: Vintage. See, in particular, Chapter 3, 'New Road: London Growing, 1800–1899'.

12 'Lecture to Art Students' delivered on 30 June 1883. See *Collected Works*: 315–16.

2

W. B. Yeats and the Ghost Club

Tara Stubbs

In an essay entitled 'Yeats and Byzantium', William Empson describes the poet's 'practical attitude to the supernatural' and suggests that we should adopt a similar attitude to reading those of Yeats's poems that appear to approach supernatural subjects (Empson, 1982: 73). But it is possible to take this argument further by suggesting that Yeats's 'practical' attitude extends beyond the 'supernatural' – that is, beyond regarding such subjects, as the *Oxford English Dictionary* defines them, as 'belong[ing] to a higher realm or system than that of nature; transcending the powers or the ordinary course of nature'. Reading through the records of the London-based Ghost Club, which Yeats attended between 1911 and 1932, there is a reliance instead on the adjective 'supranormal', an alternative rendering of 'supernormal' which, as the *OED* puts it, tends to be 'Applied to phenomena of an extraordinary or exceptional kind, involving a higher law or principle than those ordinarily occurring, but not necessarily supernatural'.

Frederic Myers, co-founder of the London Society for Psychical Research, coined the term 'supernormal' (as well as 'telepathy') in 1882. In an essay on automatic writing, Myers noted: 'By a supernormal phenomenon I mean not one which overrides natural laws, for I believe no such phenomenon to exist, but one which exhibits the actions of laws higher, in a psychical aspect, than are discerned in action in everyday life' (Myers, 1885: 30). By 'higher' Myers meant, 'apparently belonging to a more advanced stage of evolution' (Myers, 1885: 30). 'Supernormal', then, does not imply the same distinction between natural and higher realms that 'supernatural' connotes. For Yeats, the term 'supranormal' (or 'supernormal') could provide a means of aligning the phenomena of visions and psychic experiments to the actions of natural laws, as present in everyday life but only discerned by a few. Myers's argument, Yeats might also have perceived those who discerned the 'supranormal' – like the phenomena they could see – as 'belonging to a more advanced stage of evolution'.

This strength of the association between the everyday world and the supranormal/ supernormal, and between the visions themselves and those who perceived them is registered in the fact that members of the Ghost Club referred to themselves as 'Ghosts'. The Club was launched formally in 1862, dissolved in the 1870s, and then later revived, on All Saints' Day 1882, by A. A. Watts and the medium Rev. William

Stainton Moses – 'one of the most distinguished men in British spiritualist circles', as Margaret Mills Harper describes him (Harper, 2006: 239). Between 1882 and its formal dissolution in 1936, the Club had, thanks to its emphasis on exclusiveness and frequent attendance, a total of just 82 members. Each member, or 'Ghost', whether living or dead, was mentioned in a roll-call given at the meetings on All Souls' Day each year (2 November); meanwhile when members died, they were described as having 'passed on', their non-attendance at the Ghost Club attributed simply to 'losses by death'. This attitude towards the Club's deceased members might be explained by the two main doctrines of the spiritualist movement: 'the continuance of the human personality after death (whether through one or many incarnations) and the ability of human spirits to communicate from beyond the grave through sensitive individuals in this world' (Harper, 2006: 4).

There were approximately six meetings of the Ghost Club each year, mostly held at the Maison Jules restaurant, London. The Club itself disbanded on 2 November 1936, when, as the Minutes of the meeting record:

> it was passed unanimously that the Club be wound up and its archives offered to the British Museum (and if not accepted, the London Library, then the London Spiritualist Alliance, and the Society for Psychical Research). This offer was on the condition that the archives should not be opened up until 25 years after 2 November 1936. (Minutes, 2 November 1936)

The desire expressed here to keep the archives closed until November 1961 implies not only that the material is of a sensitive nature, but also that it might be mocked by others: of course many members of the Ghost Club were society figures leading 'normal' lives. Their advanced age would have meant that most, if not all, of them would have 'passed on' by 1961. At the same time, however, the naming of the Ghost Club Minute Books and related materials as 'archives', and the decision to offer these to research libraries, suggests that the members believed that their findings would eventually be of use to researchers. Interestingly, the preference for the archives to be offered first to the British Museum and then to the London Library – with the London Spiritualist Alliance, and the Society for Psychical Research being regarded as last resorts – tells us that the Ghost Club members were disinclined to think of the material as being for specialist purposes only, and that they preferred to see it as of value to a general reading public.

The story of Yeats's participation in the Ghost Club situates him within a circle of well-known London figures. These included the physicist and chemist Sir William Crookes (1832–1919) who was heavily involved with the Club for many years; the architect and illustrator Frederick Bligh Bond (1864–1945); and the naturalist Alfred Russell Wallace (1823–1913) who was in his declining years when Yeats joined the Club in 1911. From then until just after his marriage to George Hyde Lees in October 1917, Yeats was a frequent attender. After this date, he attended meetings sporadically until his final visit in 1932, that, as Margaret Mills Harper argues, was a 'rather late date' for Yeats to be 'talking about his experiences with occult phenomena', as 'communication with the spirit communicators of the Vision documents had dwindled to a mere trickle long before' (Harper, 2006: 240). Why, then, did Yeats feel the need to continue his membership of the Ghost Club even after his marriage – which gave him a ready amanuensis and assistant in spiritual matters – and after his interests in spiritual matters had 'dwindled'? By investigating the Ghost Club records archived at the British Library[1] we can see how Yeats's participation in the Club allowed him to try out his theories concerning the spiritual world before an indulgent audience, and enabled him to reaffirm some of the ideas he had expressed in his poetry and writings. Moreover, the records of the Ghost Club before his marriage – the event that, critics agree, impacted most on his spiritualist endeavours – help to clarify the extent of Yeats's involvement in spiritualist matters before the autumn of 1917.

1911–1917

From early on in his membership of the Club, Yeats appears to have used the meetings as a platform for discussing the interconnectedness of his spiritual and writing lives. For example, in June 1913, Yeats talks of his communications during a séance (held by the medium Etta Wriedt) with 'Leo the writer', probably referring to his famous spirit voice Leo Africanus, whom Mills Harper describes as a returning presence in Yeats's spiritual exercises up until the spring of 1917.[2] Then, in March 1916, Yeats describes how one of the characters of a play he has been writing while staying in Sussex has appeared to a local girl:

> Brother Yeats spoke of his having been lately in Sussex engaged in writing a play and one of the imaginary characters in this play appeared on several occasions to a girl living in the neighbourhood and, while she was dreaming. The dreams were recurred and of a terrifying kind.' (Minutes, 1 March 1916)[3]

Here the unemotional manner of reporting glosses over the fact that Yeats's observations denote a slippage between conscious and unconscious states, of waking and sleeping, within a limbo-like space. Yeats had questioned such states in an earlier address to the Ghost Club in 1911 when, describing his early forays into spiritualism, he had noted how, 'Like every other student of the subject, I have been bewildered by the continual deceits, by the strange dream-like manifestations, by the continual fraud' (Minutes, 7 June 1911). At the same time, however, the link implied in such visions between the imaginary characters of his play and 'real' people, and between Yeats's imagination and the visions of an ordinary country girl, might give his writings a spiritual resonance and lends his work prophetic power.

The attribution of psychic awareness to a country girl in Yeats's account is of course unsurprising given Yeats's Revivalist view of the important place of the peasant within Celtic spiritualism – as evidenced in his collections *Fairy and Folk Tales of the Irish Peasantry* (1888) and *The Celtic Twilight* (1893). In a well-known passage from his 1902 essay 'Away' Yeats had told stories of Irish country people, and their preoccupation with those 'men and women and children [who] are said to be "away"' – people who are constantly in the company of fairies and go about their daily lives as in a dream (Yeats, 1975: 267). Such views allowed for a synthesis between normal country people and supranormal visions. As G. K. Chesterton puts it, recounting a hypothesis Yeats once made:

> he used one argument which was sound, and I have never forgotten it. It is the fact that it is not abnormal men like artists, but normal men like peasants, who have borne witness a thousand times to such things; it is the farmers who see the fairies. (Chesterton, 2006: 147)

A common theme in the descriptions of Yeats's contributions to the Ghost Club meetings is his relation of stories of 'normal men' and women, often living in villages, and their 'supranormal' psychic experiences. In 1912, for example, he tells the story of a 'Miss Fox who lived in a little cottage in which she sometimes practised ceremonial magic' (Minutes, 9 October 1912); and during the meeting of 1 July 1914 he describes a possible 'miracle' occurring in a Scottish village:

> Bro. Yeats read an account of an investigation of an alleged miracle at [-Inverbeg?-] in which he was accompanied by Edward Feilding [sic] & Maud Gonne. It was alleged that an oleograph picture of the Sacred Heart in the possession of a village priest had dripped with blood. Bro. Yeats entered into the subject in great detail and a manuscript of his very interesting account will be added to the archives. (Minutes, 1 July 1914)

Unfortunately for Yeats, at the next meeting he is forced to concede that 'it had been ascertained that the red pigment in question was not blood of either human or canine origin' (Minutes, 7 October 1914): a case, perhaps, of the country people having the artists on?

Entries to the Ghost Club Minute Books during this period of Yeats's early (and frequent) attendances tell us as much about his gullibility as about the members' reactions to events in the outside world. For example, in an entry for 1 May 1912, Yeats describes how 'two clairvoyants quite independently had prophesied that he would be killed in a riot', but this is during a period when all those in attendance are feeling keenly their mortality (Minutes, 1 May 1912). Hence, after Yeats gives his prediction, the 'Ghosts' discuss the death of the journalist, critic and spiritualist W. T. Stead aboard the Titanic the previous month, and worry about whether the visit to England by the medium Mrs. Wriedt will be affected. Interestingly, the 'Ghosts' would read out a 'Christmas message' from Stead – sent, presumably, from beyond the grave – at the Ghost Club meeting of 8 January 1913. Throughout the period of the First World War, the 'Ghosts' devote much of their time to discussing prophecies surrounding battles, and trying to communicate with acquaintances who have been killed. At a meeting of 7 October 1914, for example, Yeats recounts – during a discussion of the war – a communication he has received from a medium:

> Bro. Yeats mentioned that from a medium he obtained on July 17 1914 a communication much in the following. Terms [:] "smoke – smoke everywhere – tramping men – high hope – a young face – thunder – oblivion" [.] Bro. Yeats submitted that this was unmistakably a battle picture. (Minutes, 7 October 1914)

Similarly, in a meeting of 1915, two 'Brothers' tell of attending two separate séances at which they heard from an unidentified man, Alfred Russell Wallace, and deduced that he must have 'passed over' while fighting in the war (Minutes, 5 May 1915). Then, at a meeting of 6 June 1917, Yeats makes perhaps his most audacious claim yet:

> Bro. Yeats spoke of War prophecies and statements received by automatic writing and mentioned one obtained by him in February last telling him to note that March 9 would be a day of some importance and indicating that it referred to activities in Asia Minor. That day was, in reality though not so publicly announced the day when the capture of Baghdad was effected. It was also the commencement of the charges in Petrograd. He also stated that he had received a psychic message that the war would end during the reign of Arcturius and Orion, that is between October next and the year end. (Minutes, 6 June 1917)

Of course, the second prediction is in essence correct – as the war did indeed end on 11 November 1918 – but the first date, predicting the 'capture of Baghdad', seems to be forcing a rather tenuous connection.

Aside from their ostensibly prophetic tone, Yeats's contributions to the Ghost Club during this period before his marriage seem to be based mainly on anecdote, as although he is attending séances and carrying out experiments, they are yielding little material. Nevertheless, he still has plenty of stories to draw upon. For example, at the meeting of 8 January 1913, Yeats takes some time recounting a tale of a clergyman and a vampire:

> Brother Yeats related an interesting experience of a clergyman who, on two occasions, in two places, saw a grotesque figure which he took to be a vampire. On the first occasion at an hotel in Paris he was alone, but struggled with the creature and drove it out of the window. On the second occasion – in another place – a friend was with him, and the two had a struggle to get rid of the creature. The hotel in Paris where the first experience took place was said to be haunted. The clergyman's companion refused to speak about the matter, which is to be regretted, as his evidence would be valuable to substantiate the story. (Minutes, 8 January 1913)

Unfortunately, many of Yeats's stories from this period end in the same way – with the inability to find evidence to 'substantiate' them. A similar situation arises in the subsequent meetings of the Club in February and April of 1913, during which Yeats tells of a story he has heard that:

> 'one of the "Titanic" victims – a lady – had since walked into the house of 2 lady friends in Wales and lived with them for a few days, wearing her sister's clothes and sleeping in the same bed as her sister, then departing as mysteriously as she had come'. This, he says, he has 'not yet been able to confirm'. (Minutes, 5 February 1913)

Yeats follows this up at the next meeting when he announces that he is 'still on the track of the victim of the "Titanic" disaster who appeared to the two friends in Wales, and he hoped to find out more about it' (Minutes, 2 April 1913). The episode is never mentioned again.

1917–1932

After his marriage to George Hyde Lees on 20 October 1917 – and the meeting of the Ghost Club that he attended on 2 November, at which he was congratulated on his wedding – Yeats attended meetings only a handful of times: on 3 December 1919, 7 January 1920, 4 May 1921, 6 October 1926 (the first 'Ladies' Night' for the Club), 1 May 1929, and 6 April 1932. And though earlier Club records indicate that Yeats had dabbled with automatic writing since around 1911, it is clear that his marriage sparked a renewed interest in the practice. Margaret Mills Harper has noted how the automatic writings that W. B. and George Yeats created at Stone Cottage in Ashdown Forest, Sussex during November 1917, signalled an 'amazingly productive first month of script' (Harper, 2006: 190). Meanwhile, in a recent essay, Clair Wills has observed that 'it was George's honeymoon discovery of her talent for automatic writing, beginning as a sly attempt to consolidate her marriage, which set Yeats on the path of his symbolic cosmology, *A Vision*, and fifteen years' joint work' (Wills, 2011: 3). In short, Yeats's marriage gave him a ready and willing amanuensis and, so, as the frequency of automatic-writing sessions increased, Yeats's visits to the Club decreased. Yet his sporadic attendance during this period suggests that he cannot quite relinquish the spiritual offerings of this London group. Moreover, the records indicate that Yeats was initially reluctant to discuss the actual circumstances of his spiritualist sessions with the Club – he rarely mentioned George, for example, nor does he describe in any detail their automatic-writing practice – implying that he was hesitant about clarifying the collaborative qualities of his project. Yeats would confess in his 'Introduction' to the 1937 edition of *A Vision* that 'On the afternoon of October 24th 1917, four days after my marriage, my wife surprised me by attempting automatic writing' (Yeats, 1962: 8), but he only acknowledges George's role once in a meeting, of 1 May 1929, when he describes how his messages over 'several years had been given through the hand or utterances when in Trance of his wife' (Minutes, 1 May 1929).

Nevertheless, what is revealed at these meetings provides important new approaches to the study of both Yeats's spiritualist practices and his writing. For instance, at the Ghost Club meeting of 4 May 1921, Yeats describes how he had been investigating different types of religion during a recent visit to the United States. The Minute Book for the meeting records that:

> Bro. Yates [*sic*] speaking of his recent experiences in the states [*sic*] said that mormonism was very similar to shintoism, & was really a system of ancestor worship, a highly organised spiritism. The mormons had temples for initiations with symbolic ceremonial, they practiced [*sic*] Baptism and marriage for the dead. They also practiced [*sic*] healing by occult means. (Minutes, 4 May 1921)

Roy Foster discusses in some detail Yeats's tour of the United States in January to May 1920, during which he gave lectures and readings in New York, Washington, Yale, Chicago, California and Oregon; addressed two Mormon universities in Utah; and by April was 'introducing the poets of the 1890s to Waco, Texas' (Foster, 2003: 163–6). Foster also notes that George, having stayed in New York for much of the trip, 'accompanied [him] to the west, where one of the last formal sessions of automatic writing took place in the improbable surroundings of a flowery bungalow hotel in Pasadena' (Foster, 2003: 169). Yeats's insight into the spiritualism of the Mormon faith, as related to members of the Ghost Club, combined with his continued automatic writing experiments during his tour, indicates that despite the gruelling nature of his travels he was keen to continue to develop his spiritual ideas, clearly seeing them as integral to his literary work. On another occasion, Yeats, having been 'abroad, and absent for some time from the Ghost Club', is described as having given 'an interesting account of Philosophical Expositions' (Minutes, 1 May 1929) – but Foster notes that Yeats 'lectured to the Ghost Club for an alleged three hours' during which 'discretion' about his spirit instructors 'was now, apparently, thrown to the wind' (Foster, 2003: 388). It is clear that with every meeting Yeats is growing in confidence; indeed his long speeches about 'Philosophical Expositions' seem far removed from his anecdotal contributions during his early years of membership.

Yeats's final attendance at the Club, in April 1932, included another long address, during which he 'referred to his intended publications of lessons in Philosophy he had received from a group of beings on the other side' (Minutes, 6 April 1932). The minutes of this meeting see the note-taker trying to keep up, as Yeats recounts the 'chief subjects' of these 'lessons':

> i. Life of the passed over. ii. History. iii. The order of human souls. iv. Cycles of incarnation. In order, presumably, that his subconscious predilections should not be aroused, his teachers imparted this knowledge to him in compartments, so much so, that he was unable, until the course was finished, to grasp thoroughly it's [*sic*] aim. He was encouraged to ask questions, provided they were exact, rapidly put, and strictly stipulations, indeed they could only be termed a very gruff lot. (Minutes, 6 April 1932)

Humorously, Yeats recounts the strange smells and visions that have accompanied his communications with his 'gruff' instructors: 'Throughout the period of instruction Bro. Yeats and his wife witnessed many phenomena, e.g. a strong scent of roses, and apparitions in mediaeval costume, at the time of their son's birth'; but this is echoed in Yeats's introduction to the 1937 version of *A Vision*, where he notes that during their spirit communications 'Sweet smells were the most constant phenomena' (Yeats, 1962: 15). Further references to *A Vision* can be perceived in the passage quoted above. In the introduction to *A Vision* Yeats confesses to his previous 'ignorance of philosophy' (Yeats, 1962: 19); here we are given concrete examples of the 'lessons in Philosophy' that Yeats has received from his spirit instructors. Likewise, the preoccupation with 'history' and the listing of four 'chief subjects' of the lessons find overlaps with *A Vision*'s reliance on 'the historical scheme' and its 'Four Faculties' and 'Four Principles' (Yeats, 1962: 18).

There are further parallels with *A Vision* at the end of the description of Yeats's contribution to the meeting, where the minute-taker notes:

> Bro. Yeats's conclusion, founded on the conception of the Universe as based on one thought, were that with this premise, it should be possible to forecast the

probability of certain events, the actual precipitation of these events being left to
the agency of human beings. These his teachers classified in 28 different types,
which he found he could easily distinguish among the people he met. (Minutes,
6 April 1932)

Interestingly, the '28 different types' of people (or characters) are actually present in
the 1925 version of *A Vision*, which pre-dates this meeting. Indeed, Yeats notes in his
introduction to the 1937 version that '[t]he first version of this book, *A Vision*, except
the section on the twenty-eight phases, and that called "Dove or Swan" which I repeat
without change, fills me with shame' (Yeats, 1962: 19). The 'Twenty-Eight Incarnations'
of *A Vision* – a 'classification of human types based primarily on the position of Will
on the Great Wheel' (Adams, 1995: 87) – are re-worked here in the '28 different types'.
But the clarity and coherence of Yeats's 'lessons' from his instructors – and their
parallels with both the later and earlier versions of *A Vision* – might be almost too
convenient: is it merely the case that Yeats is using his meetings with the Ghost Club
to promote his upcoming publication, and to give his work a spiritual credibility – as if
to counter any criticisms of his 'system'? Margaret Mills Harper asks a similar question
of the introduction to the 1937 version of *A Vision*. Pointing out that it 'is not without
its ambiguities', she notes that 'the story of the automatic script and other experiments
is told years after the fact, with the luxury of recollection and the concomitant blurring
of fact into the fabrications of memory' (Mills Harper, 2006: 86). In a similar way, it is
tempting to doubt the veracity of what Yeats tells the Ghost Club in April 1932, almost
three years after his last attendance – which was, in turn, some three years after his
previous visit – as we can neither place the dates of his involvement with the 'group of
beings from the other side' who have taught him 'lessons in philosophy', nor trace how
these lessons came about. It may be more accurate to see Yeats's reports to the Ghost
Club over this period as enhanced descriptions of séances and automatic-writing
sessions that took place over a long period of time; but we should also note that the
convenient parallels between Yeats's findings and the language of the ultimate texts
may undermine the authenticity of the findings themselves.

1919–1920: Foretelling 'the second coming'?

The very first of the meetings that Yeats attended after his marriage gives further clues
about the relationship between Yeats's spiritual practices, his stories of these practices,
and the texts that apparently emerge from them. According to Roy Foster, George and
W. B.'s first period of experimentation with automatic writing 'more or less came to an
end as a regular activity on 22 December [1919]' (Foster, 2003: 162); thus Yeats's absence
from the Ghost Club from November 1917 to December 1919 conveniently frames this
intense period of spiritual activity. Returning from his interlude of self-imposed exile
from the Club, Yeats launched into a summary of the theories he had been developing
with his wife during his absence – but made it seem that the information had been
gleaned from one source in one sitting, rather than over a protracted period. The note-
taker for the December 1919 meeting painstakingly recorded Yeats's address, crossing
out words and phrases in a bid to represent Yeats's views as faithfully as possible:

> Bro. Yeats said he had received information from a supranormal source that the whole world cloud and tribulation was but a prelude to a different state of civilization and the introduction to a philosophy of life a foundation of a new spiritual epoch. The important thing was not the present upheaval, but the reaction which would follow culminating in a kind of second coming of Christ not literal coming of a simple incarnate personality but rather of many individuals in many lands all illumined with the same spiritual influence[.] (Minutes, 3 December 1919)

This dense passage is illuminating in various ways. Whether or not we credit the circumstances in which Yeats claims he has received his information, the minute-taker's recording uses language that foreshadows the prophetic images of Yeats's 1920 poem 'The Second Coming'. Take for instance the circular motif of the 'world cloud and tribulation', that appears to apprehend Yeats's circular vision of chaos in the poem, where all is 'Turning and turning in the widening gyre', and 'Mere anarchy is loosed upon the world' (Yeats, 1990: 235). Moreover, the idea that this 'tribulation' is merely a 'prelude' to a 'different state of civilization' and the introduction to a philosophy of life' that heralds a 'new spiritual epoch' envisages the 'rough beast' of 'The Second Coming': one that 'Slouches towards Bethlehem to be born' – as a kind of awful Messianic figure for the twentieth century. Interestingly, Margaret Mills Harper notes that a dedication by W. B. Yeats on George Yeats's personal copy of the first edition of *A Vision* reads, 'in memory of all tribulations when we were making this book' (cited in Harper, 2006: 14). Again, there seems to be a specific lexicon running through the Ghost Club records, the texts themselves, and even the inscriptions Yeats has written on them.

The barely suppressed excitement of 'The Second Coming', which leaves the reader unsure whether or not the poet heralds the 'terrible beauty' of the slow-moving beast and the upheaval that will follow, finds an intriguing prediction in the details that are crossed out from the passage above. The 'different state of civilization' that the 'supranormal source' has predicted is originally described as 'higher' rather than merely 'different'; likewise its incompatibility 'with present social conditions' has been hinted at and subsequently erased. As yet, though, we are not given an image of one Messianic figure heralding Yeats's envisaged 'second coming', but rather of several: 'many individuals in many lands' are predicted to arrive, 'all illumined with the same spiritual influence' (Minutes, 3 December 1919). The crossings-out here most likely illustrate a combination of care on the part of the note-taker and uncertainty on the part of Yeats, as both try to outline a prophecy that is as yet something of a hypothesis – predicting a 'kind of second coming of Christ', the vagueness of which is arguably far from the prophetic certainty of the final poem. Within Yeats's occult beliefs, Margaret Mills Harper contends, 'a wild card of supersensual otherness remains'. Expanding on her theme, Harper adds:

> The shivering traces of another, unrepresentable world in poems like 'The Cold Heaven', 'The Second Coming', and 'Byzantium' are examples of a less readily assimilable universe. W. B. Y[eats]'s universes are neither solipsistic nor closed: they end in a face, of ghost, rough beast, or image-begetting images, but it is not our face. (Harper, 2006: 45)

Yet in consulting the Ghost Club Minute Books for December 1919, the description of the meeting between Yeats and his 'supranormal source' complicates Harper's view of the 'unrepresentable' within 'The Second Coming' in particular. Thus the 'rough beast', the image upon which the poem ends, is redefined not as a part of a vision that has little to do with our own world, but as something in itself 'supranormal': simultaneously part of our everyday world and beyond it, 'belonging to a more advanced stage of evolution'.

The confusion that Yeats's comments at the December 1919 meeting had caused, evidenced most obviously by the corrected account of Yeats's descriptions in the Minute Book, led Yeats's Ghost 'brothers' to make further enquiries at the subsequent Ghost Club meeting in January 1920. In response, Yeats took to the floor:

> Bro. Yeats [,] asked to further define his communication at the last meeting [,] said that it was impossible to express in a few simple words so vast a subject. Taking for comparison Mendel, who has reduced Heredity to a series of mathematical developments, Bro. Yeats described his theory as reducing the Philosophy of Human thought to a similar science, a natural development or law of growth of the human mind – so accurate that one could venture to a prophecy. That the whole matter as revealed to the speaker was based on certain Geometric forms, and when once the system is grasped is capable of mathematical demonstration. The expected revelation will but be identical with that already given by Christ but will represent that portion of truth he was unable to express. (Minutes, 7 January 1920)

This answer is similar in tone to the prophetic, somewhat self-important Yeats of *A Vision*. Yeats sets himself up as a kind of spiritual guide who is carrying out the work that 'Christ' could not, and who will tap into a revelation so profound that it will 'represent that portion of truth he [Christ] was unable to express'. Indeed, Yeats's speech almost appears to be a plug for the spheres, gyres and moon phases of *A Vision* – particularly in terms of the emphasis he places on 'certain Geometric forms' and his implication that once others have grasped his system it will be 'capable of mathematical demonstration'. Meanwhile, the notion of a 'revelation' predicts once again the prophetic tone of 'The Second Coming' – 'Surely some revelation is at hand' (Yeats, 1990: 235) – thus hinting at further affinities between Yeats's apparently tentative spiritual experiments and his ultimate literary works.

Of course, what is unclear here is how truthfully Yeats is explaining the actual information he received at the original spirit meeting with his 'supranormal source'. Is he clarifying his ideas, or expanding upon new ideas in order to further impress, and baffle, his audience (a collection, let's not forget, of esteemed spiritualists, scientists and public figures)? Or do his descriptions reflect instead a poet struggling to put into words the 'supranormal' images he has gleaned from his spirit sources, via his scriptor wife? Miguel Tamen provides a convenient argument to settle such debates: 'It seems … that the control of a vision implies the notion that in a certain sense we already possess, at least partially, its ultimate meaning, a foreknowledge of its ultimate consequences' (Tamen, 1998: 297). Perhaps, then, Yeats is simply reading in his spirit visions an answer to the 'ultimate meaning' he has already been searching for in his work. Or perhaps, more cynically, Yeats has embellished the first spirit meeting in order to play to an eager audience who might listen to his theories and commend his spiritual wisdom.

The exhausting and ambiguous relationship between 'supranormal source', the receipt of the information from that source, the recording of that information through George Yeats (his near-constant scriptor from the end of 1917 onwards), Yeats's report of that information to the Ghost Club, the minute-taker's record of that information, and the ultimate poem, is made even more complicated once we address the question of timing. Richard Ellmann reports that George Yeats told him that 'The Second Coming' was written in January 1919 (Ellmann, 1954: 257). However, it did not appear in print until it was published in *The Dial* and *The Nation* in November 1920: and it was subsequently published in *Michael Robartes and the Dancer* by the Cuala Press in 1921. Margaret Mills Harper, meanwhile, argues that the 'few weeks' that predated an automatic writing session of 12 May 1918 'may have seen the composition of such poems as "The Second Coming"' (Harper, 2006: 297). In his introduction to Yeats's *Vision Papers*, George Mills Harper puts the date for composition as possibly in the days after 9 May 1918, as part of a set of 'poems on system' – including 'The Second Coming', 'The Phases of the Moon', and 'The Double Vision of Michael Robartes' (Harper, 1992, Vol. 1: 21). Meanwhile in *The Making of Yeats's 'A Vision'*, Harper quotes an unpublished letter from Yeats to his friend and sometime collaborator Ezra Pound, dated 1 July 1918, in which Yeats claims to have finished the poem (Harper, 1987, Vol. II: 19). Yet the passage from the Ghost Club Minute Book that appears to predict 'the second coming' dates from December 1919: in other words, before the publication of the poem itself, but after the dates that George Yeats and Mills Harpers suggest for its composition. Bearing in mind this information, it would be too simple to dismiss Yeats's report to the Ghost Club in December 1919 as a self-promoting plug for his upcoming poem, and to suggest that Yeats is engaged in the same 'continual fraud' that he had found as a student of spiritualism in 1911. Yet the Ghost Club meeting of 3 December 1919 was the first Yeats had attended since 2 November 1917. Moreover, as we have seen from the Minutes themselves, Yeats's expositions of his theories in December 1919 were still somewhat tentative – at least in terms of the exact description of the 'kind of second coming' that he envisaged. In addition, the more certain, confident descriptions that Yeats gave at the January 1920 meeting might also imply that his theories had continued to be developed during the month between meetings.

Thomas Parkinson and Anne Brannan have noted the importance of Yeats's marriage to our understanding of his revision process. They argue that while 'the poems written before his marriage on 20 October 1917 – "Easter, 1916", for instance – make their appearance in publishable shape and show few revisions', the 'drafts of poems written from late 1917 through 1919 are carefully preserved in relative fullness, often containing very early and sometimes illegible notations' (Parkinson and Brannen, 1994: xix). For this preservation they credit George Yeats, who even rescued torn drafts after Yeats had discarded them. The (undated) drafts for 'The Second Coming' tell us that the words of the title itself – which appeared in Yeats's report to the Ghost Club as 'a kind of second coming of Christ' – do not appear in the poem's manuscripts until the fifth draft. Instead we have in drafts two and four an image of a 'second birth', while the title 'The Second Coming' does not appear until the seventh draft (Parkinson and Brannen, 1994: 147–61). Might it be the case, then, that as late as December 1919 – the date that Yeats attended the Ghost Club meeting and discussed his theories of the 'second coming' – he was still revising his ideas, alongside the drafts for his poem? Might it also be the case that the earlier dates that critics give for the poem's conception – ranging from May 1918 to January 1919 – refer to earlier drafts of the poem, which were still being reworked when Yeats attended the Club in December 1919: some 11 months before 'The Second Coming' was first published in *The Dial* and *The Nation*? Further, might it be possible that the phrase 'the second coming' – which is implicit but never explicit in the automatic-writing scripts for the period November 1917 to December 1919[4] – was only concretized through Yeats's discussions with fellow members of the Ghost Club? Whether the December 1919 meeting marked the first expression of the phrase 'the second coming' in relation to Yeats's spiritualist theories is, then, difficult to establish. Nevertheless, what the Ghost Club minutes do reveal is that this meeting signalled a moment, some months before the poem would actually be published, when Yeats outlined, in the most public way yet, the revelatory theories that had informed, or would inform, his composition of the poem. Previous to this, Yeats had apparently discussed his poem with his wife and Ezra Pound; but by December 1919, he felt able to divulge and expand upon his theories to this esoteric London society and, in turn, have them written down and recorded in the Ghost Club Minute Books.

Conclusion: 'Ridicule or true belief'?

With all of Yeats's forays into séances, automatic writing, and spiritualist practices, the question of their credibility does need to be raised. Mills Harper notes, with regard to W. B. and George Yeats's experiments:

> Inexplicably, sometimes the pen moves. This is the moment of mystery, the moment that, in retrospect as well as on the immediate occasion, may provoke either ridicule or true belief. It has done both as the tale of the automatic writing has been told and retold in Yeats studies. (Harper, 2006: 4–5)

As Harper asks later of Yeats's findings, 'Should they be granted any status besides that of fiction, self-delusion, or fraud?' (Harper, 2006: 18). Yet to reduce Yeats's involvements with spiritualism to 'cheap, brainless fakirism' – as the American poet Marianne Moore did[5] – is to miss the point. For beyond giving us opportunities for retrospective mockery, the evidence provided by resources such as the Ghost Club Archives reveals intriguing connections between Yeats's spiritual investigations and his poetic method.

Notes

1 After the dissolution of the Ghost Club, its records were deposited in the British Library. They can be accessed via the Manuscripts Department (Add. 52258–52273).

2 See Minutes of the Ghost Club, 4 June 1913, *Ghost Club Minute Book, 1910–1917,* Ghost Club Archives, Vol. VII. British Library Add. 52264. See also Harper, M. M. (2006: 317).

3 Yeats is probably referring to a Noh-style play, as he was writing these while staying with Ezra Pound in Stone Cottage, Sussex during the winters of 1913–16. James Longenbach describes this period in detail in his book *Stone Cottage: Pound, Yeats and Modernism* (1991).

4 For example, George Mills Harper traces some of the genesis of the poem to an automatic writing session of 9 April 1918, thanks to questions about spirals and circles (Harper, G. M., 1992, Vol. 1: 544–5), rather than to an explicit mention of a 'second coming' or a 'revelation'.

5 Marianne Moore to [her brother] John Warner Moore, 10 October 1915: 'To my disgust I learn that Yeats has interested himself in spiritualism and is busying himself about that to the exclusion of everything else. … [We] deplored the fact that such a cheap brainless fakirism should have secured a toehold on him' (Moore, 1998: 101).

3

'On the Pavements Grey': The Suburban Paradises of W. B. Yeats and William Morris

Adrian Paterson

The landscape of W. B. Yeats's poetry is familiar: Ben Bulben, Coole Park, Thoor Ballylee. The poet summons these landmarks with authority enough to make them obey his call, and out of the holy land of Ireland they are recruited to his own personally consecrated phantasmagoria. The apparition of 'The Lake Isle of Innisfree' marks the first of these summonses; somehow, from 'on the pavements grey', Yeats conjures an island pastoral idyll. This summons is the more remarkable because issued from city streets. As by all accounts the city in question is London, this does seem to make it, as Yeats himself considered it, a London poem. Yet the story of the poem's provenance is woven more intricately than this. In *A Transnational Poetics*, Jahan Ramazani argues that in a world of migrant modernist poets we are not to presume 'the citizenship of a poem' (Ramazani, 2009: 25). He is right I think to be circumspect, but the choice of the phrase 'citizenship' is intriguing. Deployed, perhaps, to blunt the thorny burrs of that word 'nationality', citizenship tacitly assumes a poem's adoption by a city. This does have a ring of truth: as literary objects, modern poems were – at least until the advent of the web – most often presented to their readership in a material form (by being printed in a book or a periodical) that emerged out of such centres of production: London, say, or Chicago or Paris. Poetic citizenship will be endlessly disputed; hence, all the more reason to try to determine and distinguish the mechanisms by which poems find their way into the world, especially if the poems in question act so self-consciously about these origins. Better then to look around and to examine the ground of the city, and not imagine that its terrain is even and unvaried. This chapter, as a consequence, takes as its axiom that not only the author and the text, but the material conditions of a text's production, are themselves profoundly affected by precise geography.

What follows is a tale of two poems and one city. If the poems in question have vastly different lengths and ambitions, they nevertheless share both metropolitan origins and distinctly anti-metropolitan orientations. Both, it seems, come from London and yet both appear to want to vacate the place. The two poems play a role in a larger narrative: the first as part of a much longer poetic sequence poem, and the second as a lyrical spin-off from a short poetic novel. On examining their specific incarnations, however, these poems start to pull in different directions, and finally dissent as to their place, even their mode, of belonging in the world. What stands out is that their one city, London, is anything but a homogenous entity; it is simultaneously medieval, nineteenth-century, and of the future. It is overlain by urban, suburban and pastoral topographies by turns, and all this not least because the city is being constantly refounded in the lines themselves. We cannot understand the poems without understanding something of the city, and except for a jarring hyperbole it is tempting to say that the reverse is also true.

Earth

William Morris's *The Earthly Paradise* was envisaged as a bibliographical event as much as a poem. To encompass his Chaucerian narrative poem-sequence, Morris planned a sumptuous edition, the design and typography of which were to take the history of the book to a new plane. The project was conceived in the heart of London to where Morris had reluctantly moved, (because of illness) from the Red House to live over the premises of Morris and Co.: 'in dismal Queen Square in black old filthy London' as Edward Burne-Jones put it (Burne-Jones, 1904, 2: 23). In the event, the design exceeded its bounds: although Burne-Jones completed over 70 illustrations for the book, the print and paper technologies of the 1860s were insufficiently attuned to Morris's visionary ideas, and the ever-lengthening poem was eventually published in several sober volumes between 1868 and 1870 by F. S. Ellis of Covent Garden. All that remained of a grander scheme was a frontispiece woodcut of three musicians, designed by Burne-Jones. Morris had to wait 30 years before something like the beautiful book he conceived in reaction to the grime of the city became a reality. But it is obvious that its city-born status had from the very beginning defined both the concept and the scope of the project.

In November 1888 Morris attended a lecture at the New Gallery on Regent Street, given by the printer Emery Walker for Walter Crane's Arts and Crafts Exhibition Society. Walker, who had been persuaded to speak by the artist and bookbinder T. J. Cobden-Sanderson, expounded the virtues and possibilities of book design and the hand-press, projecting magic-lantern slides of his collection of fifteenth-century typefaces. This was a moment of inspiration for Morris who, in November 1889, wrote to Andreas Scheu: 'I really think that something might be done with my books, more than has been done' (Morris, 1984–96, 3: 129). Morris's earliest works had been printed through Bell and Daldy at the Chiswick Press, and it is generally agreed that his moves to print the prose romances *The House of the Wolfings* and *The Roots of the Mountains* there from 1889 – with Walker's help in design and choosing his own paper, ink and typeface – marked his serious re-entry into thinking about book design, and made possible the subsequent 'typographical adventure' of the Kelmscott Press (Morris, 1984–96, 3: 249). Geographically speaking, there was not far to shift. Chiswick Press operated just up the river, while Emery Walker lived in Hammersmith Terrace, a few hundred yards upstream from Morris's house on Upper Mall, within sight of his despised Hammersmith Bridge. With Walker's advice and constant presence Morris spent most of 1890 preparing the ground, and by January 1891 he was ready to begin, producing from his house the first production of the Kelmscott Press: an edition of his tale *The Glittering Plain*. Further sumptuous editions of his own and others' work followed; memorable highlights being editions of Chaucer and Rossetti. The press finally closed its doors in 1898.

So it was in 1896 that an edition representing something like Morris's original wishes for *The Earthly Paradise* was finally carried out from next the Thames at Hammersmith. The colophon for the first volume proclaimed his central role: 'Printed by William Morris at the Kelmscott Press | and finished on the 7th day of May 1896' (Morris, 1896–7, 1: 203). The fifth volume admitted a sad change. Morris having died in October 1896, subsequent volumes were 'Printed by the Trustees of the late William Morris' (Morris 1896–7, 5: 247), the eighth and last acknowledging the central importance of place: 'at the Kelmscott Press, Upper Mall, | Hammersmith, in | the county of Middlesex' (Morris 1896–7, 8: 259). Despite Morris's later absence from the scene, it is rare for an author to exert so much control over the material circumstances of a text's publication. Not only did Morris supervise the printing of the volumes on an Albion hand-press, but he also designed the typeface and the borders and elaborate capitals. An extract from 'The Prologue' illustrates some of the verses' sentiments:

Forget six counties overhung with smoke,
Forget the snorting steam and piston stroke,
Forget the spreading of the hideous town;
Think rather of the pack-horse on the down,
And dream of London, small, and white, and clean,
The clear Thames bordered by its gardens green;
Think, that below bridge the lapping waves
Smite some few keels that bear Levantine staves
Cut from the yew wood on the burnt-up hill,
And pointed jars that Greek hands toiled to fill,
And treasured scanty spice from some far sea,
Florence gold cloth, and Ypres napery,
And cloth of Bruges, and hogsheads of Guienne.

(Morris, 1896–7, 1: 11)

The poem proceeds to relate the discovery by weary mariners of a western land in which imagination is set dreaming. There hoary tales of west and east, newly retold, are exchanged, forming the substance of the poetic sequence. No wonder, then, that the overall disposition of the poem suggests an abiding longing to be somewhere else, so that while the poem's London birth-pangs are manifest in these opening lines, we are urged to 'forget' the blighting 'smoke' of coal and industry, indicative of the nineteenth-century city's 'spreading' urban landscape. Instead, Morris conjures a vision of pre-industrial London with those clipped neat adjectives 'small, and white, and clean', the 'cl' crisply picked up in the 'clear' Thames bordered – note the word – by gardens green. For in this particular printed incarnation, just so is the (admittedly busy) white space housing the words bordered, even overgrown by the 'spreading' profusion of leaves and vines, a symbolic greenery that starts almost to overwhelm the text. Such devices spread and dominate alarmingly. The box title and author-line are entwined with flowers and organic tracery; the capital 'F' is ornamented, even obscured by growths that seem to emerge out of the borders. Even gaps in the text are filled in with brief organic designs, and at the end of each line dotted by a dark leaf motif. Forget the spreading of the town: this is the revenge of the countryside. Nor is this fanciful when we remember that not long before the appearance of *The Earthly Paradise*, Morris's *News from Nowhere* (1891) described a remarkably similar scene. Waking in Hammersmith, close by the Thames, John Guest emerges to an elegant, uncivilized London, with gardens blanketing much of the suburbs and city centre, and forests stretching from Hyde Park to Epping Forest. 'The leading passion of my life', Morris would assert, 'has been and is hatred of modern civilization' (Morris, 1910–15, 23: 280). Taken together, *News from Nowhere* and *The Earthly Paradise* overturn civility by constituting a gloriously overgrown garden city.

There is no question that printer and designer are self-consciously using biblio-graphic codes to play with the author's words; especially when we consider all three are one-and-the-same man. Morris evidently cared deeply about the visual appearance of his books: Harry Buxton Forman reports that for Morris's *The Roots of the Mountains* 'the verses on the title page were written just to fill up the great white lower half' (Forman, 1897: 140). Jerome McGann argues that the foregrounding of textuality in cases like this makes the book-text not a means, but an end in itself, and such stylized printed profusion is certainly 'thick with its own materialities' (McGann, 1993: 74). It also makes the poem rather hard to read: so closely printed is the text that its legibility is more-often-than-not opaque. Persistent capitals hardly render the words smoothly to the eye, especially swathed in tendrils as they are. The poem moves in rhyming couplets, although a reader might be forgiven for not noticing as such regular organization is disrupted by the visual rhythms set up by line-breaks and the inserted leaves. It is by such gestures, McGann suggests, that time-measured poetic language is pressured to become 'predominantly spatial and iconic' (McGann, 1993: 74), the book a thing in itself. Yet we should not make the mistake of thinking this is an immanent, inward-looking esoteric phenomenon. The close integration of text and book design produces a beautiful but robust object, and this fact, even the space it occupies, produces meaning. The political value attached to such making, with design, printing and bookbinding finished by hand, must always be considered. Setting itself against mass-produced Victorian values, the book embodies an opposition to the mechaniza-tion of the printing process: the reader is given the book to be handled and admired, and is therefore brought into physical contact with its makers. By drawing attention to the integrated nature of its production, such a book tries to assert its commonality, its creation by a community of craft.

Such craft is meant, of course, to recall late medieval manuscripts or early printed books that were themselves manuscript imitations. The crowded dexterity of the whole page exerts this pressure. Slowing down the eye thus brings to mind earlier reading practices. Ironically, minimizing white space and concentrating on visual blocks of text recalls a time before silent reading, when manuscripts were sounded aloud by their readership. In bringing to mind a pre-modern era, the poem's vision of early London is also brought into focus. To be sure, it is idealized, but not naively so. This is no pastoral paradise: London is instead presented as a busy mercantile centre, with luxury goods arriving, via the Thames, from around the world. And amidst it all, the reader observes Chaucer writing in his role as controller of customs in the port of London:

> While nigh the thronged wharf Geoffrey Chaucer's pen
> Moves over bills of lading – mid such times
> Shall dwell the hollow puppets of my rhymes.

(Morris, 1896–7: 12)

These lines, cunningly printed over the turn of the page in the more modest lowercase font that continues the poem, connect Chaucer's penmanship with the cosmopolitan centre of a sophisticated manuscript culture. The imported wealth of 'Levantine staves', 'cloth of Bruges' and 'pointed jars that Greek hands toiled to fill' may or may not be commonweal like the language and story-materials Chaucer also imported, but all of it required the connections of the city, and its main river artery. That everything arrives on 'green lapping waves' starts to generate an implicit rhyme with the avowed Thameside production of the book itself. And this book was conceivable, as it happened, only on the Thames at Hammersmith. Only there, within a space of a few hundred yards, could Morris find the nexus of relationships, skills, and materials which made rejuvenating and promoting such book craft possible: Emery Walker to print, Cobden-Sanderson to bind, and all the handcraft helpers of Morris's household to assist the author with his labours. Perhaps this is why the book's elaborate greenery protests so much. It was not produced in the countryside, and without quite wanting to admit it, the existence of its elaborate bibliographic codes urge as much the suburbs' revenge on the *urbs*. At the very least it marked in print the displacement of London's central publishing hub by its hands-on periphery.

Water

Shortly after Emery Walker's lecture on book craft, in December 1888, W. B. Yeats wrote from London to his friend Katharine Tynan in Dublin about a new poem (what follows preserves Yeats's punctuation and orthography):

> Hear are two verses I made the other day. There is a beautiful Island of Innis free in Lough Gill Sligo. A little rocky Island with a legended past. In my story I make one of the charecters when ever he is in trouble long to go away and live alone on that Island – an old day dream of my own. Thinking over his feelings I made these verses out of them –
>
> I will arise and go now and go to the island of Innis free
> And live in a dwelling of wattles – of woven wattles and wood work made
> Nine been rows will I have there, a yellow hive for the honey bee
> And this old care shall fade.

There from the dawn above me peace will come down dropping slow
Dropping from the veils of the morning to where the household cricket sings.
And noontide there be all a glimmer, midnight be a purple glow,
And evening full of the linnets wings.

(Yeats, 1986: 121)

Although written from London, for the moment there is precious little trace of the city in these lines. The poem presents Yeats's own celebration of a western earthly paradise, but unlike Morris's vision it seems to need no contrasting scene, no mariners to set sail and no elaborate frame tales. In what is an astonishing act of the imagination the poet just arises and goes, and readers (including Tynan herself) have ever since been carried along. Yet the poem is not brought forth *ab ovo*; likewise its earthly paradise is not a vision of nature untouched. This far west of Eden, man's relationship to the natural world is experienced through work: indeed, Thoreau's notion of 'earn[ing] my living by the labour of my hands only' (Thoreau, 1980: 17) manifestly takes a hand in the deftly spaced 'nine bean rows' and the 'yellow' 'hive for the honey bee'. Here, nature and cultivation join hands. For this, too, is a poem celebrating handcraft. The dwelling of 'woven wattles and woodwork made' is a structure in which natural materials are shaped by carpentry and weaving, and it is perhaps through such continuing careful labour that 'old care shall fade'. Just the same craft applies to the poem. Describing its genesis Yeats uses the same word as for the dwelling: 'Here are two verses I made' (not wrote, not sang). Not that the poem is finished; a good deal of rewriting is to come. But for the moment, this earthly paradise is handmade; full of growth, yes, and natural plenty, but of a nature tended by hand. Even as nature's compensation arrives in the second stanza, there is just a suggestion of the textile worker's delicate touch in its veils, glimmer, and purple glow, that taken altogether create a fine visual picture. Readers are being invited to Yeats's ideal home exhibition, which perhaps explains the 'household' cricket. Unquestionably the exhibition is tended by a householder who cares very much about the look of things. For the moment therefore the imagery is, in the main, rendered visually.

If this reminds us a little of the ideals of Morris's household, we should not be altogether surprised. The embodiment of Morris's craft-vision for *The Earthly Paradise* would arrive in the Kelmscott Hammersmith edition of his poem. Yeats's poem arrived in Dublin sent from not far away; delivered to Tynan from London, yes, but as the address revealed from '3 Blenheim Road |Bedford Park | Chiswick' (Yeats, 1986: 120). As Yeats recalled in the autobiographical 'Four Years', his whole family had returned to this district west of central London from Dublin in the late 1880s. Planned as a community village of applied arts and crafts, the garden suburb, including the Yeatses' red brick house and garden, represented as W. B. put it 'the Pre-Raphaelite movement at last affecting life'. If the romance had faded from Yeats's earlier experiences as a schoolboy 'play[ing] among the unfinished houses', some ideals remained: the community theatre survived, as did the over-elaborate red-brick church, and The Tabard, a public house that tried forlornly to remember Chaucer's London. For the Yeatses second time round, Bedford Park's faded optimism had certain compensations: 'it had some village characters and helped us to feel not wholly lost in the metropolis' (Yeats, 1999, 113).

It was here, in an atmosphere of wilting but still visible ideals, that 'The Lake Isle of Innisfree' was conceived. As Yeats's sister Lily remembered:

> In Bedford Park one evening, Helen Acosta and Lolly painting and I there sewing – Willy bursting in having just written, or not even written down but just having brought forth 'Innisfree', he repeated it with all the fire of creation and his youth – he was I suppose about 24. (Foster, 1997: 79)

In this telling, the poem represents the contribution of the eldest son to a household of Yeatsian crafts, most of them inspired and influenced by the Morrises. It was but a short walk southwards to Morris's Hammersmith residence at Kelmscott House, where Yeats was by now a regular visitor. The whole family took French lessons there, and it was there that Lily Yeats had just become an embroiderer for May Morris, working and dining there 'every day': hence her evening sewing (Yeats 1986, 111). The 'Helen Acosta' of Lily's account also worked for the Morrises with Yeats's other sister Lolly, who before long became a pioneering author of books on illustrative brushwork. And although Yeats was 'a little disappointed' in the house itself, seeing it as a collection of beautiful things rather than a unity, he nevertheless made Morris 'my chief of men' (Yeats, 1999: 131). His intellectual life at the time of writing the poem was, therefore, thoroughly interwoven with the crafts and activities of Morris's household. Morris's own 'intellect', he realized, was 'wholly at the service of hand and eye', and the fact that Yeats wanted to follow him perhaps explains the hand-and-eye emphasis of his poem's early draft (Yeats, 1999: 132). Joining the Sunday evening debates of the Socialist League at Kelmscott, Yeats became part of a small group regularly invited to supper afterwards where he 'very constantly' met Morris's frequent guests: the very same arts-and-crafts pioneers already mentioned – Walter Crane, Emery Walker, and Cobden-Sanderson (Yeats, 1999: 131). It is tempting to speculate on their conversation, and natural perhaps to conclude that Yeats was observing at first hand the discussions on book design that informed Walker's pioneering lecture and led to the founding of the Kelmscott Press. According to Yeats's later categorization of personalities, Morris had little self-knowledge: his particular achievement was rather that 'He imagined instead new conditions of making and doing' (Yeats, 1999: 133). In its own way this is what 'The Lake Isle of Innisfree' tries to achieve. Of the importance of his friendship with Morris, Yeats concluded: 'Though I remember little [of his exact talk], I do not doubt that, had I continued going there on Sunday evenings, I should have caught fire from his words and turned my hand to some medieval work or other (Yeats, 1999: 135). We should probably be thankful that he did not, but at the same time it is possible to divine in 'The Lake Isle of Innisfree' a handworked tribute to Morris and his attempts to create his own earthly paradise. This is not all that Yeats's poem represents, of course; and just as Yeats departed Morris's table we shall have to account for the poem's departure from Morris's hand-and-eye ideals. But, at the same time, there exists sufficient evidence to suggest that Yeats's verses were born out of Morris's London.

Evidently this homely poem did not arrive while the poet was at home. According to Lily Yeats, William had burst in from outside, arriving on foot from one of his tours of the neighbourhood. Exactly where he walked that day we do not know, but he left some helpful indications. His original letter to Tynan had consciously situated 'The Lake Isle of Innisfree' as part of a larger narrative. In this it is not unlike the 'Prologue' to Morris's *The Earthly Paradise*. Except that, unusually for such a consummate versifier, the 'story' to which Yeats refers is a novel, *John Sherman*, which on his father's advice he had been writing throughout 1888. Only Yeats's second book, it was eventually published in 1891 by T. Fisher Unwin under the pseudonym 'Ganconagh', attracting only modest success. The plot concerns the move of the eponymous John Sherman to London from 'Ballah' in the west of Ireland – manifestly a version of Yeats's ancestral Sligo. He lives with his family very near to where the Yeatses themselves lived; in fact rather nearer the river, in St. Peter's Square, Hammersmith. He also shares some of the poet's own habits, such as being drawn by long London walks (undertaken in large part to save money on transport). In the novel's most successful passage of self-dramatization, Yeats portrays Sherman as a man condemned like a ghost to wander a city imprinted with memories of home. It is apparent, however, that particular glimpses and sounds of the city provoke these connecting thoughts. The following passage presents many examples, but one moment, in particular, stands out:

> Ballah was being constantly suggested to him. The grey corner of a cloud slanting its rain upon Cheapside called to mind by some remote suggestion the clouds rushing and falling in cloven surf on the seaward steep of a mountain north of Ballah. A certain street corner made him remember an angle of the Ballah fish market. At night a lantern, marking where the road was fenced off for mending, made him think of a tinker's cart, with its swing-can of burning coals that used to stop on market days at the corner of Peter's Lane at Ballah. Delayed by a crush in the Strand, he heard a faint trickling of water near by; it came from a shop window where a little water-jet balanced a wooden ball upon its point. The sound suggested a cataract with a long Gaelic name, that leaped crying into the gate of the winds at Ballah. Wandering among these memories a footstep went to and fro continually, and the figure of Mary Carton moved among them like a phantom. He was set dreaming a whole day by walking down one Sunday morning to the borders of the Thames a few hundred yards from his house – and looking at the osier-covered Chiswick eyot. It made him remember an old day-dream of his. The source of the river that passed his garden at home was a certain wood-bordered and islanded lake, whither in childhood he had often gone blackberry-gathering. At the further end was a little islet called Inniscrewin. Its rocky centre, covered with many bushes, rose some forty feet above the lake. Often when life and its difficulties had seemed to him like the lessons of some elder boy given to a younger by mistake, it had seemed good to dream of going away to that islet and building a wooden hut there and burning a few years out, rowing to and fro, fishing, or lying on the island slopes by day, and listening at night to the ripple of the water and the quivering of the bushes – full always of unknown creatures – and going out at morning to see the island's edge marked by the feet of birds. (Yeats, 1891: 91–3)

The disguise of 'Inniscrewin' would be replaced by 'Innisfree' in subsequent editions of the novel that also admitted Yeats's authorship. But these thin veneers of anonymity, and indeed the many stories its author later told about the poem, cannot quite obscure the central role that Chiswick Eyot plays in provoking the thoughts that led up to the poem. It was, after all, Sherman's local walk down to the Thames and his view of the Eyot that 'made him remember an old day-dream of his'. And at least since J. H. Pollock's suggestion, made in 1935, that it was indeed this island in the Thames that summoned up Yeats's dream island of the Irish West, the subsequent passage has understandably been taken as providing the grounds for Yeats's poem (Jeffares, 1977: 355). For this reason alone, it is ground worth retreading.

Although Chiswick Eyot – the last downstream island in the Thames before it opens out to estuary – is now rather overgrown, it still matches Yeats's keen eye. Covered with osiers, coppiced willows that once produced thin branches for weaving baskets or building panels, it remains a perfect location for a dwelling 'of woven wattles made'. It was here that the poet came to harvest perfectable material for the craft of the imagination: indeed, the island rests very close to the natural point for a walker to arrive at the river from Bedford Park, so the growths, the weavable materials it yields are rather easily accessible to this particular frequent walker. Furthermore, the island lies only two hundred paces west of Kelmscott House, and despite the river's gradual curve it can be seen from the windows. In fact, the river at this point provides an obvious route connecting Bedford Park with Morris's London home; on any given Sunday, Yeats could have walked down to the riverbank and continued past the island, nodding to Emery Walker's house in Hammersmith Terrace before arriving at Morris's door. Hardly surprising then that Yeats should associate an island poem with Morris and his making.

In his visionary encounter with the island, John Sherman has been 'set dreaming a whole day by walking down one Sunday morning to the borders of the Thames a few hundred yards from his house'. This Thameside spot was nearer still to Morris's house, and if Sherman had Yeats's inclinations he would have ended this whole Sunday's dreaming at the same riverbank with a visit to Morris's Sunday evening gathering, island vision and poem still playing in his head. It is perhaps something of a stretch to associate Sherman's experience on the 'borders of the Thames' with the borders of Morris's bookcraft (at this moment barely begun), but the same 'Clear Thames bordered by its gardens green' that Morris conjured in *The Earthly Paradise* certainly inspired the cultivation of Yeats's watery vision. Even Yeats's 'lake isle', a Middle English archaism of the kind soon to be deleted from his verse, connects with the old name kept by Chiswick's island. 'Eyot' is a later variant of the Old English 'ait', a small island, found usually in a river. By such old reckoning Innisfree has the marks of a river isle, and so it appears that after all Yeats really had turned his hand to something almost medieval.

In this atmosphere 'The Lake Isle of Innisfree' emerges as the most suburban of poems. Its citizenship is not entirely in question, but if we are to claim it as a London poem, we have to be very careful about which city we are imagining and where exactly the poem is placed; especially as at this time Yeats was unquestionably a poet of the suburbs. We might then conclude that the poem discreetly acknowledges but remains distinctly uncomfortable about its suburban genesis, and that it seeks to be somewhere else. That it mostly succeeds is part of its enormous imaginative achievement, but at the same time it would always carry the bruises of its own birth.

The associations provoked by the cluster of places around Hammersmith, Chiswick, and Bedford Park, were crucial to Yeats's development, as his 'Four Years' quite openly admits. Judging by the accounts in both *Autobiographies* and *John Sherman* it is obvious that such questions of geography had been carefully considered. For one thing, Sherman's fictional house on St. Peter's Square is placed exactly halfway between Chiswick Eyot and Morris's Hammersmith residence, a positioning that seems designed to render geographically the central antithesis that the novel attempts to dramatize. Put at its simplest, it is one of place. Sherman's decision about where to live and thrive is the central question of the novel. His choice is between 'Ballah' and London, and the novel plays with these antitheses, not only as opposites, but as opportunities for symbolic doublings. So Sherman has a choice of countries, cities, homes, and jobs. For a time working unhappily as a clerk in the city, even his choice of sweethearts (between a loving homely Irish girl and a flighty, flirty London socialite) is starkly emblematic. In such a fiction this tug-of-war can produce only one winner, and of course, after some accidents and perambulations, Sherman returns to Ballah and Mary Carson. His imaginative return to the island on the borders of the Thames in Hammersmith prefigures a physical return to Ireland. Fortunately for the reader, this pattern is complicated by the Reverend William Howard, who acts as Sherman's double, stepping in to take over his London love affair. They are best friends who disagree: Howard's opinion of Ballah seems to be unvaryingly sour, characterizing it as of the 'squalid eighteenth-century'. However, his opinions are not to be dismissed entirely. The pairing of Howard and Sherman intimately dramatizes something like the choice that Yeats himself felt he had to make. His own returns to Ireland were anything but final. The outcome, therefore, of this choice could be by no means so clear-cut.

Discussing their ideal futures, as young men are wont to do, Sherman's imagination discovers something like an Anglo-Irishman's easy paradise: I should have a house in the country; I should hunt and shoot, and have a garden and three gardeners … a small house with a green door and a new thatch, and a row of beehives under a hedge (Yeats, 1891: 46)'. While his gardeners add an amusing touch, the image of a modest domestic enterprise wins out: the house, after all, is small and the beehives suggest a fruitful, if frugal, state of life, as indeed exists on Innisfree. Howard, by contrast, paints a picture of himself as aesthete and intellectual:

> I have also planned my future. Not too near or too far from a great city I see myself in a cottage with diamond panes, sitting by the fire. There are books everywhere and etchings on the wall. On the table is a manuscript essay on some religious matter. (Yeats, 1891: 47)

The airy vagueness about the essay's subject suggests that even for the clergyman this is really an aesthetic vision that owes much to Morris's example. His Hammersmith house was indeed neither too near nor too far from London, and the window panes Howard desires recall not only fashionable vicarage medievalisms, but Kelmscott House itself. The Oxfordshire original, described in the text and then depicted on the frontispiece for Morris's Kelmscott Press edition of *News From Nowhere* (1894), has, not diamonds, but the small square panes that Morris preferred. Still, it is hard not to see all this domestic décor as representing something that Yeats desired: his London flat in Woburn Buildings would in due course contain books and prints by Blake and Rossetti, and, of course, plenty of manuscript essays on the table.

Although Sherman's vision wins out, the novel manages to dramatize a real tension. Sherman himself walks west to Chiswick Eyot, when he might equally have gone east to Kelmscott House. Such an easterly drift into aestheticism was something Yeats portrayed his central character as determined to resist. But as Richard Ellmann astutely remarked, the poet 'has cut himself definitely into two parts ... Yeats is both characters' (Ellmann, 1987: 81–2). And it is notable that even before he has left Ballah, the as-yet untravelled Sherman's sense of metropolitan conditions is precocious:

> In your big towns a man finds his minority and knows nothing outside its border. He knows only the people like himself. But here one chats with the whole world in a day's walk, for every man one meets is a class. The knowledge I am picking up may be useful to me when I enter the great cities and their ignorance. (Yeats, 1891: 47)

Such sharp awareness of the separation of strands of society likely in 'big towns' and 'great cities' is remarkable for such an ingénue, and in fact seems to reflect, already, an experience of city living. Moreover, the local knowledge to which Sherman refers was proving useful, especially for a poet selling himself as an Irishman in London. Yeats had written warning Katharine Tynan that they must capitalize on their exotic relation to the London literary marketplace. And as Richard Finneran reminds us, the above passage echoed sentiments expressed by Yeats himself in an essay called 'Village Ghosts' that he produced for W. E. Henley's *Scots Observer* of 11 May 1889: it eventually appeared in *The Celtic Twilight* (Yeats, 1893: 29). The same sentiments about the city's claustrophobic exclusivity were expressed, again, in another letter to Tynan:

> Hey ho, I wish I was out of London in order that I might see the world. Here one gets into one's minority among the people who are like one's self – mystical literary folk, and such like. Down at Sligo one sees the whole world in a day's walk, every man is a class. It is too small there for minorities. (Yeats, 1986: 116)

That personal note evident in 'mystical literary folk' indicates plainly the poet's own professed dissatisfaction with the kind of coteries into which he felt he was drifting. Writing to Tynan he was presenting a self-conscious, exaggerated stance. And a contradictory one in that these were precisely the coteries that might provide him with paid work. Yeats played this game as well as any: he had sent Morris's daughter May a copy of his first volume of poetry, *The Wanderings of Oisin*, and coming upon Morris by chance under Holborn Viaduct, Morris promised to help: '"you write my sort of poetry," he said' (Yeats, 1999: 135). Yet if the ideas Yeats shared with Sherman divulged a class-consciousness forced upon him by the dynamics of the city, they also figured a desire for a classless society conspicuously in line with socialist principles. As it happened, these were principles he first encountered at Morris's Sunday evening meetings.

In *Autobiographies* Yeats definitively describes himself as a socialist under Morris's influence: 'I did not read economics, having turned Socialist because of Morris's lectures and pamphlets' (Yeats, 1999: 135). And it was at Morris's table that he 'always' met 'certain more or less educated workmen, rough of speech and manner' (Yeats, 1999: 131). So even Yeats's veneration of small-town Ireland owed a good deal both to urban living and suburban socialism as it existed in London. 'The Lake Isle of Innisfree' represents in some sense a working out of these contradictions: an attempt to reconcile homely socialist ideals and anti-metropolitan rhetoric learned at Morris's hearth with an uncertain but growing sense of national sentiment.

In Yeats's musings about minorities and coteries we can observe the beginning of a reaction against Morris. Yeats's frustrations gradually turned into an attack on the assumptions of Morris's suburban circle, encouraged perhaps by the kind of English patronizing gaucheness that Morris sometimes displayed in dealing with his working-class guests; an attitude that Yeats records, with his embarrassment, in his *Autobiographies*. All this exposed a wider disillusionment with Morris and his ideals, a disillusionment that would eventually be expressed on national, and indeed material lines. How to square the exclusivity and expense of Morris's artistic projects with his socialism has long been an occasion of argument. It was a contradiction that Morris himself acknowledged but never accepted as inevitable. In its descriptions of the ease and delight in making beautiful things enjoyed by individuals or small groups of willing handworkers not coerced by capital, *News from Nowhere* certainly makes an attempt to explain and justify his position. Just at that moment Morris felt himself under attack: in response to anarchist advances, in November 1890 Morris's Hammersmith Branch of the Socialist League seceded to form the Hammersmith Socialist Society. Yeats's ground for dissent, as later articulated in *Autobiographies,* was the uncertain position of religion in a Socialist future. But his entry into the argument was contemporaneous, and oriented rather differently. He made his intervention in *The Providence Sunday Journal* of 26 October 1890, in an essay that, significantly, represents his only true art review. Entitled 'An Exhibition at William Morris's', the piece was as the text makes clear not an account of a display mounted either at Kelmscott House or Morris and Co., but a review of the second, 1890 exhibition at the Arts and Crafts Exhibition Society, housed in the same New Gallery on Regent Street where two years before Morris had been inspired by Emery Walker's bookcraft lecture. For Yeats, however, there was no doubt that Morris was the presiding spirit of the exhibition, and no apparent doubt about his protean pre-eminence; the article describes how the arts of decoration have been revolutionized under 'the leadership of William Morris, poet, Socialist, romance writer, artist and upholsterer, and in all ways the most many-sided man of our times'. It also however skewers Morris by noting that he 'had turned aside a little from his dreams of a Eutopia of Socialism for the poor, to create a reality of art scarcely less beautiful for any rich man who cares', noting 'these heavy tapestries and deep-tiled fireplaces' and 'hanging draperies and stained-glass windows' all 'murmur[ed] of the middle ages' (Yeats, 1970: 183). It is Yeats's discussion of bookcraft that makes clear his dissatisfaction with the economics of Morris's project, and the unequal access to such beautiful things. Dismissing typical nineteenth-century book covers as 'pretentious and foolish' – 'gilding smeared hither and thither in conventional forms' – he admires the simplicity of the new designs, but not without reservation:

These Cobden Sanderson [*sic*] books are, however, simple and artistic, but also not cheap. ... There seems to be no reason why the cover of books should not be designed by good artists and yet remain not altogether beyond the purse of the poor student for whom, after all, books chiefly exist. (Yeats, 1970: 184)

If Yeats did not study economics, the economics of book production certainly exercised him a great deal. Sharing Morris's distaste for the usual conventions of nineteenth-century design and printing, he nonetheless worried about the exclusivity imposed by the expense of Morris's elaborate books, or those produced after his example. And Yeats was not alone: Cobden-Sanderson was starting to develop his own reservations about the extravagance of Morris's book designs. A bookbinder who set up at 15 Upper Mall, Hammersmith, opposite the Kelmscott Press, Cobden-Sanderson was in the process of moving from bookbinding to book designing and printing. In a lecture entitled 'The Book Beautiful: Calligraphy, Typography, Illustration' given under Morris's auspices at the Art Workers' Guild on 3 June 1892, he tried to articulate his differences. He thought Morris's type too heavy, and his respect for meaning, for the value of the communicative power of words insufficient. When it came to printing poetry in particular, he could not share Morris's insouciance about verse form:

Thirdly, and I think this a real blemish, I dislike the dislocation of the verses apparent in his books of poems, for the sake of decorated margin or initial letter. In such case the verse, which as I have said, has an organic structure of its own, is broken up anyhow, is perfectly destroyed and with it its message to the eyes and to the mind. (Tidcock, 2002: 35)

Such sentiments would lead Cobden-Sanderson to set up with Emery Walker the Doves Press, a press now famous for the elegant clarity of its typography and layout. Yeats, also a passionate believer in the 'organic structure' of verse, responded to the contradictions he detected in Morris's project in two ways. For one thing he came to share Cobden-Sanderson notions of simplicity in book design. When buying the simple hand-press and establishing with his sisters on the outskirts of Dublin what would become Dun Emer, later the Cuala Press, he used Emery Walker as his chief adviser, and produced within the unified text-blocks Walker favoured the same clear text Cobden Sanderson demanded. This was a suburban project that, again, had its origins in Hammersmith, but it was one that sought always to be humbler than Morris's establishment of an earthly paradise in print. Each book would insist also upon its Irish origins. Yet with even more significance for the development of Yeats's poetic project, a nagging doubt had emerged perhaps on the banks of the Thames, as Yeats contemplated the limitations of even the finest printing presses. Morris's whole-hearted attention to design left words and letters as visual counters to be rearranged. Yeats had no intention of thus 'throw[ing] poor words away'; wholehearted attention to their sound might restore verses' organic structure and allow them to live. This would lead to a rejection of the book itself as a vehicle for presenting poetry.

Fire

It can come as something of a surprise to realize that one of the aristocrats of high modernism began with such apparently egalitarian principles. Yet really it should not. Yeats's attacks on middle-class living were self-lacerating, but they formed an essential and even orthodox part of the literary movement that was taking root in Ireland. Witness Douglas Hyde, writing in the April 1890 number of *The Nation*:

> It is an irreparable loss that there has never arisen a poet in Ireland who might do for us what Burns has done for Scotland or Schiller for Germany … who might, in other words, form an intellectual bond of union between the upper and lower classes, and whose strains might be equally familiar to cabin and drawing-room. (Hyde, 1890: 105)

This hardly represented revolutionary socialism although, as Hyde would find to his dismay, such language might promote eventual national revolution. But if it tacitly accepted existing class differentials, the notion of drawing together classes of men and women through poetry represented an enormously powerful ideal. And there is no doubt that Yeats to some degree hoped to be such a poet. The early draft of 'The Lake Isle of Innisfree' had made an attempt to build a cabin by hand from the drawing-room. Yet however skilled the hand-press, Yeats began to believe that achieving this ideal simply through print was impossible. The 'strains' of which Hyde spoke pointed to other methods, not without considerable strains of their own.

For we have still really to consider the final version of Yeats's poem. It was published very shortly after Yeats's ambivalent review of the arts and crafts exhibition in W. E. Henley's *National Observer* on 13 December 1890. This marked it in two ways as a London poem. The journal was no longer the *Scots Observer* of Edinburgh, seeking with its name change the status of a national organ, a paper of record emanating from the metropolis. For those in the know, it marked Yeats as one of Henley's young men. Henley, by now editor for Methuen & Co., lived not far from this west London suburban nexus, close enough to arrive on foot, according to Yeats: 'some quarter of an hour's walk from Bedford Park, out on the high road to Richmond' (Yeats 1999: 120). So the poem's emergence into the light was as a result of the kind of literary coterie Yeats was seemingly concerned, in letters and in print, to be seen to reject. Peter D. McDonald has considered in fine detail the meanings of the poem's 1890s print manifestations. He suggests that a different poet emerges in periodicals from the Yeats who in his own books was determined to project the image that he was an author with some control over the text's reception (McDonald, 1999: 204). I would add only that an awareness of the limitations of this control surfaces as anxieties about the nature of the book and of printed text – even within the poems, texts, and paratexts, themselves. All the specific incarnations of 'The Lake Isle of Innisfree' thus become worth considering. For after the text appeared in Henley's *National Observer* such anxiety is I think reflected in a new emphasis on aurality. Here is the revised poem in its entirety:

'The Lake Isle of Innisfree'

I will arise and go now, and go to Innisfree,

And a small cabin build there, of clay and wattles made:
Nine bean-rows will I have there, a hive for the honey-bee,
And live alone in the bee-loud glade.

And I shall have some peace there, for peace comes dropping slow,
Dropping from the veils of the morning to where the cricket sings;
There midnight's all a glimmer, and noon a purple glow,
And evening full of the linnet's wings.

I will arise and go now, for always night and day
I hear lake water lapping with low sounds by the shore;
While I stand on the roadway, or on the pavements grey,
I hear it in the deep heart's core.

(Yeats, 1989: 74)

Each addition made to the poem contributes, it would seem, to a new awareness of sound. The first stanza's close now turns away from anodyne personal reflection ('this old care shall fade') to sound instead the experience of solitary living 'alone in the bee-loud glade'. In turn, this confirms a sense that the 'linnet's wings' of the second stanza must be heard rather than seen, rhyming as they do with the cricket who 'sings'. The slow dropping of peace in this incarnation becomes, therefore, as much an aural occurrence as it was previously an artistic vision of veils and light. Such aural attention had always made up Yeats's imaginative recourse to the island: John Sherman's daydream had conceived of him 'listening at night to the ripple of the water and the quivering of the bushes – full always of unknown creatures' (Yeats, 1891: 93). But these subtle changes, handmade on the poem and printed in London, wrought an object of new sonic sensitivity and intensity.

This is especially evident in the newly added third and final stanza. This is the stanza that places the poem, and underscores the meanings of its sensory attention. Here the quality that forever remains in mind is exclusively aural, as 'always night and day / I hear lake water lapping with low sounds by the shore'. These lines seem to remember 'the green lapping waves' of the 'Prologue' to Morris's *Earthly Paradise*; as we have seen the poem's origins on the shore of the Thames make this nod conceivable. However the sound of waves on the river next to the Chiswick Eyot were as often as not caused only by boats going by. This emphasis on the particular solitary sounds of lake water distances itself from the characteristic qualities of Morris's intellect, 'wholly at the service of hand and eye'. The speaker has shut his eyes to his surroundings; his obsessive auditory concentration suggests a craft put wholly at the service of the ear. The power of these lines as an aural mnemonic is fairly indisputable: the verbal sounds themselves do seem to register deeply upon consciousness. Lily Yeats's account of hearing the poem for the first time when 'not even written down' emphasized its sounded quality: 'I felt a thrill all through me and saw Sligo beauty, heard lake water lapping' (Foster, 1997: 79). The new final stanza places the poem by placing the poet: he stands 'on the roadway, or on the pavements grey', and he does so as a figure who listens. It is made plain, as this poet-figure goes to the island in imagination, that only an astonishing imaginative power has the heft to transport him where we must follow. And how is this managed? The answer is by the ear: 'I hear it in the deep heart's core'. The poem itself embodies an imaginative act aurally perceived, aurally conceived, and perhaps, if the circumstances were right, aurally transmitted.

Pavements are inescapably urban things; the archaic 'roadway' might just as easily refer to the countryside. It is left in to fill the metre, yes, and perhaps as a quiet memory of the poem's more leisured beginnings in suburban London, but it echoes with its own redundancy. Soon Yeats would not invert syntax like 'pavements grey'; but in a last hurrah for Tennysonian straddled adjectives he borrows one to damn metro-politan culture. The phrase also craftily tries to fix the poem as an inner-city poem. Finally, despite his mentor's hatred of modern civilization Morris had only moved to the suburbs. Even Chiswick Eyot was an island, after all, that at the lowest tide could be reached by crossing the muddy clay bed of the river; hardly a place to 'live alone in the bee-loud glade'. The place of the poem's birth was inescapably suburban: access to the riverbank was (and, in fact, is still) heavily restricted by a series of private gardens across the street from the houses; suburban property rights asserting themselves in a manner unfitting to a socialist rural idyll. Chiswick would thereafter be written out of the poem's history. Ramazani argues that the modernists translated geographical displacement 'into a poetics of dissonance' (Ramazani, 2009: 25). With the poem's emphasis on 'peace' and the careful concord of its lines perhaps it is better to say that here the geographical displacement tries to enact a poem of great resonance – that in sound can be found the peace the city lacks. Whatever, it is a transposition that works entirely through sound, and requires the expert casting of an aural imagination, which is perhaps why Morris and Chiswick would no longer play such a part in it.

Much more might be said about this, but one final thing to notice is the poem's renewed concentration on rhythm. Its ragged lines have been purified into carefully weighted, considered cadences; finished in a form that speaks the sense. If we like, we can imagine this work being done not at a desk but as Yeats in his customary habit paced the roadways of the suburb chanting to himself. In the end it matters little. However they have been achieved, these tweaks and adjustments that contract and spread certain lines have transformed what was a rough sketch into an aural artefact. This in any case was what Yeats took from the poem's achievement; and as he later memorializes this, it is fascinating to observe him reconceive the whole ground of its imaginative genesis:

> when walking through Fleet Street very homesick I heard a little tinkle of water and saw a fountain in a shop-window which balanced a little ball upon its jet, and began to remember lake water. From the sudden remembrance came my poem 'Innisfree', my first lyric with anything in its rhythm of my own music. (Yeats, 1999: 139)

If rhythm is what makes the poem, where Yeats found his 'own music' requires an explanation. Now the explanation must come from the sound of water. Not that this is entirely unconvincing: the pattern of London observations recorded by John Sherman includes a comparable connection, where 'delayed by a crush in the Strand' the sound of the 'faint trickling of water' is transmuted into language, 'suggest[ing] a cataract with a long Gaelic name' (Yeats, 1891: 91–3). This name however does not make it into the poem. For Innisfree's specific genesis I find John Sherman's explicit visual rhyme with Chiswick Eyot more convincing. But to what degree Yeats really allowed these memories to lap around the poem is less important. What matters is that he has conspicuously and consciously recast the poem's beginning, founding a powerful myth of origin. Not only here has the central city overwritten the suburbs, but Fleet Street has overwritten the Strand. Conceivably this is but a slip: the two streets do run one into the other. This is however a dangerous assumption to make of such a considered and self-correcting artist. It is surely significant that his *Autobiographies* place the poem's aural inspiration at the heart, then as now, of London's newspaper culture. 'The Lake Isle of Innisfree' is recorded as emerging magnificently from such a heart of darkness: 'I hear it in the deep heart's core', declares the closing line, now defiantly disclosing an exclusively aural imagination as against Fleet Street's print obsession, and indeed the poem's own newsprint manifestations. Gone, therefore, are any suburban associations, and gone too is any sense that the poem might not have been so aurally imagined from the beginning. It has been lifted from Morris's suburban milieu of craft and print culture into a brave old world of resistance against what Yeats would call 'dead words on dead paper'.

It must be added that this reappropriation of 'The Lake Isle of Innisfree' fits into a pattern of broader weave. Just two months after its first publication in the *National Observer* of 28 February 1891, Yeats reviewed Douglas Hyde's *Beside the Fire: A Collection of Irish Gaelic Folk Stories*. He gave high praise to Hyde's scholarly erudition, and especially his phrasing 'the result is many pages in which you can hear in imagi-nation the very voice of the *sennachie*, and almost smell the smoke of his turf fire' (Yeats, 1970: 188). Rather than displacing 'six counties hung with smoke' by a hand-press, it was through the voice that one might return to the smoking turf fire of an imagined rural community. To achieve this manoeuvre imaginatively required above all intimacy with sound.

It was becoming Yeats's habit, in what he later termed his Irish 'propaganda' of the late eighties and early nineties, to set in opposition Irish and English poetry. 'Poets may be divided roughly into two classes', he asserted. The first class consisted of poets in the Romantic tradition who tended to be 'personal and obscure'. The other was the 'bardic class', containing those 'who sing of the universal emotions': 'they do not write for a clique, or leave after them a school', he claimed, 'but sing for all men'. As we might anticipate, 'to this latter class belong ... almost all our Irish poets' (Yeats, 1970: 105). This unwavering boundary laid between popular and obscure, communal and personal, Irish and English poets we should now disclaim as simplistic, but for Yeats it was not only a national distinction. He was groping towards a differentiation he could believe in, with, it must be said quasi-socialist tendencies that cut across what he chose to see as English class distinctions, and expressed itself finally in opposing the allegedly oral tradition of Ireland to the printed tradition of England. It was along these lines that battle was drawn, and into which 'The Lake Isle of Innisfree' and Yeats's attempts to influence its reception was pitched. Rendered more comprehensively, the distinction would remain with him: 'English literature', he wrote in 1906, 'is yet the literature of the few: Irish poetry and Irish stories were made to be spoken or sung, while English literature, alone of great literatures, has all but completely shaped itself in the printing press' (Yeats, 1959: 206). Holding this in mind, it is evident that 'The

Lake Isle of Innisfree' both in its becoming, and in subsequent explanations of its beginning, was being aligned with a specifically aural sensibility, which might imply an oral articulation. Because it was aurally inspired it was a poem to be heard, even to be spoken: its print manifestations would only tell half its tale.

Not only was this a truth in which Yeats could believe: it was something that he forever associated with Morris. The following passage comes from his essay 'Literature and the Living Voice', drafted not long after he had received a present of the Kelmscott Press edition of Chaucer for his fortieth birthday. It casts Morris and all his craft of eye and hand as writing for the reader, not an audience, a trap into which the current writer was not to be drawn:

> Modern literature, above all poetical literature, is monotonous in its structure and effeminate in its continual insistence upon certain moments of strained lyricism. William Morris, who did more than any modern to recover mediaeval art, did not in his *Earthly Paradise* copy from Chaucer – from whom he copied much that was naïve and beautiful – what seems to me essential to Chaucer's art. He thought of himself as writing for the reader, who could return to him again and again when the chosen mood had come, and became monotonous, melancholy, too continuously lyrical in his understanding of emotion and of life. Had he accustomed himself to read out his poems upon those Sunday evenings that he gave to Socialist speeches, and to gather an audience of average men, precisely such an audience as I have often seen in his house, he would have been forced to Chaucer's variety, to his delight in the height and depth, and would have found expression for that humorous, many-sided nature of his. I owe to him many truths, but I would add to those truths the certainty that all the old writers, the masculine writers of the world, wrote to be spoken or to be sung, and in a later age to be read aloud for hearers who had to understand swiftly or not at all and who gave up nothing of life to listen, but sat, the day's work over, friend by friend, lover by lover. (Yeats, 1959: 206)

For Yeats, Morris's *Earthly Paradise* was a product of a determinedly graphological culture. Even in its most fabulous hand-produced and manuscript-imitating volumes – and we observe that Yeats talks of what it might mean to 'copy' Chaucer – this was ineluctably a print-bound culture too. Morris's straightforward pursuit of socialist ideals is seen as misdirected and unfulfillable. If he had spoken he might instead have found an audience; of workers, of lovers, of 'average men'. This too smacks of idealism: it was not that Yeats's own projects of speaking or singing poetry produced unified communities or lasting records. Yet it was still an ambition into which he flung his life and his verse: the recasting of 'The Lake Isle of Innisfree' shows how early this began.

Air

Yeats's verse-speaking projects returned to where he had begun. In September 1931 Yeats was invited by the BBC to give a reading of his poems for broadcast, starting with 'The Lake Isle of Innisfree' 'because you would expect me to begin with it'. The BBC studios were then crammed into the Savoy Hill buildings, on the Victoria Embankment of the Thames between Hungerford and Waterloo bridges, and had not the poet at the time been encased in a small soundproof booth, he would have had wonderful views up and down the river as he read. Perhaps because he was right on the Thames, or more probably because he had always associated the poem with his Pre-Raphaelite forebear, Yeats prefaces his reading by reference to Morris.

Aware that the traffic of the Strand passed only a few yards from the studio door, Yeats retells the old tale of the poem's watery aural inspiration, this time reverting to the Strand. It is with corresponding sonic attention he insists on reading his poems with 'great emphasis upon the rhythm'. Intriguingly he finds his justification in the Morris of: the William Morris of 'hand and eye'. He recalls Morris's angry comment on leaving a lecture hall after hearing a poem of his ('Sigurd of Volsung') recited that it gave him a devil of a lot of trouble to get that thing into verse. Says Yeats 'it took me a devil of a lot of trouble to get in to verse the poems I am going to read which is why I will not read them as if they were prose' (Yeats, 2000: 224). Morris is here recast as a man for whom sound matters. His love of sagas and even the nominal tale-telling of the Earthly Paradise allowed him to be hailed as part of an oral tradition to which Yeats is the heir. Yeats's wavering reading, going up and down in a melodic line, becomes an audible tribute to Morris. This performance of the lyric with 'its own music' is the consummation of a process which has transformed 'The Lake Isle of Innisfree' from a handmade artefact to an aural phenomenon. Broadcast across London, the rising cadence of the closing line in Yeats's reading ('I hear it in the deep heart's core') seems to insist this is a tradition which lives and beats even in the very heart of the city.

If the suburban attachments of this tradition were quietly forgotten, its relationship to Morris was audibly revivified. Remarkably, this was not the only aural tribute to Morris hosted by the BBC that year. Gustav Holst's commissioned piece for wind-band, 'Hammersmith' (Op. 52), was on 23 April 1931 played through at the BBC's Broadcasting Studio number 10; an orchestral performance at Queen's Hall in November was conducted by Adrian Boult[1]. The piece was 'the result', Holst wrote, 'of living in Hammersmith for thirty-nine years on and off and wanting to express my feelings for the place in music' (Short: 291). Like Yeats his feelings for the place were inextricable with feelings for Morris. As a young man Holst had joined Morris's Hammersmith Socialist Society and dined with Bernard Shaw at the same table as Yeats. Holst was remembering a Morrisian socialism that, like Yeats's, turned to community and aurality: before Morris's death Holst had formed the Hammersmith Socialist Choir, and had even driven around Hammersmith playing the harmonium on a cart distributing socialist pamphlets. The 'good-tempered' bustle of these Hammersmith streets is present in the music in passages of quirky scherzo rhythms. Still Holst, like Yeats, returned finally to the sound of water: most memorable is the eerie ground bass motif that begins and ends the piece, representing, said Holst, 'the background of the river, that was there before the crowd and will be there presumably long after' (Short: 292). Beneath all these 1931 performances the ebb and flow of water draws us back to Morris's riverside.

As Yeats had put it long before, Morris, '"The Idle Singer of an Empty Day"', 'has neither sung nor wrought idly' (Yeats, 1970: 184). Here Yeats draws out the distinction of maker and singer with deliberate effect; but what he said was true in as far as Morris's influence went further than we might think. One of his triumphs was to affect the genesis and subsequent orientation of one of the most celebrated poems in the English language. Morris's making helped Yeats understand that the direction of his craft lay towards song, or at least in the sounds of the spoken word. All this began beside the Thames with the making of a poem that opened its ears to water. If we read aright we can still hear Morris's poem beating in the heart of Yeats's. In helping thus to build Yeats's 'isle of bliss' it is fitting Morris should have the last word:

So with this Earthly Paradise it is
If ye will read aright, and pardon me,
Who strive to build a shadowy isle of bliss
Midmost the beating of the steely sea,
Where tossed about all hearts of men must be;
Whose ravening monsters mighty men shall slay,
Not the poor singer of an empty day.

(Morris, 1910–15: 3:2)

Note

1 For additional information about Gustav Holst, I would like to record my debt to Annika Forkert of Royal Holloway, University of London.

4

Shaw the Londoner: Politics, Polemics and *Mrs Warren's Profession*[1]

Michelle C. Paull

When Bernard Shaw arrived in London in 1876, just in time for the funeral of his sister Agnes, he knew no one but his mother, Lucinda Elizabeth, and her lover, George Lee. By 1892, he was a local councillor for the Borough of St. Pancras and had been asked by the Fabians to consider running for the Parliamentary seat of Battersea. While the swiftness of Shaw's transformation from unknown Dublin land agency clerk to doyenne of the London political scene is perhaps surprising, it was certainly no accident. His success was, in large part, a tribute to his phenomenal determination and, as Michael Holroyd puts it, a 'passion for improvement' (Holroyd, 1998: 50) that characterized his early life. His vibrant personality and striking good looks – six-foot-tall, slim, with bright red hair – attracted much attention and an enthusiastic response from many who met him. But Shaw's skill as an orator, allied to his relentless personal drive, determination, and energy were matched by an acute understanding of London's economic and social problems. Infused by his already considerable awareness of the consequences upon the poor of low wages, debt, and high rents – during his time as a land agent in Dublin he 'met people of all conditions' (Holroyd, 1998: 52) – Shaw brought to London a social awareness allied to a keen political intelligence that set him up for his later encounters with the Fabians.

For all Shaw's Irish heritage, his early plays in particular are infused with an understanding of people and society from the perspective of, in Tom Herron's phrase, the 'other capital'. Early preparations for his writing career took place in that most literary of London venues, the Round Reading Room of the British Museum. William Archer recalls sitting next to him there, noting that Shaw's reading material was, as ever, a combination of the academic and the artistic – *Das Kapital* in French and the complete musical score for Wagner's *Tristan und Isolde*. The Round Reading Room 'became his club, his university, a refuge, and the centre of his life for almost a decade' (Holroyd, 1998: 84). Such was his thirst for knowledge that during these years he ordered more than 300 books, including the entire *Encyclopaedia Britannica*.

His transition from politics to theatre is not as long a journey as it might seem, and the continuum between Shaw's two public worlds – London politics and London theatre – is evident not only in the action and content of his plays but also in the language in which they are constituted. The language of his early theatrical writing – notably, the declamatory expressions and the Socratic dialogic technique – finds its origin in the experience of public speaking that he gained in London's radical political circles. Shaw was ever the magpie: in Dublin he had taught himself the piano from a technical handbook (through sheer force of will he learned to play *Don Giovanni* in its totality) and as a land agent he remodelled his 'sloppy and straggled' handwriting into the small and compact style of his predecessor. Adaptable to his environment, Shaw characterized himself thus: 'I made good in spite of myself' (Holroyd, 1988: 52). Adept at utilizing whatever came to hand from his immediate surroundings (Barthes' *bricoleur* springs to mind here), it is unsurprising that his experience of the London political scene would have a direct impact on the ways in which he expressed his ideas in his theatrical and literary work. Indeed, at times it can appear that the strident, opinionated, rhetorical flair of the podium feeds a little too easily into Shaw's early dramatic voice, sometimes taking the place of compelling theatre.

Shaw was first introduced to the power of oratory and the importance of the staged voice at a range of political meeting-houses and small political societies. On his arrival in London, he was initially unemployed, having resigned his well-paid position in Dublin in order to make the move to England, and while he was far from poverty-stricken, at the same time he had no obvious way of earning a living and was unsure how long the money he had would last. Until he secured freelance work as a drama critic, visits to the theatre were rare and so he looked elsewhere to find entertainment and a way to pass his evenings. He began to attend public lectures and political meetings that, if not entertaining in the theatrical sense, were at least free. One of the first societies that Shaw joined was the London Dialectical Society, giving his first paper there – on 'Capital Punishment and Life Imprisonment' – in early 1882. Speakers were questioned at the end of the session and faced frequent heckling from the audience, but rather than being intimidated Shaw realized how easily he could cope with this kind of intellectual disputation (Holroyd, 1988: 126). It seems that he retains this idea of the question-and-answer session in his early plays – including *Mrs Warren's Profession* (1893) – almost offering the audience the opportunity to ask questions of his work and to interrogate the views of the on-stage characters.

As Shaw attended a wider range of political meetings, he began to search for his own distinct political direction. A notable development occurred when, after hearing the American economist Henry George speaking on land nationalization in September 1882 at the Memorial Hall in Farringdon Street, he was encouraged to read Marx, to adopt the cause of Single Land Tax, and to spend – by his own admission – four years studying 'abstract economics' (Holroyd, 1988: 129). As well as developing his political consciousness, Shaw was also finding – in quite literal terms – his political voice: 'he spoke at clubs ... he tried out his voice at the Bedford Debating Society ... he joined discussion groups in Hampstead' (Holroyd, 1988: 129). His diaries between 1885 –1894 record a frenetic period of activity, much of it taken up with public speaking. He became increasingly in-demand in this capacity and began 'drawing capacity audiences at nearly one hundred lectures a year', often working eighteen hours a day, seven days a week to meet all his commitments (Shaw, 1965: 105–6). After giving serious consideration to throwing in his lot with the Social Democratic Federation, he veered away from this organization, partly because of his personal antipathy towards its leader H. M. Hyndman and partly because he did not share Hyndman's vision that social change could occur only through the rising up of the working class. Instead, Shaw favoured social change led by the bourgeoisie, 'not because of snobbery but because I wanted to work with men of my own mental training' (Holroyd, 1988: 131). And so, in May 1884, he turned his attention to the recently-formed Fabian Society. After reading their tract 'Why are so many people poor?' he attended a Fabian meeting that led to life-long friendship with Sidney and Beatrice Webb, the couple who did much to develop the policies and the profile of the Fabian society in its early days. The Webbs helped to transform the Society into a well-organized political group, under-pinned by cogent intellectual argument and with a strong commitment to scholarly research as a means of gathering evidence of the actual conditions of the poor in London and around the country. The Webbs advocated economic co-operatives rather than individualist capitalism and it is precisely this exploration of the financial exchange underpinning the capitalist economy that Shaw elaborates in *Mrs Warren's Profession*.

Shaw's friendship with the Webbs led to his own increasing importance within the Fabian movement. In 1884 he was tasked with drawing up 'A Manifesto' for the Society, that was swiftly followed by a tract addressed 'To provident landlords and capitalists: a suggestion and a warning' (1885), and eventually he moved on to defining the ideals of the Fabian movement in his 1890 tract, 'What Socialism Is'. By 1892 he was writing the 'Fabian Election Manifesto' and thereafter his titles and interests become more didactic: the forty-second Fabian Society tract, 'Vote! Vote!! Vote!!!' was published in 1892, and the distinctly Shavian-entitled tract, 'Socialism for Millionaires', appeared in 1901. While Shaw took on the task of defining the intellectual and political positions of the society, he also, in his capacity as Chairman of the Publications Committee, 'revised and edited most of the tracts drafted by his colleagues' (Shaw, 1965: 106). Thus he would have read or heard (many were given as public lectures) most of the Society's tracts before beginning to write *Mrs Warren's Profession*. Of particular relevance in this respect were Sidney Webb's investigations into the conditions of workers in London in his tracts, 'Figures for Londoners' (1889) and 'Facts for Londoners' (1889), the latter influencing Shaw's own tract 'Women as Councillors' (March 1900) in which he defends the right of women to have representation on the new Borough councils.

Such details show a writer and thinker in the years leading up to the creation of *Mrs Warren's Profession* as constantly engaged in political and polemical discourse, and as increasingly well-armed with research material relating to the economic and social deprivations of Londoners; particularly of London women. Always active at Fabian society meetings, he was asked to join the Executive Committee in January 1885. He was regularly included in committee business – the Minutes of 3 June 1886, for example, record that Annie Besant, Hubert Bland, and Shaw were 'authorised to act on the Vigilance Committee re the Stratford contest'.[2] Thus his presence in the upper echelons of the Fabians also brought him into direct contact with active feminists such as Annie Besant who would inform him of the particular economic conditions of London's female working-class. In 1888, when Besant organized an 'entertainment' to support the fund for women strikers at the Bryant and May match factory in Stratford,

East London, Shaw himself joined in and performed in one of the amateur theatricals at the event.

But what was it that the professional theatre provided for Shaw that the political platform did not? What local and national politics could not indulge was Shaw's inclination towards irony and reflective self-criticism. Politics required definitive answers, absolute confidence of solutions, and little opportunity to deviate from the party line (a line that he himself was largely responsible for establishing). Shaw was not short on confidence but his awareness of cant was never far away. Commenting to Harley Granville Barker on Nigel Playfair's performance of Hodgson in *John Bull's Other Island* in 1904, he remarks that the actor needs some instruction in 'political windbaggery' (Shaw, 1957: 96). Shaw has often been accused of plenty of windbaggery in his own plays, but he is always aware of the potential for falsity in all political posturing, which he later delineates very carefully in *John Bull's Other Island* (1904).

It may seem strange to look back to a play written nearly a decade before *John Bull's Other Island* in order to examine Shaw's representation of political speech and public posturing, particularly when the latter play is so replete with examples of the ridiculous logic of political pontification. But Shaw is rehearsing the beginnings of his political speech-making style in *Mrs Warren's Profession*. This play is the first to respond directly to the economic imperatives for political change that through his intense involvement with the Fabians Shaw had begun to recognize as necessary. *Mrs Warren's Profession* adopts an internationalist view of the political imperative for economic change, a view that would find its elaboration in the more focused and specifically-national representation of the economic and political case for Irish Home Rule in *John Bull's Other Island* a few years later.

Shaw was also highly aware of the persona he had to present to the public in his role as a local politician:

> You know my line ... I am Honest George Bernard Washington who cannot tell a lie ... I am a leading publican ... a teetotaller, an imperialist a protectionist, a socialist, an Irishman of Yorkshire family of Scotch descent. In short, all things to all men.[3]

It seemed, however, that this universal persona was popular. By 1891 *The Sunday World* was able to claim:

> Everybody in London ... knows Shaw, Fabian Socialist, art and musical critic, vegetarian, ascetic, humourist, artist to the tips of his fingers, man of the people to the tips of his boots. (Shaw, 1965: 106–7)

Such celebrity status was partly accorded Shaw because of his love for, and mastery of, the word: both written and oral. But it should not be forgotten that his initial literary attempts were as a novelist. During his years studying in the British Museum and working in local politics, Shaw wrote five novels (all rejected by publishers). He also spent almost twenty years as a theatre and music critic for, amongst others, *The Saturday Review*, *The World*, and *The Pall Mall Gazette* before seeing any of his own plays produced on stage in London. In short, it is this pre-eminence of the literary word rather than theatrical performance that characterizes Shaw's approach to his writing for the theatre. This priority – of the word over public performance – is captured by Shaw's friend, the actor Cedric Hardwicke. Hardwicke, who appeared as The Archbishop of York in a 1923 revival of *Back to Methuselah*, recalled Shaw attending rehearsals in Birmingham:

> Shaw's rehearsal methods were founded on experience and developed by the cold logic of his mind. With his manuscript beside him, he had worked out in advance all the important stage business, so that he knew not only what he wanted every speech to convey, but also precisely where it was to be spoken.[4]

By scrupulously plotting the stage positions in advance, Shaw allows the actors to concentrate solely on the significance and the delivery of the lines: lines supplied to them, of course, directly by Shaw himself. In this sense Shaw views actors as his puppets: he positions their bodies on the stage, he interprets the script for them, he tells them how to convey the lines, especially the most important lines – those lengthy monologues and declarative speeches – that are so characteristic of his work. There is a distinct sense that a production of one of his plays is less a theatrical undertaking than a ventriloquized literary recitation. Hardwicke's account of Shaw's directorial style leaves us in no doubt about the potential problems faced by actors attempting to perform a production that was only partially designed for public consumption. The issue of 'bracket acting' only adds to this perception. Hardwicke explains that

> what is known as 'bracket acting', which is one of the misfortunes an actor suffers all too frequently at the hands of modern playwrights. They pepper their scripts with such stultifying instructions as (turning pink) and (smiling inwardly) in an effort to add some tenuous literary quality to their work.[5]

For all the detail and length of his 'stage directions' Shaw, according to Hardwicke, was remarkably cavalier towards their influence on the actual performance of his plays. In fact, Hardwicke claims that Shaw directed his actors away from the written guidance of the stage directions set out in the published versions of the plays:

> The published plays of Shaw contain their share of what on the face of it is bracket acting. He refused to allow any actor to take such instructions seriously. 'The trouble is', he once explained to me, 'that you are trying to follow those directions of mine. They are meant for the general reader, not for the performer.'[6]

So on paper, Shaw contrives a performance for his reader, writing his plays so that they can be read like novels. On stage, he constructs a similarly literary performance for his audience. In this respect, Shaw's plays work against the truism of most academic theatre departments: *viz.* that plays are written to be performed, not simply to be read. He looks to a wider audience than those actually present in the theatre, and like Ibsen, he knew that readers would often have access to his works in print long before (and after) they were publicly performed.

Mrs Warren's Profession, however, suffered a tortuous process to become a published text and only struggled into print after a 'mangled and mutilated' version of the play suffered a public reading at the Victoria Hall in March 1898 in order to give Shaw copyright over a printed version of the play. Playwrights' ownership of copyright could be established only once a public performance had taken place, and so as Shaw's original version of *Mrs Warren's Profession* had been refused a license by the Lord Chamberlain, George Redford, the playwright was forced to create a bowdlerized version, changing Mrs. Warren's occupation to a thief and cutting four acts to three. The Lord Chamberlain allowed this 'female Fagin' version of the play to pass for performance that, in turn, enabled Shaw to publish the complete play afterwards in its original form.[7] In fact, *Mrs Warren's Profession* had been originally published in the 'Plays Unpleasant' series of 1898, long before any performance of the full play.

Although the play was written with Fabian dogma very much in mind, one gains a definite sense that Shaw's target audience are people teetering on the brink of involvement in political action. There is a real sense of Shaw inciting political action, of him provoking public awareness of what he regards as the degraded condition of women in the advanced capitalism. As a feminist play *Mrs Warren's Profession* reflects to a large degree Shaw's own considerable involvement in feminist politics in 1890s London, and beyond. The impact that Shaw made as a speaker at various political gatherings had led Annie Besant to attend a debate at the Dialectical Society in Oxford to argue against him. Instead, she found herself so convinced by his arguments that she asked him to nominate her for membership of the Fabians (Holroyd, 1998: 168). And Besant was not the only feminist activist to be swayed by Shaw's rhetoric. Emmeline Pankhurst noted that the character of Mrs. Whitfield in *Man and Superman* had 'strengthened her purpose and fortified her courage'.[8] There is little doubt that Shaw himself was fully aware of his work as contributing towards the feminist political movement. In the 'Author's Apology' to *Mrs Warren's Profession* he makes it abundantly clear that the audience he wants most to address is female:

> I simply affirm that *Mrs Warren's Profession* is a play for women; that it was written for women; that it has been performed and produced mainly through the determination of women that it should be performed and produced. (Shaw, 1970: 253)

And it is with outrage that he expects women (and men) to respond to such insouciant economic arguments as Sir George Crofts presents to Vivie in justification of his investment in her mother's business:

> Why the devil shouldnt I invest my money that way? I take the interest on my capital like other people: I hope you don't think I dirty my own hands with the work. Come! You wouldnt refuse the acquaintance of my mother's cousin the Duke of Belgravia because some of the rents he gets are earned in queer ways. You wouldnt cut the Archbishop of Canterbury, I suppose, because the Ecclesiastical Commissioners have a few publicans and sinners among their tenants. Do you remember your Crofts scholarship at Newnham? Well that was founded by my brother the MP. He gets his 22 per cent out of a factory with 600 girls in it, and not one of them getting wages enough to live on. How d'ye suppose they manage when they have no family to fall back on? Ask your mother. And do you expect me to turn my back on 35 per cent when all the rest are pocketing what they can like sensible men? (Shaw, 1970: 331)

The political language of the Fabian speechmaker is here. Corruption at the highest levels of society, the factory owner's fat profits, the argument that everyone else is doing it: all capture the voice of the politician basing his rhetoric on facts. The character of the Crofts' amoral city gentleman investor is present, but his language is informed by that of Shaw the politician and as a result, it almost outweighs Crofts' city persona. Both the politician and the investor are satirized through such blending of their speech-making, but the influence of the podium is profound. For Shaw the habits of the political proselytizer die hard. As a result of his early experiences of attending and speaking at public lectures and meetings, he did not see much of a distinction between informing a crowd at a political meeting and entertaining an audience in a theatre. As a voice in the public domain, his job was to juggle both roles, and he saw his playwriting as an extension of the public lecture platform of his early years.

The psycho-geography of the writing confirms *Mrs Warren's Profession* (1893) as a London play, since Shaw began work on it after walking in Regent's Park and Primrose Hill and completed the manuscript 'between visits to the Jaeger Wool Shop and the British Museum … camping from time to time on wayside seats to complete the speeches' (Holroyd, 1988: 292). The play is also written during the period when Shaw began his role as a councillor and he claimed that the inspiration for the play came as a direct response to his experience of life in London. Around the time of writing he was also involved in the protest against police attempts to close down a speaker's corner in Dod Street in East London, pledging he would risk imprisonment to defend the right to free speech. As it happened, no arrests were made and the police retreated, leaving intact this site for public speaking. But it was threatened again two years later when Sir Charles Warren, Chief of the Metropolitan Police, summarily closed down Trafalgar Square to further protest meetings. London's unemployed, anarchists, communists and radicals alike were due to gather to protest primarily against the Government's Irish policy. This ban on public protest in the area transformed the protest into one to protect the right of free speech. Shaw took an active interest in the proceedings, studying the act that Warren had used to close the Square and coming to the conclusion that the actions of the chief of police were illegal. Alongside William Morris and Annie Besant, Shaw addressed the crowd just before they set off to Trafalgar Square for these famous 'Bloody Sunday' protest riots in November 1887 (Holroyd, 1988: 184–5).

Mrs Warren's Profession speaks of its London origins in the same way that *Heart of Darkness* (1899) reflects London, and like Conrad's story, the play resonates internationally in that Shaw links the destructive reach of London-based capitalism with its international consequences, just as surely as Conrad reveals the human and cultural degradations underpinning European expansionism. While writing *Widowers' Houses* (1892) Shaw had read about prostitution in the London newspapers and he had studied Charles Booth's monumental study, *Labour and Life of the People In London* (1891), that only recently had gone to a second edition (Holroyd, 1998: 290). Since the 1870s 'continental' brothels had been licensed and one of the great scandals of the Victorian period was the discovery that young British women and girls were being exported to Brussels and Vienna to work in these officially sanctioned establishments. The economic link between Europe and England via prostitution was clearly in Shaw's mind as he began to write his play.

More specifically, Shaw claimed that the idea for the play came from a conversation he had had with Janet Achurch, the actress who played Nora in the first London production, at the Novelty Theatre in June 1889, of *A Doll's House* and with whom he instantly fell in love. Achurch was already married to Charles Carrington who played her stage husband Torvald Helmer but this did not deter Shaw whose fascination with Achurch in these early years undoubtedly led him to focus on Ibsen's work with a determined vigour. He saw Achurch in *A Doll's House* five times in fewer than three weeks. Intoxicated with Achurch, he pledged to work solidly during her absence from England (she and her husband were soon to embark on a two-year acting tour in Australia) and indeed he did, becoming, by his own admission, 'a mere arguing, committeeing, writing, lecturing machine' (Holroyd, 1998: 256). He wrote to Achurch regularly while she toured Australia, telling her of his own volume *The Quintessence of Ibsenism* and 'Still After the Doll's House', the short story he had written as a kind of literary answer to the sequel of the play, written by Walter Besant that Shaw disliked. Shaw was already displaying what would become his familiar literary and dramatic pattern: engaging in literary repartee (here with Besant's work) and engaging in debate (in this case a virtual conversation with Ibsen about the position of women within society) of which *Mrs Warren's Profession* is the outcome.

This pattern of dramatic dialogue between one dramatist and another emerges through the connection between Ibsen, Achurch and *Mrs Warren's Profession*, for Shaw finds a way of continuing a discussion which he sees unresolved by Ibsen's play through writing his own work. Clearly the subject matter of the women imprisoned by their economic circumstances had not been changed or resolved by Ibsen's play and Shaw was aware that there was still much to do to achieve female economic equality. The risk, implied in Ibsen's play, that marriage could become a kind of legalized prostitution, finds its logical conclusion in *Mrs Warren's Profession* where the convenience of marriage is removed, to allow a rigorous debate about the social and moral position of women and the economic rationales for the social imbalance between the sexes. But it was his new-found Fabian friends that substantially influenced his writing of the play. Shaw went to stay for three weeks in the Wye Valley with Sidney and Beatrice Webb, and during the stay read them the first act of the play. Beatrice had made a substantial contribution to Booth's *Life and Labour of the People of London*, and her advice to Shaw (that he should 'put on stage a real modern lady of he governing class – not the sort of thing that theatrical and critical authorities imagine such a lady to be') resulted in Shaw's rejoinder: 'I did so: and the result is Miss Vivie Warren' (Holroyd, 1998: 292). Shaw wanted Achurch to play Vivie, and re-inscribing the Ibsen connection still further, wanted Mrs. Warren herself to be played by a fellow Fabian, Mrs. Theodore Wright, who had played Mrs. Alving in the first London production of Ibsen's *Ghosts*.

The play in its final version thus came about as a result of the direct intervention of Fabian politics into the structure and focus of the characters, and as such it can be read as a direct expression of Fabian political understanding of London. Rebutting criticism in *The Daily Chronicle* that he was overly influenced by the work of De Maupassant or Ibsen, Shaw issued a corrective. In a letter dated 28 April 1898 the playwright specifically draws attention to his London location and civic responsibilities as the main sources of inspiration for his work:

Allow me to give you a few instances of the real living influences under which I work. I live in the parish of St Pancras, and am a vestryman thereof. St Pancras contains a quarter of a million inhabitants. An appalling number of them living in single-room tenements.[9]

While it may seem that Shaw is about to delineate the trauma of living in a tenement building, much as his fellow playwright and friend Sean O'Casey would go on to do, he explains to the readers of *The Daily Chronicle* the economic inequality faced by women every day on the streets of London, using the most basic example of human need – the public convenience. Shaw notes that this service is freely available to men, but that in his parish women were charged a fee to use the facilities. While it is clear that he is not linking public toilets and prostitution, he is pointing out that he needs no French satirist or Norwegian realist to teach him anything about the absurdity of the economic divisions and inequalities between men and women in present-day London. It is here, evident in the daily life of women, seen at its most prosaic level in the provision of facilities for the most basic human need. Women have to pay – men do not. This is an issue that is elaborated in *Mrs Warren's Profession*: why is there this inexplicable economic distinction between the position of men and women in society? What are the logical consequences of such inequalities? Are the needs of men greater than those of women? And what impact do such divisions have upon the society of which we are all part? It is this sense of communal responsibility for the state of the nation that Shaw is still keen to stress in his programme notes to the production at the Strand Theatre, London on 3 March 1926, when his work is still subject to the accusations of being derivative and passé. Shaw presents his audience with a conundrum: we all are complicit in allowing Mrs. Warren to 'justify herself' through 'commercial principles' and this justification is 'not only possible but unanswerable'. Shaw also broadens his reach to expand the continuing economic exploitation of women beyond the specificity of prostitution *per se* and back towards the wider economic exploitation of women, in this case, in the workplace, that Mrs. Warren herself had drawn attention to:

> If this play no longer had any relation to life I should not trouble the public with it now ... But the truth is that the economic situation so forcibly demonstrated by Mrs Warren remains as true as ever in essentials today. ... When the war came the late Mary Macarthur found women 'doing their bit' for twelve hours a day at twopence-half- penny per hour. ... [I]t convicted us that, twenty years after the date of my play, of making the wages of virtue lower than the wages of sin at a moment when the nation needed its virtue very urgently.[10]

The economic prostitution of women is almost directly named by Shaw and he is troubled by the betrayal of women who have given their labour freely, only to find that they are not being rewarded fairly. Shaw thus poses the moral problem of this continued economic imbalance for women as the essential fact of his play and comments to the audience and reader pointedly at the end of his author's note: 'I cannot pretend to feel easy about it. Can you?'[11]

As Shaw's comments make clear, the play presents prostitution as a social question, a question of economic and political difficulty. As an audience we may not feel sorry for Mrs. Warren or her daughter Vivie, but that is not their dramatic (or textual) purpose. Their function is to draw us towards an understanding of why the economic and political system upholds the argument of a woman in Mrs. Warren's position; an argument that is entirely logical and consistent with an economic system based on inequality. What most concerns Shaw is not what Mrs. Warren is but what she represents. As his address to the audience underlines, Mrs. Warren can argue that her point of view is both socially acceptable and intellectually sound, because in the context of the political system surrounding her, it is. And this, for Shaw, is what should disturb his audience as much as it disturbs him. Mrs. Warren owns and manages brothels in Europe and so she is both a capitalist and an enabler; as Shaw explained to R. Golding Bright, 'Mrs. Warren. is much worse than a prostitute. She is an organism of prostitution' (Shaw, 1965: 566). Clearly, Shaw does not want his audience to feel a great deal of personal sympathy for Mrs. Warren who is a figure to be reviled, not replicated.

The oratory of the public speaker inflects the tone and style of Shaw's prefaces to his plays and even characterizes his characters' dialogue, especially in the early plays. There is an arch quality to some of the speeches of Shaw's characters – a self-reflective, almost Brechtian style of self-awareness. The use of the preface in itself encourages a kind of literary-critical engagement with the subject of the plays, rather than an emotional response allowing an easy identification with the characters. The Prefaces, which were later published in separate volumes as essays in their own right, demonstrate that Shaw remained aware that he had a readership for his work, not only a theatrical audience.[12] Certainly a new preface was added to the edition of *Mrs Warren's Profession* published in 1902 after the first public performance by the Stage Society (that, as a private members' club, could avoid the stricture of the Lord Chamberlain's censorship and mount two performances of the play). Shaw was conscious that his readers must be addressed with new material, much as his audiences must have new plays. In this sense he attempted to set up a dialogue with his readership just as he did with his audiences at the performances of his work. But he also used his Prefaces as a means of replying to his critics; their post-performance heckling was answered in print in just the way that he would have done in a political debate. For example, in response to Sisley Huddleston's critique of the play and his suggestion that there had been significant changes in factory practice by the time of the 1924 Parisian production of *Mrs Warren's Profession*, Shaw addresses the critic by name:

All that Mr Huddleston can claim is that some attempts have been made to prevent lead poisoning and phosphorous poisoning in the factories where Mrs Warren's 'respectable' sisters worked. If that consoles him it does not console me, nor make the lesson of my play obsolete. It still remains true as it was in 1894 that we praise female virtue highly and pay it poorly, and pay female vice highly whilst we deplore it verbally.[13]

The ethical and moral problems of a woman seduced by materialism cannot fail to strike the audience throughout Mrs Warren's speech. In the following example, Vivie asks her mother whether or not marriage to a labourer or even working in a factory would be preferable to prostitution. Her mother replies 'indignantly' in a speech that tumbles maternal responsibility and moral outrage into an inverse dilemma:

> What sort of mother do you take me for! How could you keep your self-respect
> in such starvation and slavery? And what's a woman worth? What's life worth?
> Without self-respect? (Shaw, 1970: 314)

Shaw is not concerned to emphasize Mrs. Warren's personal suffering or anxiety
about her circumstances. He presents her instead as a woman who has made a logical
economic choice, for how could she have made any other? As she points out to her
daughter, Vivie, when she finally explains why she turned to prostitution:

> It can't be right Vivie that there shouldn't be better opportunities for women. I
> stick to that: it's wrong. But it's so, right or wrong; and a girl must make the best
> of it. (Shaw, 1970: 314)

It is this sense of resigned acceptance that Shaw feels is most dangerous to women
and should cause outrage amongst his audience. When women like Mrs. Warren
co-operate with the system of their own oppression, then how is the inequality of their
position in society to be challenged? Mrs. Warren has absorbed the logic of social
advancement and opportunity through economic power and Vivie's resistance seems
absurd to her. When Vivie returns the cheque for her mother's monthly allowance,
Mrs. Warren is keen to explain to her daughter what she is missing and outlines the
benefits of her own economic position compared to her daughter's role working in the
legal profession. The benefits should be clear to Vivie, if only she will reach out and
take them:

> It means a new dress every day; it means theatres and balls every night; it means
> having the pick of all the gentlemen of Europe at your feet; it means a lovely house
> and plenty of servants; it means the choicest of eating and drinking, it means
> everything you like, everything you want, everything you can think of. And what
> are you here? A mere drudge toiling and moiling for your bare living and two
> cheap dresses a year. Think it over. (Shaw, 1970: 350)

Like a fantasy Fairy Godmother (albeit with the moral logic of Beelzebub) Mrs.
Warren offers her daughter a fairytale existence of everything she believes a woman
could desire. The only downside is the moral origin of the wealth, about which the
merest quibble is regarded as illogical foolishness by Mrs. Warren:

> Where would we be now if we'd minded the clergyman's foolishness? Scrubbing
> floors for one and sixpence a day and nothing to look forward to but the
> workhouse infirmary. Don't you be led astray by people who don't know the world
> my girl. The only way for a woman to provide for herself decently is for her to be
> good to some man who can afford to be good to her. (Shaw, 1970: 314)

Shaw's intense provocation in the language here is that of the podium not of maternal
concern. Vivie would not listen to any advice from her mother because it would not
work effectively for her characterization – there is little empathy or understanding
between the two women. Vivie has been brought up in a series of boarding schools and
taught by tutors, and as she explains to Praed 'I hardly know my mother ... I only see
her when she visits England for a few days' (Shaw, 1970: 279). Vivie has a curious but

unsurprising emotional detachment from her mother. She is almost an observer of a strange woman in her midst, a woman who has a biological claim to her but little claim to emotional support or advice. This conversation between mother and daughter, the mother offering some friendly advice, is not compelling in a human sense. There is no sense that Mrs. Warren is aware of the moral dilemma of her daughter (or herself). The conversation has more of a tone of the financial adviser and client and must be read as the inverse of every maternal advice given to Edwardian women by their mother. There is a definite Brechtian sense that Shaw hopes his audience will rise up and abuse Mrs. Warren for such thoughts but also that they immediately call for social change to make this kind of logic impossible to sustain as reasoned argument. The idea that prostitution is a viable profession for women is horrific, but that it is perfectly logical within the society is the real target of Shaw's criticism. Since it is not possible to defend an idea that is both logical and morally repugnant, the audience must be forced to accept that a society that produces this combination must be changed. This kind of speech is much more like debating rhetoric than drama. Consider, for example, the following discussion of the distinction between poverty and wealth in Shaw's Fabian tract 'What Socialism Is', written just three years before *Mrs Warren's Profession*:

> Poverty means disease and crime, ugliness and brutality, drink and violence, stunted bodies and unenlightened minds. Riches heaped up in idle hands mean flunkeyism and folly, insolence and servility, bad example, false standards of worth, and the destruction of all incentive to useful work in those who are best able to educate themselves for it. Poverty and riches together mean the misuse of our capital and industry for the production of frippery and luxury whilst the nation is rotting for want of good food, thorough instruction, and wholesome clothes and dwellings for the masses. What we want in order to make true progress is more bakers, more schoolmasters, more woolweavers and tailors, and more builders: what we get instead is more footmen, more gamekeepers, more jockeys, and more prostitutes. That is what our newspapers call 'sound political economy'. What do you think of it? Do you intend to do anything to get it remedied? (Shaw, 1890: 2)

Shaw foreshadows his use of the direct question to the audience in his theatre criticism, a style that, as we have seen, he deploys to respond to a critic of the 1926 production of *Mrs Warren's Profession* in *The Daily Chronicle*. Though the style is more densely packed, the rhetoric remains recognizable and the comparison between what riches can bring – 'frippery and luxury' – seems a proleptic nod to Mrs. Warren's narrative obsession with the material objects her money can buy for her daughter later used in the play.

Ellen Terry, one of the first people to whom Shaw sent a copy of the play, was distinctly anxious about the political style (and length) of Mrs. Warren's speeches. Shaw, however, writes to correct her:

> You are wrong, believe me, about the long speeches. The easiest thing to do in public is a monologue. … Why does nobody ever fail as Hamlet? Because he has long speeches. Remember the nation is trained to hear sermons. The real difficulty in that scene is not Mrs Warren's talking but Vivie's listening. … I've made

speeches hours long to casual wayfarers who could go away when they pleased; and they've all stopped for at least half an hour ... They would not have stood ten minutes of duologue. (Shaw, 1965: 795)

Shaw's specific recollection of his political speech-making past is significant. He is clearly thinking back to his own experience as a public political speaker – the monologue is what he can deliver most easily since he is remembering his own public speaking. But he is also directly drawing attention to the design and structure of his speeches, based upon the experience of speeches he has made at political and debating societies. To convince your reader you have to lecture them, Shaw suggests: a practice he had honed to perfection in his early London years. Although actors may occasionally differ on the matter, Shaw doesn't think the audience will find listening particularly onerous. At a political meeting the audience are ready to listen carefully, alert to ask the speaker direct questions afterwards. Theatregoers may not be as keen to be attentive.

So, Shaw is attempting to encourage the development of a new kind of theatre audience, one that will be more ready to listen in the style of a political meeting and become attuned to their role in responding to the issues he raises. Small wonder then that the connections to Brecht are evident in Shaw's early work. For W. B. Yeats, however, this kind of speech-making was all that Shaw as a dramatist could do well. Shaw, he asserted:

has a very unique mind, a mind that is part of a logical process going on all over Europe but which has found in him alone its efficient expression in English. He has no vision of life. He is a figure of international argument. (Foster, 1998: 506)

While it might seem remarkable that Yeats should criticize Shaw for having 'no vision of life', at the same time he correctly highlights that quality of detachment from humanity that is so much a feature of the playwright's early work. Yeats finds an unlikely ally in a much later assessment of Shaw's work from Germaine Greer, who is similarly dismissive of Shaw's attempts to engage with 'a vision of life' in *Mrs Warren's Profession*. Greer finds Shaw's focus on prostitution curious since, as she points out, the play does not answer the question 'what is prostitution?' Instead, she argues, 'Shaw could get no nearer the correct etiology of whoredom than the feeble Fabian diagnosis that women are overworked, undervalued and underpaid (Greer, 1970: 22). Greer is actually asking a question that the playwright avoids. Shaw was not interested in the definition of prostitution *per se* – the theme was simply a metonym for his observations on the economic and political deprivation of women merely because of their gender difference. What is interesting about Greer's analysis is that it also reveals Shaw's lack of emotional engagement with the human aspect of the theme of prostitution. Just as Yeats had suggested Shaw does not have a 'vision of life', Greer notes that when it comes to characterization, 'Shaw refrains from making his spectators desire his heroine but the whole structure of the play relies upon their prurience for its interest' (Greer, 1970: 19). The recognition of the complete lack of emotional involvement between audience and characters is made all the more clear when Greer refers specifically to the 'spectators' not 'the audience'. Again, the Brechtian overtones are clear.

This emotional detachment in Shaw's early plays stems from his experience of public speaking. The debating society dynamic is alive and well in *Mrs Warren's Profession*: in the performance of the play one can sense Shaw waiting for his audience to respond, to critique, and to question, just as his political audiences did during and at the end of the public debates in which he took part. Shaw's early work for theatre is less play and more political polemic. His audience is wider than those in the theatre; he addresses readers as well as theatre-goers; and although he is personally respectful of actors, he saw their main job as to speak *his* words, not act *their* roles. This emotional detachment may be one of the reasons why critics questioned whether *Mrs Warren's Profession* remained relevant to contemporary audiences of the mid-1920s. Shaw always seems surprised that he had to defend his play from such criticism. But in the detachment of the personal from the political, Shaw removed a timeless human connection between the audience and his play. *Mrs Warren's Profession* does retain a continuing relevance to us, for as Greer puts it, 'prostitution is universal in a capitalist society in that all talent, all energy, all power is a commodity with a cash value' (Greer, 1970: 22).

As such, Shaw's play should resonate with us all until the end of capitalism. But our sympathy doesn't stretch to Mrs. Warren or Vivie because Shaw has not allowed us, as a theatrical or literary audience, to experience any personal connection with them. Instead, we now watch or read *Mrs Warren's Profession* because of Shaw himself, and because of what the play tells us about his development as a dramatist. In the final analysis we are perhaps listening to Shaw as he might have wanted us to – strident, controversial, witty and thoroughly informed, but at the same time guarded and at one remove from personal engagement with his characters.

Albert Hunt's review of a 1989 London revival of *Mrs Warren's Profession* is one of the few to note the value of this Brechtian dimension in Shaw:

> Shaw ... introduces each scene by reading his extremely detailed stage directions. The effect is one that Brecht, who admired Shaw, would have appreciated. ... We are constantly being reminded that we are watching situations being played out. And this is precisely how Shaw must have wanted his play to work. (Hunt, 1989: 66)

Certainly, Shaw never speaks of his characters' feelings for and emotions towards one another. Writing in 1924, when the play gained its first public performance after being subject to censorship for the previous 30 years, Shaw remains at pains to stress the economics underpinning the play as a means of stressing that the moral position of women in society is in direct correlation to their financial status. His argument is not about whether as a daughter Vivie would ever abandon contact with her mother or the emotional suffering that Mrs. Warren might face at the hands of her daughter. In his 'Preface' and 'Replies to his critics', Shaw always maintains the persona of the public political speaker. In response to suggestions that his play is out of date after the 1914–18 War and that the situation of women is no longer circumscribed by such conditions, Shaw points to the example of the women working in the munitions factories many of whom had been 'working twelve hours a day for 2 1/2d an hour under the impression that they were saving their country instead of making huge profits for their employers'

(Shaw, 1970: 364). He is anxious to stress that the conditions he had identified are still thriving and is keen to stress the links to the international sex trade as well:

> It still remains as true as it was in 1894 that we praise female virtue highly and pay it poorly, and pay female vice highly while we deplore it verbally. We flog white slave traffickers of the male sex (thus protecting Mrs Warren against male competition); but we do not raise the wages of women to the point at which they would be independent of prostitution. That is the root of the matter. (Shaw, 1970: 365)

Shaw himself directed the first unexpurgated private performance of *Mrs Warren's Profession* at the New Lyric Club Theatre in London. The Stage Society production featured Shaw's friend Harley Granville Barker in the role of Frank Gardener. The first review of this private performance concentrated not on the subject matter at all, but on Shaw's ability as a dramatist. The reviewer in *The Times* remarks that Shaw has written 'a series of explanations', not a play.[14] While it may well be fair to characterize these explanations as somewhat detached, they are not without a degree of passion. Ronald Eyre commenting on his own production of *Mrs Warren's Profession* identifies a powerful emotional rhythm in Shaw's speeches, which cannot be used by the actor consistently throughout their delivery of the lines. For Eyre, Shaw's speeches contain all the energy of an immediate outburst of emotion, which might be dramatized simply by the use of an expletive in the work of another dramatist. In Shaw, however, this intensity lasts for the entire speech, but as an actor you cannot maintain that level of heightened emotion in your performance of the speech – because there is a danger of emotional overload for the audience and the actor and the power of the speech as a whole could be jeopardized. Simply, the speeches are too passionate for verbatim speech (or what passes for such in stage realism). The actor cannot speak exactly what is written at such a constant emotional high so they have to find a way to contain the emotion for a more dramatic delivery suited to theatre, rather than the impassioned emotional constancy required in a political speech. Yet Eyre also identifies the interweaving of detachment and observation within Shaw's writing:

> the inner process which in some other play might come out in one expletive is elaborately verbalised here. But what you cannot do is put the passion of the expletive into the whole speech. You have to find some cool way of serving it up. (Eyre, 1989: 20)

It is significant that Eyre uses the phrase 'verbalized' not 'dramatized' here. He recognizes the extent of the emotional passion in the words – and that there is too much of this trauma for one speech. So the lines have to be delivered by the actors less in the declamatory style they seem to demand and instead in a more reflective, observational style. This is the only way to cope with the verbal power of the speeches in performance, while not losing their theatrical context entirely.

Victor Merriman suggests that 'Bernard Shaw's works are most productively understood as artefacts of a sustained, unrivalled, public intellectual engagement with Ireland and the world' (Merriman, 2010: 216). For modern audiences raised on the visual rather than the verbal, Shaw's political and polemical plays may prove more difficult to recover. What would Shaw make of devised, visually inflected versions of his work by modern physical theatre companies such as Complicite and Kneehigh for example? Is this why so little of Shaw's work has been adopted by contemporary physical theatre companies? Shaw has not yet achieved the kind of revivals afforded in recent years to Wilde, Coward or Rattigan. This may not be because of his Irishness or lack of it, not because of his politics or polemics, but because he is a voice, a public speaker in the age of the soundbite.

Notes

1 Material by George Bernard Shaw reproduced with kind permission of The Society of Authors, on behalf of the Bernard Shaw Estate.

2 Fabian Society, 'Minute Books 23 December 1885–21 January 1887', C1: 6.

3 Bernard Shaw letter to William Crooks MP 27 February 1904, quoted in R. H. Hamilton (1980) 'Bernard Shaw's Reflections on Being a City Councilman', *Public Administration Review*. (40) 4 July/August: 317.

4 *Back to Methuselah* programme, National Theatre, London 31 July 1969: 23.

5 Op. cit.

6 Op. cit.

7 See Leonard W. Conolly (2004) 'Mrs Warren's Profession and the Lord Chamberlain', *The Annual of Bernard Shaw Studies*. 24: 46–95.

8 Robin Cook (2004) 'The Power of an Unreasonable Man', *The Guardian* (Review Section). 2 October: 36.

9 Letter to the Editor of *The Daily Chronicle*, 30 April 1898 in, see Shaw (1970) *The Bodley Head Bernard Shaw Collected Plays with their Prefaces*. London, Bodley Head: 267.

10 Bernard Shaw (1970) Author's Note in Programme for London production of *Mrs Warren's Profession*, The Strand Theatre London, 3 March 1926, *George Shaw Bodley Head Collected Plays*. London, Bodley Head: 366.

11 Op. cit.

12 Borges, an admirer of Shaw's work, discovered the plays through reading them, rather than seeing productions. Argentinian productions of Shaw's work would have been rare, but Borges continued to be drawn to Shaw's work through the word rather than any theatrical production: 'When I was still a young man in Buenos Aires I read George Bernard Shaw's *The Quintessence of Ibsenism*. I was so impressed that I went on to read all of his plays and essays and discovered there a writer of deep philosophical curiosity and a great believer in the transfiguring power of the will and the mind.' See Peter Gahan (2010) 'Bernard Shaw and the Irish Literary Tradition', *Shaw: Annual of Bernard Shaw Studies*. 30 September: 3.

13 Anon. (1924) 'Mr Shaw Hits Back', *Evening Standard*, 15 September.

14 Anon. (1902) 'Review of *Mrs Warren's Profession*', *The Times* 7 January: 12.

5

'A World of Difference': London and Ireland in the Works of Katharine Tynan

Whitney Standlee

Aware of the allure that emigration held for many of his literary compatriots, W. B. Yeats would emphasize throughout his career the importance of remaining in, and writing for, Ireland. His most famous convert to the enticements of Ireland and its mythic west was, of course, the young John Millington Synge, who at Yeats's urging returned from Paris in the late 1890s to live on, and write of, the Aran Islands. A decade earlier, however, he had attempted to cast a similar spell over another Irish writer he admired: his close friend and fellow poet Katharine Tynan (1859–1931). In one of the most intimate of the many letters he wrote to Tynan, Yeats expressed both his reluctance to turn to prose as a literary medium, and the centrality of Ireland to what he perceived as their mutual poetic project:

> When you write, always tell me what you are writing, especially what poems, the journalism interests me more dimly of course, being good work for many people, but no way, unless on Irish matters, good work for you or me. ... Much may depend in the future on Ireland now developing writers who know how to formulate in clear expressions the vague feelings now abroad – to formulate them for Ireland's not for England's use. (Yeats, 1953: 102–3)

Yeats would not have felt the need to insist, as he did with Synge, on Tynan's residence in Ireland. She had lived in the same Irish farmhouse for nearly all of the 30 years of her life and, to Yeats, she appeared to be an indelible part of the national literary landscape and as bound to the project of creating a new type of Irish literature as he was.

Yeats's emphasis on remaining in or returning to Ireland as a prerequisite for writing Irish national literature is curious, coming as it does from a man who spent most of the first 57 years of his life living in and around London. It is nonetheless evident that Yeats believed literature 'for Ireland's use' was not likely to be produced from a space of expatriation. Tynan's own case acts as an indication that Yeats may not have been so very mistaken in his concerns that geographical distance from Ireland might lead to a form of emotional detachment. Within a few years of Yeats's letter being written, Tynan would emigrate from Ireland to London, and on arrival there she would veer widely from the path they had hitherto charted together. To understand this parting of the ways, it is necessary to comprehend something of the intimacy of the relationship that existed between Yeats and Tynan. So important was he to her in the 1880s, the decade in which both their careers began to flourish, that any comprehensive study of Tynan's work must necessarily include something of Yeats'. Yet the converse is also (and just as) true, and Tynan's contribution to Yeats's professional development should not be underestimated.

Tynan and Yeats were introduced in 1885, when Charles Hubert Oldham, then a student at Trinity College Dublin but shortly to become editor of the *Dublin University Review*, brought the young poet to one of the literary gatherings that Tynan held at her family's farmhouse, Whitehall in Clondalkin, County Dublin. It was an unlikely friendship from the first. Tynan was six years Yeats's senior, devoutly Catholic, and spoke with what Douglas Hyde referred to as a 'frightful brogue' (Day, 1974: 87). Yet their first meeting came, significantly for Yeats, immediately following the publication of her inaugural volume of poetry, *Louise de la Vallière and Other Poems* (1885). The book quickly made Tynan's name. *The Irish Monthly* devoted more than ten pages in various editions to singing its praises, referring to it as a 'true work of art', while an admirer in *The Ampleforth Journal* would assert that upon its publication 'the whole Irish world broke into rapturous delight'.[1] Yeats, meanwhile, had yet to make his mark on the literary establishment, in Ireland or elsewhere.

It was to Tynan's literary reputation that Yeats was drawn rather than, as might be expected, vice versa. Recognizing in Tynan 'a link to the world of literary editors', Yeats actively cultivated the friendship, and the two soon became the closest of confidantes.[2] During the latter half of the 1880s and into the first years of the decade that followed, the pair often exchanged in their frequent letters drafts of various projects-in-progress for comment and critique. It is in these letters that many of Yeats's early poems – including 'The Wanderings of Oisin', 'The Lake Isle of Innisfree', and 'When You Are Old' – first appear, often in rudimentary form, and it was together with Tynan that Yeats edited what was in essence the first published volume recognizably attributable to the Irish Literary Renaissance: *Poems and Ballads of Young Ireland* (1888).

The imperative role that Lady Augusta Gregory would later play as Yeats's facilitator and sponsor was initially undertaken by the combination of the poet Ellen O'Leary and Tynan. Of the many women who nurtured Yeats, they would be the earliest and most formative. O'Leary took it upon herself to look after Yeats's physical well-being, and her importance to the poet's maintenance and protection is detailed in Tynan's reminiscences:

> Between Ellen O'Leary and W. B. Yeats there was a charming and touching friendship. She loved Willie in a motherly way, because he was young, because he was not very robust, because he knew so little how to take care of himself. Willie would never know when he had missed a meal though he might feel a vague discomfort: when he was wet and weary, when he was too thinly or heavily clad, when he had a hole in his shoe, though the water squished in it. (Tynan, 1924: 100)

At the same time, it fell to Tynan to assist in cultivating and nurturing his poetic sensibilities, and she did so with indefatigable enthusiasm. Whitehall was, in essence, his first Coole Park – a home in the countryside to which he would often retreat for weeks at a time to immerse himself in the discussion and writing of poetry. Tynan would become his earliest reviewer and for many years remained his most diligent and fervent advocate in the press. Thus, when Yeats wrote, 'I had about me from the first a little group whose admiration for work that had no merit justified my immense self-confidence', he undoubtedly had Tynan and O'Leary uppermost in his mind.[3]

Moreover, the traces of Tynan's influence are recognizable in Yeats's poetic output. *The Wanderings of Oisin* (1889), for example, grew out of a project, inspired by John O'Leary and encouraged by Alfred Perceval Graves, that had begun with her own Ossianic poem, 'The Pursuit of Diarmuid and Grainne' in 1887, and at least one of his poems, 'In Memory of Robert Gregory' (1919), is perceptibly indebted to her work.[4] In his 'Introduction' to Tynan's *Collected Poems* (1930) George Russell ('A. E.') maintained that 'Katharine Tynan was the earliest singer in that awakening of our imagination which has been spoken of as the Irish Renaissance' (Russell, 1930: vii) and Yeats himself acknowledged Tynan's importance both to the direction his poetry would take and to Irish literature more generally when in 1908 he publicly credited her with being one of the triumvirate[5] who embarked on a venture 'to reform Irish poetry' and thereby kindled the Literary Revival (Yeats and Johnson, 1908: 3).

The genesis of Tynan's nationalist inclinations likewise predated by a number of years her associations with the Revivalist cohort and may in fact have acted as an early influence on Yeats's own cultural politics. She admits to having developed her political conscience when the appearances of her poetry in periodicals and newspapers lent to her a sense of civic responsibility, and it was in 1878, the year that her first poem was published in *Young Ireland Magazine*, that she found herself 'taken up with a new interest in the shape of active politics' (Tynan, 1913: 71). Her passion for affairs of state was further invigorated by what she describes as the 'romantic force' of the personalities of the Land League's leaders, Michael Davitt and Charles Stewart Parnell (Tynan, 1913: 72). Angered at their arrests in 1881, she became an active member of the Ladies' Land League at its inception – in fact, it was Tynan who suggested the organization be called the 'Women's Land League', a name that was rejected for being 'too democratic' – and formed, during the period of her involvement, a friendship with Anna Parnell, its effective leader (Tynan, 1913: 75). She would remain adamantly and publicly Parnellite ever after, although ten years later her loyalties to Ireland's 'uncrowned king' would be severely tested during the split of the Irish Parliamentary Party precipitated by the revelation of Parnell's affair with Katharine O'Shea. Tynan evocatively describes the damage inflicted on her career during the period of the party schism in a notable letter, written a month after Parnell's death, in which she reacts to the news that even her long-time mentor Father Matthew Russell, editor of the Jesuit-owned literary periodical *The Irish Monthly*, was being forced by anti-Parnellites to distance himself from her and her work:

> I'm feeling now as if I was a wicked person since this morning when I got a letter from Father Russell telling me he couldn't do anything for my poems … in the *Irish Monthly* because of the part I'd taken in politics. It isn't his will but stronger wills outside. He told me for the first time that last December two of

his subscribers returned the *Irish Monthly* because I had something in it. I'm sure those two were priests and I shall say for the future that for intolerance and un-Christian uncharitableness priests take the cake.[6]

Her affection for Parnell and for the Home Rule cause remained intact, but this experience and others which mirrored it would lead to many changes in Tynan's political opinions, in her literary life, and in her relationship to Ireland.

In many ways, the trajectories of Tynan's and Yeats's careers can be seen to run counter to one another. While he spent many of his formative years in involuntary exile in London, longing for just the type of Irish countryside retreat that Tynan had always inhabited, she was orienting her literary aspirations on the English capital. As early as 1884, she revealed the magnetic attraction the city held for her when she wrote to Matthew Russell to request a letter of introduction into a London literary household: 'You will understand that I am very anxious to make some literary friends,' she confessed. 'To get into a London literary circle is my earthly ambition.'[7] Considering options for the publication of her first book of poetry later that same year, she was resoundingly dismissive of Dublin and the prospects there. 'I should not go to [the Dublin publishing house M. H. Gill and Son] unless as a dernier resort,' she asserted to Russell, adding that:

> publishing in Dublin would not please me very much – I have always thought that to publish there is almost to ensure that the book shall be still born … and I am ambitious enough to wish for a larger audience than the Ireland of to-day.[8]

To Tynan, Dublin was little more than a literary backwater. To write for a living meant to be near the literary epicentre of the English-speaking world, and that was London.

The household into which Russell introduced Tynan – that of the Meynell family, who had earned his advocacy by being converts to Catholicism – existed at the hub of London's literary life. Wilfrid Meynell was a prolific writer and the editor of the magazine *Merry England*, while his wife Alice was a poet, journalist and essayist with substantial publishing connections herself. Between them, they had contributed to the majority of London's most widely read publications and had links to nearly all of the city's prominent editors. The friendship between Tynan and the Meynells was immediate and close; it would prove to be both enduring and enduringly important. Generous with their time and in the exercise of their influence, they quickly found Tynan's first volume of poems its publisher, Kegan Paul, and they introduced her to Henry Cust, editor of the *Pall Mall Gazette*, the newspaper that was to become the most important outlet for her work.[9]

Tynan's memoirs of early visits to London and the milieu into which her friendship with the Meynells promptly placed her vividly evoke the sense of a city teetering on the brink between mannered literary Victorianism and the antithetic movements of the *fin de siècle*. Her recollections of her first introduction to Oscar Wilde in 1884 at his mother's home on London's Grosvenor Square, for instance, reads in retrospect as an eyewitness account of the emergence of decadence. In Tynan's evocation, Speranza's candlelit drawing room is decorated for the occasion in aesthetic and eccentric style as a shrine to her son: 'Presently came Oscar,' Tynan writes of his grand entrance, 'and growing accustomed to the darkness one could see how like he was to the photographs of him which were all about the room, full-face, half-face, three-quarter face … He came and stood under the limelight so to speak, in the centre of the room' (Tynan, 1913: 149). Juxtaposed against her accounts of the rise in prominence of Wilde, and emblematic of an ongoing and seismic shift in the established literary order, Tynan also and almost simultaneously bears witness to Christina Rossetti's decline. On their first meeting in 1885, she would find Rossetti in old age still faintly recognizable as the model for the portraits that her brother, Dante Gabriel, had painted. Yet in her descriptions of the poet's cloistered existence in a 'dreary' house on Bloomsbury's Torrington Square devoid of gardens, grandeur and any sense of the loveliness that suffused its occupant's poetry, Tynan hints not only at Rossetti's retreat from the literary spotlight, but at an incipient, almost Miss Havisham-like seclusion and decay (Tynan, 1913: 183).

Like Yeats and his Rhymers' Club colleagues, Tynan was swept up in the tide of literary change that was occurring in London in the final dozen years of the nineteenth century. By the late 1880s, her reputation in the city had grown, her professional circle widened, and her literary allegiances altered. Despite the fact that she remained resident in Ireland, she travelled regularly to the English capital, attending events such as women writers' dinners at the Criterion Restaurant and finding herself in the company of, and sharing sympathies with, members of the pro-suffrage Pioneer Club and 'New Woman' writers, such as Mona Caird and Sarah Grand. By the early 1890s, she was no longer publishing her poetry through Kegan Paul but with the Bodley Head, the firm that had issued many of Oscar Wilde's works, the 'Keynotes' series of decadent novels, and the infamous *The Yellow Book* literary journal.

Just a few years later, however, financial pressures had forced Tynan into an altogether different corner of London life. Of those events that altered her economic position and, with it, her literary status, the two most important occurred simultaneously in 1893: her move from Dublin to London and her marriage to Henry Albert Hinkson. That her husband was unsuited to regular employment was made evident to her just a year into their marriage, when Hinkson was obliged to resign his position as a teacher at a boys' school, for misbehaviour.[10] At the time, Tynan was eight months' pregnant with their first child, and just weeks after his dismissal, the child was delivered stillborn. Hinkson next tried his hand at journalistic work and managed to write and publish several novels, none of which were a significant source of income for the family. He studied law, was called to the bar and authored what was then the definitive tract on copyright; yet his attempts at legal practice were abortive, and his one viable source of regular income over the course of his 26-year marriage to Tynan in fact came only when his wife's long-term friendship with Lord and Lady Aberdeen resulted in his appointment as Resident Magistrate for Mayo in 1914. Yeats's sister Lily reported the events to her father:

> now [that Hinkson is gainfully employed] I hope poor K. T. will be able to write less and now will write the good stuff she can write – drink has him by the hand these many years, she is likely to have him in handcuffs in Castlebar – all the same I am glad. K. T. was being worked to rags to keep the whole family – a good deal of debt too I know.[11]

As Lily Yeats suggests, it was indeed Tynan's work that afforded the means of 'boiling the pot' for her family throughout their years in England (Tynan, 1916: 353).

It was, therefore, at the point of her relocation to London that the seeds of Tynan's literary fall from grace were planted and where a partial answer to the question of her increasing distance from Yeats may be found, for from this point forward her work necessarily became more popular, and thus less reconcilable with his vision of what literature should be and what it was meant to achieve. Thereafter, she turned with ever more regularity to the writing of prose, and in 1895 issued the first of the approximately 100 full-length volumes of fiction she would produce over the course of her lifetime. Although she would still find herself in this altered stage of her career chatting at garden parties to J. M. Barrie or hearing of her work being praised by Joseph Conrad, her own London circle by the turn of the century largely consisted of an admixture of the women – Meynell, Marie Belloc Lowndes, L. T. Meade (Elizabeth Thomasina Meade Toulmin Smith) and May Sinclair (Mary Amelia St. Clair) – whose intensely professional writing lives she had found herself emulating (Tynan, 1908: 181). She was to claim that her first decade of residence in London was spent in the company of writers and publishers whose preoccupations were more often financial than literary. It was a place and time during which conversations were concerned with 'prices per thousand and biggest circulations, and all the crowded rooms shrieking like parrot-houses at the Zoo, and the gist of it the making of books and the prices to be obtained for them' (Tynan, 1922: 287). The London literary scene she had been so eager to enter quickly began to pall against her memories of the Irish circles in which she had once moved so prominently: 'Far other was the little and memorable movement in Dublin,' she would write, 'a pure movement, in which money and worldly success were never dreamt of' (Tynan, 1922: 287). Tynan would repeatedly claim that she was forced by circumstance to side with London and Mammon, but that her affections remained firmly in Dublin.

Although English commentators would continue to perceive in her post–1893 work a partiality towards Irish interests and the Irish people – a reviewer in the *Manchester Guardian* accused her of punctuating her volumes with the 'glib repetition of stale calumnies on English statesmen' and of exhibiting a 'hysterical' form of Irish bias[12] – it is evident that Tynan's relocation to London had the effect of distancing her from the Irish Revivalists. In his comprehensive survey of the Celtic Revival, Ernest Boyd would criticize the literary course that Tynan followed from 1893 when he argued that the whole of her talent had been revealed and spent in her first three volumes of poetry (Boyd, 1916: 107); thoughts that are foreshadowed by the comments of William Patrick Ryan in his *The Irish Literary Revival*:

[Tynan's] power is unquestioned, her nature is Irish, but her art and standpoint are sometimes English, strange to say. This is even evident in her Gaelic excursions. … She has not entered eagerly into the spirit of our present movement, preferring to work apart, and on her own lines. (Ryan, 1894: 117)

Both Ryan and Boyd, preoccupied by a collective Irish literary project the centrality of which they assert in at times self-aggrandizing ways, inevitably perceived in the newly independent Tynan a writer in decline. In actuality, there is little evidence in her poetry, when viewed as a corpus, to suggest that her literary powers diminished over time, and Boyd's opinions are further tainted by his obvious anti-Catholic bias, particularly when he asserts that Tynan's religion had already precluded her from the realms of poetic greatness:

> Interesting though she may be as the only important Catholic poet in Ireland, Katharine Tynan will hardly rank with the best writers of the Literary Revival. ... Irish Catholicism is necessarily a shallow vein of inspiration, and even at its best, it has not created, and cannot create, great poetry. (Boyd, 1916: 112)

That Yeats shared in the assessments of Boyd and Ryan with regard to Tynan's poetic output is implicit as early as 1895, when his tepid remarks about her work and its lack of 'Gaelic' passion in the third of a series of four articles he published on 'Irish National Literature' in *The Bookman* suggest that his disillusionment had by then already begun (Yeats, 1895: 168). The message conveyed by these men who were convinced of the overarching importance of the Revivalist movement – like many of Ireland's political movements, a predominantly Anglo-Irish Protestant one – is that Tynan's work after 1893 was too far removed from the Literary Renaissance's communal ethos to hold merit; that it simply was not 'Irish' enough.

Yeats and the Revivalists can be seen to exhibit an anti-English bias that Tynan did not share. From the time of her relocation to London, her texts evidence her shifting sympathies and an assimilation of what might be termed 'English' social and political viewpoints. Post–1893, she would often use her work as a means to investigate the position of the individual struggling to reconcile dichotomous consciousnesses: provincial and metropolitan, traditional and modern, Irish and English. From the appearance of her first novel, Ireland as Tynan portrays it offers scant opportunity for alteration or advancement, particularly to its women. Nearly all of her Irish female protagonists begin their fictional journeys from positions of disempowerment: they are disinherited, abandoned, unmarriageable or orphaned, with little or no hope of remedying their financial distress in their home country. London is figured as the place of economic opportunity, where women such as Biddy O'Hara in *The Dear Irish Girl* (1899) and Alicia MacNamara in *The Adventures of Alicia* (1906) find themselves readily employed and inhabiting 'bachelor girl' flats teeming with successful working women on whom they can model themselves. Almost entirely free of the prejudices that are endemic in Ireland, London is portrayed as a space of unhindered social mobility. 'In this greater, freer country, the artist was the equal of any one', Tynan would write in her 1908 novel *The House of the Crickets*. appending this assertion with a characteristically antagonistic statement aimed at those who perpetuated the stifling class-based prejudices she believed were endemic to her homeland:

> When one had succeeded, people would not gather in a corner and whisper and point out that, despite all the great success, that man or that woman had sprung from so low an origin ... All that belonged to the narrower, more provincial life over there [in Ireland]. (Tynan, 1908: 181)

Professionally, Tynan's experiences appear to have been in keeping with such fictional representations. So quickly did she become ensconced in the city's journalistic circles that, in 1896, she was asked by Henry Cust to take over the writing of the column 'Wares of Autolycus' for his *Pall Mall Gazette*. In agreeing to take it on, she inherited the avid readership of its previous writers, Alice Meynell and Elizabeth Robins Pennell, and thereby became one of the most popular and prominent (albeit anonymous) female voices in London. Tynan's contributions remain among the most readable in a series that had, by the time she ascended to its helm, been in existence for three years and included more than eight hundred separate entries. Its subject matter ranged from political commentary to domestic concerns, from gossip to gardening, but the aesthetic of the column was highly literary, and through it Tynan would adopt the position not only of a writer on London, but in essence also of a London writer.

These 'Autolycus' pieces remain compelling not only for revealing the literary standards she was able to achieve on an almost daily basis, but also for the manner in which they document her growing familiarity with, and aversion to, urban existence. Anti-industrialist in her viewpoints, she often uses the column as a means to critique the city's modernization. Her 'Reflections' entry of June 1896, for instance, begins with a deceptively simple description of the mirrors which endure in nature or have survived from the ancients, and then proceeds to compare these to what are for her London's faultlessly engineered yet soulless innovations on the same theme:

> The figure and the shadow have a companion; a third, a visible creature who leaps from the mirror to the stream, is scattered and shattered by a ripple, turned to the most inventive burlesque by the minute contortions of a Neapolitan looking-glass, and restored to decorous precision and robbed of all its separate character by the perfect plate glass of London. (Tynan, 1896b: 10)

Her distaste for the 'gradual' and 'insidious' homogenization represented by the plate glass window also enacts an expression of grief concerning the simultaneous normal-izing and systematizing processes that the city and its inhabitants are undergoing all around her (Tynan, 1896a: 4). Musing on the advent of electricity to her home in the same 'Autolycus' entry, she waxes nostalgic about the bells and candles which had only the day before rung and flickered with their own individual personalities, and derides the 'ostentatious vulgarity and hard mechanicalness that conceal mere emptiness about electric bells and light' (Tynan, 1896a: 4). Finding herself living in a rapidly changing London, she begins to long for the city she had first become acquainted with, the one which had seemed in her younger days to be full of wonder, to offer her a 'first peep into the big world' (Tynan, 1913: 135). Her earliest glimpse of a seemingly driverless motor-car would confirm both the pace of change and the dehumanizing mechanization of the city. Watching the car move through the streets, she realizes she is 'looking at a disappearing London' (Tynan, 1916: 182).

As Tynan's prominence as a journalist and novelist grew, her depictions of London act as evidence that the city's charm was quickly dissipating under the burden of overwork. By the first decade of the twentieth century, she would regularly portray it in much the same manner as did Yeats when, from his position of exile on London's 'pavements grey', he wrote of hearing the lapping of 'The Lake Isle of Innisfree'.[13] From her own urban vantage point, she begins to view Ireland as an unspoilt, pastoral utopia in contrast to the greed, grime and greyness of London. In the many of her poems that compare the two spaces through an interplay of light and shadow, innocence and experience, London always wears the dismal and jaded aspect, as in 'Compensation' in which the city's 'yellow streets' and 'poor sad people / Trudging to their task in a pallid gloom / Below the black house-walls' are sharply offset by the shimmer of her native land: 'And I for the sun at last and going home!' (Tynan, 1914: 57). Work, weariness, and immorality are figured as innate components of life in the city, her altering perceptions of which are at times recognizably attributable to her own changing professional output and position. In 'The Philosopher', London is rendered by the speaker, a returned Irish exile, as the money-driven and prosaic counterpoint to her poetic homeland:

> They haven't too much honour over there, I find.
>
> The country where small money is is better to my mind
> They don't be dramin' money and a man has got the time
>
> To look to seas and mountains and to turn a rhyme.
>
> (Tynan, 1914: 40)

Images of the city's inhabitants weighed down by work and care – 'heavy with money-getting' – would become a feature of her London poems for years.[14]

Throughout her discursive writings, too, the city is depicted as a malignant force, gradually seeping into and encroaching upon the English countryside. She tells us in her memoirs that her home in Ealing was bordered on its country-facing side by sheep pastures, but even in these spaces where the city sprawl had still to reach, these were not the 'innocent country fields' of her childhood (Tynan, 1916: 137). Dotted with 'half-built or newly-built houses, as yet unoccupied' which 'suddenly started up in front of, behind' her as she made her way homeward, the fields wear a sinister aspect: 'We had heard strange stories of the creatures who sometimes dossed in those empty houses, untroubled by the police' (Tynan, 1916: 136–7). The centre of London, in Tynan's recollections, is more ominous still. It is a miasmal place, occluded by 'fogs of a thick blackness ... days of it sometimes when gaslight and lamplight went on all day and night' (Tynan, 1916: 181), and where nature has been tainted by industry: 'the blackness of the trees in their stems and branches, the blackness of the earth which seemed to have been mixed with soot; ... the curious phenomenon that one could not even pluck a flower without having one's fingers soiled' (Tynan, 1912: 146). Describing her annual returns to Ireland, she would view her time there as a period of revivification – 'the change that should enable us to go on living again' (Tynan, 1912: 143).

As long as she remained outside Ireland, it remained in her imagination unchanged and unchanging: positively in its aspect, far more negatively in its attitudes. 'The way with Ireland,' she would write, 'is that no sooner do you get away from her than the golden mists begin to close about her, and she lies, an Island of the Blest, something enchanted in your dreams' (Tynan, 1912: 159). She admitted that the reality of her homeland often turned out to be very different than her visions of it from afar. So, too, would it be with the people who actually lived there. Over the course of her period of exile, she would see her work intensely scrutinized by her nationalist compatriots in particular: the 'touchiness of my own country-people,' she would state, 'was always a trouble' (Tynan, 1916: 261). By the mid–1890s, she found herself falling foul of both John B. Yeats, and her oldest and dearest literary friend, Father Matthew Russell. Defending herself against Mr. Yeats's accusations that her work was 'anti-Irish', she pointed to the difficulties inherent in her position as an Irish person writing from an English location:

> if you protested mildly against the many shibboleths concerning England you were told that you have become Anglicised by long residence in England, and if you hinted at an Irish fault a whole avalanche of reproaches were hurled upon you. (Tynan, 1916: 318–19)

More troubling still, was Russell's public admonishment of her literary themes. It was in 1896 that the editor of *The Irish Monthly* took her to task for not writing of 'her own people': 'Let her be true to Ireland', he stated in a review of her novel *Oh, What a Plague is Love!*, 'and leave English life to the successors of Anthony Trollope.'[15] In her response to Russell, whose critique had obviously rankled, Tynan would betray the very anti-Irishness she was attempting to defend herself against:

> They always think in Ireland that all praise falls far short of their merits. That is why I suppose our literature is one-eyed. It is not so in any other literature of the world so far as I know. And why can't I write an innocent little English love-story if I want to? It will keep my pot boiling which is more than any countrymen will. It is likely to put more in the pot than any other of my books anyhow.[16]

Here, through references to her feelings of abandonment, Tynan reveals that the old wounds Ireland had inflicted on her career remain unhealed, and simultaneously discloses the degree to which she has assimilated London's attitudes toward writing and its purpose. In her poetic versions of Ireland and in her true-life reassurances of the purity of its literary movement, financial concerns were supposed not to figure. To her, however, money appears by this time to have mattered very much.

Russell's fellow Jesuit Stephen J. Brown would judge her work differently, asserting that, because she had come to know 'both countries by long residence', her novels ably highlighted the differences between Ireland and England in a manner that reinforced the need for separatism and aided the cause of Irish Nationalism (Brown, 1935: 645). Viewed with the impartiality that hindsight lends, her texts do indeed leave little doubt that the deepest of her affections were reserved for her native country, and she would often and unequivocally assert the differences between the city she inhabited and the land of her birth: 'between London and Ireland, so far as atmosphere and feelings of things is concerned,' she would write in 1909, 'there is a world of difference' (Tynan, 1908: 1). Yet it is an indication of the degree to which her political views had been altered by long proximity to the English that her stance on the Boer War was always pro-British, and intensified after the death of a 'very English and very loyal' friend at the hands of the Boers (Tynan, 1913: 347). She admitted to having 'lived long enough in England to be concerned for the success of British arms' and did not side with her fellow Irish Nationalists who took an actively pro-Boer stance (Tynan, 1916: 210). Tellingly, she would record her own response to 'Mafficking' with little sense of detachment:

> suddenly, out of the darkness and quietness of the night, came a voice – the voice

of one who ran. It was as though someone ran with a torch. The voice was crying 'Mafeking is Relieved!'

We rushed out into the street. ... Then suddenly in the main road the indescribable noise broke out. It went on all night – London making carnival. The sober Briton had lost his seven senses for once. ... It was the reaction from the Black Week – that week in December of Magersfontein, Stormberg and Colenso – the weeks since in which things had been going as fatally ill for the British arms as could well be imagined. (Tynan, 1916: 214)

Further to this, there is no indication that she supported one of the largest demonstrations of Irish Nationalist solidarity during the Boer War period: this was the protest staged by Maud Gonne and Inghinidhe na hÉireann (Daughters of Ireland) against Queen Victoria's state visit to Ireland in July of 1900. Tynan had not, she would admit, been among Gonne's friends (Tynan, 1913: 363).

Like many of the diasporic Irish characters featured in her fiction, Tynan was to find that the decades she would eventually spend in England had left her occupying a political position somewhere between 'Irish' and 'English' which could be difficult to reconcile. 'I was a Sinn Feiner to my English and Scottish friends, and even dared to call myself so', she suggested, admitting at the same time that her 'Sinn Fein friends' would think her 'sadly lacking', and ascribing this lack to her migrancy: 'a long period of years lived out of the country has taught me that no cause and no people are altogether black or altogether white' (Tynan, 1922: 135). She would return to Ireland in 1911, believing her homecoming to be permanent, but once there, the degree to which 18 years of London life had altered her relationship to Ireland and her fellow Irish people were made manifest. She found herself living in what was for her an irretrievably 'changed Ireland', occupying a vastly different social stratum to the one she had left ('we returned to the Anglo-Irish having gone away from the Celts') and faced with the unexpected and 'appalling' poverty of Dublin (Tynan, 1919: 1 and 8).

With the advent of the First World War, she would feel both her isolation and the ideological differences with her Irish neighbours even more keenly. The apathy with which many Irish people viewed the war effort would arouse a sense of derision in her which is evidenced in many of the pages of the war diary she began keeping in the summer of 1914. In it, she would criticize young and able-bodied Irish men who worked on Dublin's shop counters rather than enlisting in the British army and refer derisively to the Irish Volunteers she witnessed on their marches through Dublin as men who were 'playing at soldiers ... & feeling doubtless very superior persons & patriots – because – they know no better, let us hope'.[17] Tynan's intense advocacy of the war effort would lead her to write a body of First World War poems that enjoyed 'an extraordinary vogue' in Britain, and the approximately 100 letters per week she was at one point receiving from war-bereaved readers attest to the extent of her popularity (Tynan, 1919: 175–6). As the fighting dragged on, her sons, each in his turn, would enlist in the British army and serve as officers with recognized distinction, despite the fact that the eldest was just 20 years of age by the time of the armistice. In much the same way as she had once longed for Ireland, she began during the war years to yearn for the comfort of like-minded friends who were as 'enthusiastically pro-Ally' as she was (Tynan, 1919: 204). Letters from London became 'news from the great world', while her home in Mayo was referred to as 'this place where nothing ever happens'.[18]

The events of Easter 1916 had the effect of briefly refocusing her attention on the cause of Irish independence. Like many Irish people, she was shocked into a renewed fervour for nationalism by the swiftness and cruelty of England's retribution on the Rising's leaders. Yet even at this juncture, when her focus was overtly on Ireland's woes, her responses were informed and intensified by her experiences of having lived in London and amongst the English: 'To me any bloodiness between England and Ireland was unthinkable', she would write three years after the Rising, her dismay and disappointment still palpable:

> All that belonged to the bad old days, and here was '98 come again, and the people who were my own people were being shot and deported by the people with whom we had lived in amity and affection for eighteen long years.' (Tynan, 1919: 205)

Back in Ealing for a visit when the Treaty of Versailles was signed, she would hang an Irish flag from her upstairs window (Tynan, 1922: 98).

By the time her 1922 memoir, *The Wandering Years*, was published, Tynan's relationship to her homeland was undergoing yet another revision. Due to a delay in publication, she was forced to append her original ending to the volume – an image of 'the happy days of the truce' – with a qualification:

> at the moment of writing (May, 1922) Ireland is more than ever in the melting-pot, and what is to emerge from it God only knows. I make this statement to anticipate the critic who might say that I jested while a dearer Rome was burning. The Irish always jest even though they jest with tears. Instead of ending at a happy moment I end at the saddest; but Hope is at the bottom of the Pandora's box of Irish troubles, and I believe proudly and firmly in the ultimate destinies of my country. (Tynan, 1922: 386–7)

A year later, following the assassination of Michael Collins and the escalation of fighting between the pro- and anti-Treaty factions in Ireland, Tynan would evidence her increasing disillusionment with her Irish countrymen in her personal letters: 'Those wretched rulers of Ireland & the whole ignominious affair!' she would write to her friend, the London-based novelist Frank Mathew, on 21 December 1923. 'How one detests it all.'[19]

Contiguous with this mounting estrangement from Ireland, Tynan's values had steadily diverged from those of Yeats. Although she had readily forgiven him his public disavowals of her work, and he had endured, with good grace, her injudicious publication of his personal letters in 1913, they had come to realize that there were points on which they might never again be compatible. It was in fact her pro-British stance during the war that became the primary site of contention between the two of them, as she would note in a journal entry in October of 1914: 'I am carried back to an evening two months ago when I talked with a distinguished writer about the War & we disagreed so sharply that I felt the old friendship would never be possible again.'[20] By 1919, Tynan was referring to Yeats as 'A Strayed Poet' with a 'muddling philosophy', and he had long since ceased to take notice of her work altogether

(Tynan, 1919: 78–9). The degree of their estrangement is marked most poignantly by his refusal to write an introduction for her *Collected Poems*, published in the year before her death. By then, he was loath to draw any attention to their early and intense literary kinship.

The insular attitudes Yeats had promoted in his early letters to Tynan – his advocacy of poetry 'for Ireland's not for England's use' – anticipate the rhetoric of separatism, of Irish-Irelandism, that was prevalent in Ireland by the 1920s. For Tynan, whose long years of exile in London had led her to acknowledge the grey areas and points of overlap between Irish and English interests and perspectives, such attitudes were artificial and untenable. She would make what was arguably the most revealing statement about her personal disenchantment with the ever more irreconcilable factions in her homeland by leaving the country permanently in 1924, remaining disappointed to the last in what had transpired after the Free State was formed. In the final decade of her life, Tynan would reconcile herself to London, her adopted city, through her recognition that, once in England, Irish people often found common ground; that in London there somehow existed a more cohesive sense of Irishness than was then possible in her homeland. 'When Irish people meet in England, they don't bother about difference in politics', she would assert (Tynan, 1922: 89). 'In Ireland, dog may eat dog. Never out of Ireland' (Tynan, 1922: 274).

Katharine Tynan died in Wimbledon in 1931.

Notes

This research was funded by an Arts and Humanities Research Council (AHRC) Doctoral Studentship (www.ahrc.uk).

1 'New Books', *The Irish Monthly*: 331 and McLaughlin, 'Katharine Tynan', *The Ampleforth Journal*: 277. See also 'Katharine Tynan's Poems', *The Irish Monthly*. 12 (138): 618–24, and 'Miss Tynan's "Louise de la Vallière", & c', *The Irish Monthly*. 13 (145): 377–82.

2 Foster, *W. B. Yeats: A Life*. I: 54.

3 Foster, *W. B. Yeats: A Life*. I: 39.

4 See Innes, *Woman and Nation in Irish Literature and Society*: 126–7. Yeats's 1919 elegy to Robert Gregory features the lines, 'Soldier, scholar, horseman, he,/As 'twere all life's epitome' and 'Our Sidney and our perfect man', that recognizably echo these lines in Tynan's 1913 poem, 'George Wyndham': 'Soldier, poet, courtier/He was these and more than these. ... Sidney's brother, Raleigh's twin'.

5 The other two in the triumvirate, according to Yeats, were Lionel Johnson and himself.

6 Letter from Katharine Tynan to Mary Gill (14 November 1891), Papers of Katharine Tynan, John Rylands Library, Manchester Box 16, Folder 3.

7 Letter from Katharine Tynan to Father Matthew Russell, S. J. (24 January 1884), Papers of Father Matthew Russell, S. J., Jesuit Archive, Dublin'.

8 Letter from Katharine Tynan to Father Matthew Russell, S. J. (4 December 1884), papers of Matthew Russell, S. J.

9 Letter from Kegan Paul to Wilfrid Meynell (24 February 1885), Papers of Katharine Tynan, Box 12, Folder 17.

10 Letter from Katharine Tynan to Father Matthew Russell, S. J. (29 May 1894), Jesuit Archive, Dublin, Papers of Father Matthew Russell, S. J.
11 Letter from Lily Yeats to John Butler Yeats (10 October 1914), Yeats Correspondence, Ms. 31,112 (23). My sincere appreciation to Janet Wallwork of the John Rylands University Library, University of Manchester, for calling my attention to this letter.
12 'New Books', *The Guardian* (Manchester): 5.
13 Yeats, 'The Lake Isle of Innisfree', *The Collected Poems of W. B. Yeats*: 44.
14 See, for instance, Tynan, 'The Foggy Dew', *The Wind in the Trees*: 71 and 'The Grey Streets of London', *Innocencies*: 55.
15 Anon. (1896) 'Notes on New Books', *The Irish Monthly*. March: 168.
16 Letter from Katharine Tynan to Father Matthew Russell, S. J. (8 April 1896), papers of Matthew Russell, S. J.
17 Katharine Tynan, *A Woman's Notes In War-Time*, entry for 16 April 1915, Papers of Katharine Tynan, Box 13, Folder 1.
18 Tynan, *A Woman's Notes in War-Time*, entry for 21 July 1915, Papers of Katharine Tynan, Box 13, Folder 1.
19 Letter from Katharine Tynan to Frank Mathew (4 July 1923), Papers of Katharine Tynan, Box 16, Folder 4.
20 Tynan, *A Woman's Notes in War-Time*, page numbered '57', Papers of Katharine Tynan, Box 13, Folder 1.

6

Pádraic Ó Conaire's London – A Real or an Imaginary Place?

Pádraigín Riggs

Pádraic Ó Conaire ('Patrick Conroy') had been living in London for almost two years when his first short story was published in the Gaelic League paper, *An Claidheamh Soluis*, in December 1901. The writer was 19 years old and was employed as a 'boy copyist' at the Board of Education in Whitehall. Ó Conaire continued to live in London for the next 14 years, the most productive years of his life as a writer, returning to Ireland in 1915. For the years following his return to Ireland until his death in 1928, he had no permanent home but moved around the country, mainly between Galway, Dublin and Wicklow, eking out a meagre existence from his writing and from some short irregular teaching posts, and dependent for much of the time on the charitable assistance of friends.

Ó Conaire wrote exclusively in Irish. His published *oeuvre*, written between 1901 and 1927, the year before his death, includes some 400 short stories and some 200 journalistic essays. Most of this material initially appeared in newspapers and journals associated with the Irish language revival movement and the nationalist political movement. A total of 20 collections of his short fiction and essays were published as books, with many items appearing in more than one collection. In addition to this material, Ó Conaire wrote one novel, *Deoraíocht* (1910), and six short plays.[1] He also wrote a number of collections of stories specifically for schoolchildren.

The fact that Ó Conaire produced his best work, all in the Irish language, during his 15-year sojourn in London is something of a paradox. While he was not a native speaker, Ó Conaire's relationship with Irish was hugely significant throughout his whole life. Born into a prosperous middle-class family in Galway City in 1882, he was exposed to both Irish and English in his domestic environment. His father, Thomas Conroy, was from the Irish-speaking area of Rosmuck in Connemara, and his mother, Kate MacDonagh, was from Galway City. The family would have spoken English amongst themselves but Irish would have been used in the family's public house where many of the customers were Irish speakers from the West. The young women who were employed as domestic servants in the house, and who looked after the young Pádraic and his brothers, were probably Irish speakers from Connemara.[2]

Thomas Conroy emigrated to America in 1888, abandoning his wife and three children. Kate immediately assumed control of the family business but she died suddenly in 1894 and, following her death, the children were sent to Rosmuck, to live with their paternal grandparents. The Conroys of Rosmuck were prosperous merchants, who conducted much of their business from boats throughout the Connemara Gaeltacht. This family also spoke English in the house but Irish was, necessarily, the language used in all dealings with the local population. Exact details of the amount of time Pádraic spent in Rosmuck are unclear but he appears to have attended school for part of that time on the nearby small island of Annaghvaan, where a family relative was employed as a teacher. Ó Conaire dedicated his novel, *Deoraíocht*, to this teacher who, he claimed 'first taught me my Irish letters'.[3] Following the death of their grandmother in 1896, Pádraic and one of his brothers were sent to stay with a maternal aunt in County Clare. Some Irish was still spoken in this part of Clare and even though English was probably the language of the home, the school at Reneen that Pádraic attended for a short time was one of the small number of schools where Irish was taught. Within two years, he was uprooted again, this time to be sent to Rockwell College in County Tipperary, a large boarding school run by the Holy Ghost order. He was enrolled in the seminary, the intention being that he would become a priest, but when the seminary closed, in August 1898, he was transferred to the order's other boarding school, Blackrock College, in Dublin. We know that he took Irish as a subject while at both of these colleges. Irish or 'Celtic' had been introduced as an extra subject for the Intermediate Certificate from 1879, though the subject was taught outside of normal school hours and the Holy Ghost priests – a French order – were amongst the small minority who opted to teach the language. In July 1899, he was asked to leave Blackrock – for reasons unspecified – without having completed his final examination. In January 1900 he commenced work in the civil service in London. By the age of eighteen, therefore, Ó Conaire had been uprooted no less than six times. On each occasion, his domestic environment was English speaking but he was exposed to Irish either in the community or in school. In London, the capital city of the British Empire, Patrick Conroy would find himself, for the first time and, again, paradoxically at the centre rather than on the margins of an Irish-speaking environment.

The Gaelic League had been established in Dublin in 1893 and, three years later, a branch of the organization was founded in London.[4] Conroy was enrolled as a member of the London branch at 8, Adelphi Terrace, Strand, on 13 December 1900 and the organization played a central role in his life until he returned to Ireland in 1915. Through his association with it he came to know Irish emigrants from all social classes: native speakers of Irish, scholars of the language, and those who joined the League in order to learn the language. He became an active member of the League's various sub-committees, he participated in its cultural activities, and he taught Irish at its classes throughout London.[5] He was respected as an accomplished speaker of Irish, as a committed activist on behalf of the language, as an inspiring teacher and, above all, as a successful writer. It is significant that his only permanent address while he lived in London was that of the Gaelic League on Adelphi Terrace. The domestic instability he experienced for the first eighteen years of his life seems to have set a permanent pattern because although he fathered four children with Mary McManus between 1905 and 1911 (there is no evidence that they ever married) the address is different on each of the children's birth certificates. When he left London in 1915, he followed in his father's footsteps by abandoning Mary and the children, although he did return on a few occasions to visit them towards the end of his life.

He had hoped to live as a full-time writer – supported by the Gaelic League – when he returned to Ireland, but by 1915 the organization had taken a new direction and providing maintenance for a writer was low on its list of priorities. He received a small allowance from the League's Executive for about 15 months in return for articles he produced for *An Claidheamh Soluis,* but these contributions appear to have ceased by March 1917. By now he was no longer in receipt of a regular income – however meagre – from his civil service post in London and his drinking was becoming increasingly problematic. Eventually his health failed and he died destitute in Richmond Hospital, Dublin in October 1928. If he left papers, books or personal effects behind when he returned to Ireland in 1915, no record of them remains. The house in Lambeth, in which Mary McManus was living, was destroyed by a German bomb in April 1945. Mary and her infant grandson were killed in the incident.

Exile is a recurring theme in Ó Conaire's writings, but only the short story, 'Nóra Mharcais Bhig'[6] and the novel *Deoraíocht*[7] focus on the situation of the exiled Irish in London. Initially, both stories were read by reviewers as realistic depictions of the plight of the Irish emigrant. 'Nóra Mharcais Bhig' tells the familiar story of an innocent young woman from a small town in the West of Ireland who, having been seduced and abandoned by her lover, runs away to London. She is obviously pregnant, though that is not explicitly stated, and soon she finds herself alone and penniless in the big city, until a 'kind man' rescues her. One night, many years later, as she is on the street, she sees the young man who first seduced her and she flees from him, taking refuge in a church where she is rescued by a priest and helped to return home to her unsuspecting parents. She struggles to adapt to her former life until, on a warm summer day, she accepts a drink from a local young man. Later that day, her father discovers her on the side of the road, drunk, and he tells her she must return to London where she learned such behaviour. The story concludes poignantly with the heartbroken father painting over the name on the side of his boat, the name of his beloved daughter who had helped pay for the boat with the remittances she had sent from London.

Although London is named in the story, descriptions of the city are somewhat general and the city's streets, buildings and landmarks are never named. In place of specificity, the city is evoked; such as here, when Nora encounters her former lover in the West End:

> She was walking the streets one night, having sent a letter, containing a small sum of money, back home. It was eleven o'clock. The people were emerging from the theatres in their thousands, and she was staring at them. Some of them stared at her and at women of her kind. That stare that reveals the desire and greed that cause human destruction, that give rise to war, that have provided poets and story-tellers with material from the days of Troy down to the present.[8]

Significantly, the reference to love, so powerful that it is portrayed in literature as a cause of war and destruction, is equated with the lustful desire that the prostitute inspires in her client. Nora's lover is mentioned on two occasions in the story, and on each occasion he is associated with an idealized notion of love that conflicts with the sordid reality that is Nora's situation:

> Because of the way she had loved him she was forced to leave Ros Dá Loch and her friends and family and go out into the big world. The affable young man who used to spend his holidays in Ros Dhá Loch was dearer to her than anyone she had ever known! And what wonderful stories he told about the way they lived in the big towns across the sea! How she loved those stories! And when he told the foolish girl that he had never met anyone anywhere that he loved more than her, how ecstatic she was! And the fine house they would have in some big town when he would be a doctor!

Reality for Nora is an overcrowded slum dwelling in a backstreet in the big town across the sea. The transition from the small town in the West of Ireland to London symbolizes Nora's internal transition from a state of blissful innocence to that of bitter disillusionment. The surreal description of her journey – her first train journey – is the stuff of nightmare:

> As she sat in the train she was alarmed to see that rivers and bays, lakes, mountains and plains all rushed past her while she herself did nothing. Where were they all going? What life lay ahead of her in the strange foreign country to which this weird carriage was taking her? She was panic-stricken. Darkness was falling on plain and hill. Her mind went blank but she felt as if she were riding some wild animal; she could hear its heart thumping beneath her with rage; it was a dragon with fire coming from its eye; she was being taken to some dreadful wilderness – to a place where the sun never shone and rain never fell.

The London of this story is not so much a geographical place but rather an internal state; Nora in London is to Nora in Ros Dhá Loch as Stevenson's Mr. Hyde is to Dr. Jeckyl:

> Nora thrived after her return home. In that person known as Nora Mharcais Bhig in Ros Dhá Loch there were, in fact, two separate women, the gentle young woman who spent time in England, earning money which she sent home, and another woman unknown to everyone at home, who lived a life of torture in a foreign city. ... And the two were in permanent conflict.

The 'gentle young woman' is simply an idealized version of Nora, the young woman whom her father imagines to be free from the self-destructive characteristics of her feckless brothers. The conflict is, in reality, between this idealized version of Nora – the only version that her family and neighbours in Ros Dhá Loch can conceive of – and the real Nora, the vulnerable, wayward young woman who has the same rebellious nature as her brothers. Nora's traumatic migration to London represents the inevitable transformation that occurs when her repressed personality emerges and this transformation is irreversible, as her failure to readapt to life in Ros Dhá Loch after her sojourn in London demonstrates.

This story was regarded by critics as a contemporary social document, highlighting the predicament of the innocent Irish country girl who came to grief when she succumbed to the temptations of the big city. Through his innovative use of free indirect style, however, Ó Conaire deliberately avoids presenting a documentary narrative and succeeds, instead, in revealing the motives and conflicts of the protagonists, making a symbolic use of the geographical locations, Ros Dhá Loch and London, in order to represent the internal rift. This was exactly what he had advocated in his 1908 prize-winning essay 'Seanlitríocht na nGael agus Nualitríocht na hEorpa'[9] when he said: 'It is worth examining any action performed by an individual in order to show the reason for it, whether that action be good or evil. [Modern writers] do not try to impose a message.'[10]

Deoraíocht is Ó Conaire's only novel. Because the story is narrated in the first person and because there are certain similarities between the narrator and the author – both were born in Galway and both now live in London – the book appears initially to be an autobiography. However, the narrator is named as Micil Ó Maoláin who, following an accident (he is knocked down by a car), has lost an arm and a leg, and whose face has been so disfigured that he is unrecognizable from his former self. Pointedly perhaps, the accident occurs when he is out on the streets looking for work. Having squandered the 250 pounds (paid in gold coins) he received as compensation for his injuries, he is destitute and accepts a job as a freak in a travelling show, owned by 'the Little Yellow Man'.[11] One of the other freaks in the show is 'the Big Fat Lady'. The story consists of a series of apparently disconnected events, in the course of which Micil succumbs to increasing self-contempt and despair alleviated only by alcohol, by the passing company of friends, and by the occasional scrap of food. Micil's narrative culminates in his violent death as he sits in a London Park waiting for something to happen. But he is not simply waiting: he is writing, he is committing to paper what will turn out to be his final moments. Cursing a man who had rejected him as a potential employee, Micil writes:

> I no longer have the energy to strike a man, or the courage. All I can do is curse you – my curse upon you George Fott! ... Maybe my curse might have more effect were I to write it down on paper ... and I have written it here, sitting under an oak tree, in the middle of a park, in London, England, on this beautiful spring morning on the nineteenth day of April in the year nineteen hundred and seven.
>
> ...
>
> I am waiting for the return of the pleasant company that I had sent away so as to visit George Fott. But they are not coming back; nothing is coming except gloomy thoughts, dark gloomy thoughts, and the delerium of hunger ...
>
> ...
>
> But the dark thoughts do not torment me all the time. I got a couple of pence yesterday for holding a horse and I bought a bit of cheese and some bread. I drank a glass of beer. I went into the park and sat under the oak tree. A kind of merriment came into my heart. I could feel the blood coursing through my veins. There were a lot of people in the park, but they had no notion of how happy was the cripple who was singing heartily under the oak tree. (Ó Conaire, 1994: 149–50)

This montage of competing sensations and thoughts are the final words that Micil commits to paper, but they are not the final words of the novel. Deploying the found document trope of the kind used by James Hogg in *The Private Memories and Confessions of a Justified Sinner* (1824), by Vladimir Nabokov in *Pale Fire* (1962) and, more recently, by James Robertson in *The Testament of Gideon Mack* (2006) another, anonymous, but eerily knowledgeable voice concludes the narrative by announcing not only the discovery of the document we have been reading, but also the death of its author in the most pathetic and ambiguous of circumstances. Set out in enboldened italics, we enter – via this new narrator's brief and partly ventriloquized contribution – into eerie, uncanny territory:

> This poor man was found dead under an oak tree, in the middle of a park, in London, England. Some of these pages were in his pocket. There was a pistol beside him which had never been fired. It was only a toy which had failed the man who carried it. Beside him also was an old knife, an old blunt chipped knife – the knife that had killed him.
>
> … And little had my poor friend thought that the pistol bought from the sailor would fail him — but had not life itself failed him? (Ó Conaire, 1994, 150)

Notwithstanding the sheer strangeness of its concluding tableau, and its fragmented and, at times, seemingly aleatory narrative (the book has, in fact, been described as the first example of Irish modernism, and it is certainly informed by European and British strains of modernist concerns and technique), *Deoraíocht* was read at the time of its publication as a documentary about emigration. For example, Pádraic Pearse writing in *An Claidheamh Soluis*, said:

> It is a story of Irish life in exile, not the successful life of the men and women who through industry and moral worth lead praiseworthy lives, but the life of the beaten, of the hopeless, of the forgotten children of our country who, as a Scotch writer says of the less fortunate exiles of his own race, leave home and never return. … The exile life of those who go under has never before been pictured as it is pictured here, never before in Irish, and never so well in English.[12]

'E. O S', writing in *An tÉireannach*, the London paper of the Gaelic League, said:

> This book is about the emigrant whose life is destroyed and who cannot recover. Anyone who is familiar with London and with the lives of the English and the Irish who live there will recognise this as an accurate depiction of the awful life endured by the Irish of this city.[13]

Seven years later, when *Deoraíocht* was at the centre of a controversy between Fr. Peter O'Leary (An tAthair Peadar Ua Laoghaire) and the National University of Ireland concerning the suitability of the book as a textbook for the matriculation examination, Douglas Hyde wrote in defence of the book:

> The truth is, if this book were properly understood, it would be obvious that this is a homily against people emigrating from Ireland and settling in a big city, failing and finding themselves hungry. That is what the author himself did; he left Connemara and went to London.[14]

The title, 'Deoraíocht' ('Exile') encouraged this response – emigration was a prominent issue at the time. Four years before the publication of the novel, the Haverstock Hill school of the Gaelic League had produced a play entitled *An Deoraí* (*The Exile*), by Lorcán Ó Tuathail, the main objective of the production being to provide anti-emigration propaganda. In 1908, Mícheál Ó Conchúir won second prize in the Gaelic League Oireachtas literary competition for a 'short novel' entitled *Scéal an Deoraí* (*The Exile's Tale*) and this was published in two instalments in *An Claidheamh Soluis* in 1909. Ó Conchúir's exile was based in America. The style and structure of Ó Conaire's novel are inconsistent with the style and structure of a social document, however. In his preface to the 1973 edition, Mícheál Mac Liammóir stated:

> *Realistic* is the description used by many critics but that is not entirely accurate. The book is profoundly realistic but, as far as its structure and style are concerned, it is not realistic but, rather, has that quality described by painters as *primitif*.

Eleven years later, a new interpretation was suggested by Tomás Ó Broin in a study entitled *Saoirse Anama Uí Chonaire* (*Ó Conaire – A Liberated Soul*). According to Ó Broin, *Deoraíocht* is an example of Expressionism, and he suggests, as putative models, Jarry's *Ubu Roi* and Strindberg's *Till Damascus*. He admits, however, that:

> *Deoraíocht* contains so many features of Expressionism that it can be described as a consummate example of that movement. However Ó Conaire's sources are not easy to identify. The book bears a striking resemblance to certain plays that were written after 1910, but all we can say is that the authors may all have drawn on the same sources as Ó Conaire.[15]

Read in the wider context of Ó Conaire's fiction, *Deoraíocht* is another story of thwarted love. It is possible to identify three corresponding triangular relationships in the story. In each relationship there is a young man, a young woman and her father. In the first triangle we find Micil, Máire Ní Laoi, the woman he left behind in Galway whom he had hoped to marry, and Máire's father (described as Micil's 'uncle'). In the second triangle we find a character called 'Seoirse Coff', who is the freakish persona that Micil assumes in the travelling show, with the Fat Lady and the Little Yellow Man (who, it transpires, is the father of the Fat Lady). In the third triangle, we find Willie Reilly (a character in a historical ballad that 'Seoirse' is reading one evening after the show, when the Fat Lady appears to offer him a plate of food, the Cooleen Bawn (Willie's beloved) and Squire Folliard (the father of the Cooleen Bawn).

The first 'triangle' forms the main storyline: Micil has left his home in Galway in order to find work in London, so that he can earn enough money to marry his cousin, Máire Ní Laoi, but Máire marries someone else – the marriage having apparently been arranged by her father, who disapproved of her relationship with Micil. When the travelling show visits Galway, Micil (heavily disguised as 'Seoirse') is shocked to see Máire in the audience and misunderstands when she calls out 'Micil!' until he realizes that Micil is the name of her husband. Here, as in a number of other scenes in the book, Micil contemplates his ideal love scenario, but, as in the case of Nora, the ideal makes a mockery of the character's real situation.

The second 'triangle' contains a trio of grotesque characters but the relationship between them mirrors that of Micil, Máire and her father. Seoirse Coff is the name given to Micil by the Little Yellow Man, after he has dressed him in a hideous costume, calculated to exaggerate his disfigurement and make him even more repulsive, so that Seoirse becomes a separate persona. The Fat Lady, who is defined by her colossal size, declares her love for Seoirse and the Little Yellow Man decides to exploit this declaration by presenting the bizarre couple to his audience as a pair of lovers. Invoking literary sources, from the contemporary songs of Thomas Moore to the traditional story of Deirdre and Naoise, he entertains the audience with the love story of the two freaks:

> 'The fattest woman in the world', he said. 'Twenty-seven stone in weight. The Fat Lady who married the Mad Man who killed eight men in Germany with a knife! Look at the traces of blood! And are they not the happy pair? Ah, all you young women, isn't love a wonderful thing? The great Irish poet, Thomas Moore, was not far from the truth when he said that there is not in this wide world a thing as powerful as it. … Ah, is it not as permanent as the hills, as glorious as the sun?…
>
> Has it changed in the least from the way it was in the time of the brave Sons of Usna? It has not, my friends! The Mad Man has his own Deirdre. He has, and he loves her more than …' (Ó Conaire, 1910: 52–3)

Once again, the idealized scenario, as portrayed by the poets and storytellers, is contrasted with the terrible reality.

The third triangle further accentuates this discrepancy. Micil (alias 'Seoirse') is relaxing after the show, reading a book, when the Fat Lady appears with food for him. She insists on knowing what he is reading and when she sees that it is a collection of verses she recites the following lines:

> 'Rise up, Willie Reilly', she says, 'and come along with me,
> I'm goin' to leave my father's house, and quit this countiree,
> To leave my father's houses, his dwellings, and free lands,
> And go along with Reilly, as you may understand.'

This ballad was well known at the time *Deoraíocht* was published. It had been included by P. W. Joyce in his *Old Irish Folk Music and Songs*, published in 1909 and William Carleton had written a novel based on the Willie Reilly story.[16] Details of the background are given by Joyce as follows:

> The event commemorated in this ballad occurred towards the end of the eighteenth century, and the scene is near Bundoran, beside the boundaries of the three counties, Donegal, Fermanagh and Sligo, where the ruined house of the great Squire Folliard is still to be seen. The proper family name is Folliot, but the people always pronounced it Folliard. The whole story is still vividly remembered in the district; and Carleton has founded on it his novel of 'Willie Reilly'. The penal laws were then in force, and it was very dangerous for a young catholic Irishman to run away with the daughter of a powerful local Squire. The song, with its pretty air, was known and sung all over Ireland, so that it has clung to my memory from my earliest days. (Joyce, 1909: 230–1)

It can be fairly assumed, therefore, that the ballad would have been familiar to readers of *Deoraíocht* and that the few lines quoted would have been sufficient to evoke the full song, that in Joyce's version runs to 15 verses. According to the story, Willie Reilly, a young Catholic, seduced the daughter of the Protestant Squire Folliard. Reilly was arrested and charged with stealing jewels and 'many a precious thing'[17] from the young woman and he faced the death sentence. But his 'Cooleen Bawn' was present in court, and she spoke up in his defence, declaring that she loved him and that it was she who forced him to run away with her. Reilly is acquitted and though the couple do not marry, she gives him a ring as a token of her love 'that [you] may think of my broken heart when in a foreign land'. The similarities between the Willie Reilly story and the Micil / Máire love story of *Deoraíocht* are clear, particularly in the reference to the 'foreign land'. As a love story, the Reilly story may not have an ideal ending, but unlike Máire Ní Laoi, the Cooleen Bawn offers Reilly a token of her everlasting love even if she is unable to marry him.

As we saw in the case of 'Nóra Mharcais Bhig', the geographical locations in *Deoraíocht* – in this case, Galway and London – are, again, internal states. Each place is defined as the obverse of the other – that is, 'Galway' is a place that is not London and 'London' is a place that is not Galway. Although London is named, its placenames and landmarks are entirely absent from the text; the city representing the present, and Galway the past (as well as some ideal, imaginary time). Micil attributes his misfortunes to the fact that he was forced to go to London, and it is more than tempting to regard his disfigurement and disability as a metaphor for the emotional damage that he suffered as a result of losing Máire. Thus, London is synonymous with loss and damage – when it is described it is very often in abject and grotesque terms – while Galway is synonymous with a state of innocence and hope, a kind of *Paradise Lost*. When Micil returns to his native Galway, it is in the persona of Seoirse Coff, and the unexplained urgency of his return to London seems to correspond to Nora's banishment back to that city because the person each has become is incompatible with the person each had been formerly.

Deoraíocht is more complex than *Nóra Mharcais Bhig*, which adheres to the restrictions of the short story form, and is less amenable to interpretation – as the diverse attempts at interpretation testify. While the three triangles give some coherence to the disconnected series of incidents that make up the narrative, there are a number of secondary themes that are less easy to accommodate within the confines of a single story; foremost among them, the theme of language. Although the story is purportedly set in London (and not in the Irish-speaking London of the Gaelic League where Ó Conaire found his spiritual home) there is just one reference to the fact that the language being spoken is English. There is a scene in a public house, where Micil, having squandered his money apart from the last half-sovereign, makes a deal with a sailor whereby he parts with his money in return for a pistol and both proceed to spend the money on drink. Micil quickly becomes excited and he begins to talk volubly. He says:

> I began to talk. I began to recount marvellous stories to the lusty sailor at my side, and of course, the stories were all about myself.

I was speaking in English at first, but it was not long before I changed to Irish, without realising it. (Ó Conaire, 1910: 16)

This is an important point in the overall narrative because it is at this point that the Little Yellow Man first makes an appearance and proposes that Micil work for him in his show. It is clear that nobody understands the language Micil is using but the sailor tells the Little Yellow Man that he is a German, with a colourful past that explains his mutilated body. Micil begins to conform to the role that has been assigned to him and utters a blood-curdling bellow. He is amazed when a woman responds, speaking to him in Irish, saying: '"You are a strange German, you, who have been speaking Irish all night"!' The speaker is another grotesque character, The Big Red-haired Woman, who resembles one of Maupassant's kind-hearted whores and whose subsequent relationship with Micil alternates between that of mother and that of jealous lover. Claiming to have come from the West of Ireland, she also functions as Micil's link with his Irish past. However, her role in the overall story is not clear.

One other episode, that has no apparent connection with the narrative as a whole, occurs after Micil has returned to London following his short visit to Galway with the travelling show. He is penniless and profoundly despondent and has had virtually no human contact for some time and he decides to venture into the street. He sees a group of men – vagrants, like himself – standing by a wall and he decides to speak to them:

'Was Alf Trott here today?' I asked. (Alf Trott was the name of the Little Yellow Man.)

They were surprised when they heard me speak to them.

'Trott – Trott – Alf Trott', and he repeated the name twenty times as if he were trying to bring somebody to mind.

The others heard the question I had put.

One of them began to repeat the word 'Trott' again and again, as if he were enjoying the sound. Another began to repeat 'Trott – Trott – Trott' also and yet another began repeat 'Trott – Trott – Alf Trott'.

They were all fascinated by the word. Some of them declared that he had been there that morning. Others swore that he had not been there or for a couple of days. I thought they would come to blows.

'Is he not the big fat man who plays cards here every evening?' said one of them

'That is not he', said another 'but the little thin man who is always with him'.

'Trott is not the name of the fat man', said the first man I spoke to, 'but it is Cox'.

'And the little man is called Box. I know him well', said I, mockingly. 'They are called Box and Cox.'

This surprised them. It had not occurred to them that they might be called Box and Cox. A dispute started about the pair. One of them knew where Cox worked. Another knew for a fact that he never did a day's work in his life. I didn't

want to hear any more. I left them there, arguing about Cox and Box and Trott.'
(Ó Conaire, 1910: 73–4)

The comic aural effect of the monosyllabic names serves to highlight the meaning-lessness of the exchange between the speakers. Significantly, this is one of the few episodes in the story where Micil actually attempts to engage in a verbal exchange with anybody – his normal mode of communication is his 'special bellow' that is taken a degree further by Seoirse, and is calculated to alienate and frighten rather than to engage in a verbal exchange.

It is possible that *Deoraíocht*, which was apparently produced in some haste in time for the Oireachtas literary competition (in which it won first prize) in 1909, was a combination of more than one story: indeed, there was a question of publishing it initially in parts rather than as a whole. As suggested above, Micil's story can be read as a story of thwarted love – a theme that is to be found throughout Ó Conaire's fiction. The damage caused by the accident (details of which are very vague and even implausible) affect Micil's mobility and apparently annihilate his former identity by destroying his face. These circumstances do not, however, fully explain why his attempts at verbal communication invariably fail (apart from the occasions when he relates to the Big Red-haired Woman from the West of Ireland). The theme of frustrated communication is to be found in other stories by Ó Conaire, most notably in 'Aba Cana-Lú!', written at around the same time as *Deoraíocht*.[18] This story, set in an imaginary oriental country, is about a people who have been annihilated by their enemies, apart from one very old man, who has survived the disaster because he was in prison. On his release, he goes in search of his people, but not only have they all been wiped out but the country itself has been destroyed also. He hears a voice calling him and, convinced that it is the voice of his son, he follows it. When he eventually finds the source of the sound he discovers that it is just a parrot, and he dies broken-hearted. This poignant and powerful story is a metaphor for the loss of the Irish language. It seems plausible, therefore, that Micil's impairments – both physical and verbal – that are a consequence of his forced migration from Galway (representing Irish-speaking Ireland) to London (representing an Ireland where Irish has been replaced by English) should be read as a metaphorical account of the trauma suffered by Irish-speaking Ireland following the seismic language shift that occurred in the country in the nineteenth century. And this trauma is not simply left behind by the migration to London of Micil and his fellow countrymen and countrywomen. In one of the most explicit descriptions of the world of Irish migrants in London, Micil relates in almost sociological terms the life of the inhabitants of 'Little Ireland' that area of North London encompassing Kilburn, Cricklewood and Camden Town. Describing the way in which the area appears like a Munster-in-minature, Micil describes how this

> small population of exiles in a foreign city kept up the manners and customs of the people of the ancient Irish nation. The Irish heritage of language, music and literature which rich people at home had abandoned in their efforts to imitate the English, who would have as soon have seen them at the bottom of the sea, was kept alive by these people. They understood, in their own way, that a race should

guard the culture which had come down to them from their ancestors and they guarded it like a precious jewel. (Ó Conaire, 1994: 105)

What is fascinating here is the way in which the narrative articulates the continuation of a tradition occurring in this migrant population that runs parallel to (but seems infinitely less self-conscious than) the orchestrated attempts at national redefinition of the revivalists at 'home'. Here in this 'foreign city' 'authentic' Gaelic culture is alive – at least for the time being: for Micil is not starry-eyed about its future:

> The adults kept up their habits, customs and language. But their sons and daughters
> … gradually abandoned the language and a lots of its musical and literary culture.
> Their grandchildren lost both the language and the culture, and seemed to have
> retained only the worst of their racial characteristics. And many, naturally, inter-
> married with the English. People who breed animals will tell you that when one
> breed is crossed with another, the offspring will inherit the worst characteristics of
> each. Others, however, take the opposite view. (Ó Conaire, 1994: 105)

London in *Deoraíocht* is, in the final analysis, a place of loss, a place where the migrant's human identity is erased. As one who writes, Micil is in that relatively fortunate position of being able to articulate his sense of self, even if that articulation is a record of irredeemable loss. But *Deoraíocht* speaks not just of its narrator's fate; it looks wider to the fate of that stratum of London society that Fanon calls the 'wretched of the earth' for whom any sense of identity, of dignity, of worth is destroyed by the sheer harshness of material and economic conditions in the other capital. In a scene from which the narrator and the reader never fully recover, Micil describes the scene in which huge numbers of surplus labourers kill time in a park in the centre of the city. In a scene reminiscent of the 'grove of death' scene in Conrad's *Heart of Darkness* (indeed, Conrad's story is explicitly referenced by the narrator of *Deoraíocht*) we are led in the midst of a warm autumn morning to a dark corner of the park:

> That corner was so crowded you would not have room to move in it. It was black
> with people all lying on the ground. They were all homeless, vagrant people.
> Most of them were lying face down on the ground. Some of them lying on their
> backs, their faces to the sky. Some asleep. Others awake. A man here cursing and
> swearing loudly enough to split the rocks of the Burren.
>
> …
>
> I could only liken this corner of the park to some huge hateful giant who was
> suffering from some hideous loathsome disease, a dreadful disease that was
> rotting his flesh, and gnawing it to the bone, visible in great black spots erupting
> from his skin. … I, too, started sunning myself on the breast of that diseased,
> detestable giant.
>
> …
>
> A withered leaf falls on my forehead. I let it stay where it fell. Another falls on my
> mouth. They are now falling about me thick and fast. And the homeless men who
> dot the grass around me seem like huge withered leaves, fallen from some great
> tree … (Ó Conaire, 1994: 83)

Lying there on the ground among the leaves and the insects and fellow human beings (who are not, in fact, identified explicitly as Irish people) Micil is hardly distinguishable from the detritus that gathers on the streets and parklands of the city. In this complex interweaving of abjection and pleasure, of desire and despair, of persistence and atrophy, Micil's vision of London as the 'City of Darkness' (Ó Conaire, 1994: 23) achieves its most intense articulation. The other capital is revealed not as a place of opportunity or of hope, but rather as a realm of nightmare in which the traumas visited upon the colonized are replayed time and again in all their grotesque horror.

Note on the text

Although some of the material in this chapter has already appeared in my book, *Pádraic Ó Conaire: Deoraí* (1994), the contents of the book are not accessible to those who cannot read Irish.

Notes

1 The plays were collected and published in a single collection entitled *Bairbre Rua agus Drámaí eile* by Pádraig Ó Siadhail in 1989.
2 Two young women, employed in this capacity, Nóra Ní Cheallaigh and Cáit Bhreathnach, are specifically mentioned as having spoken Irish to Pádraic when he was a small child. See Riggs, 1994: 12.
3 'Duitse, a Mháire Ní Thuathail, an scéal seo, mar is tú a mhúin na litreacha Gaeilge i dtosach dom' / 'This story is for you, Máire Ní Thuathail, because it was you who first taught me my Irish letters.'
4 According to Mark Ryan, the London Gaelic League was formed after a lecture given by Douglas Hyde in October 1894 to the Irish Literary Society in London. Frank Fahy, who had established the Southwark Literary Club back in 1883, was the first president. The League was initially given the use of premises at 8, Adelphi Terrace by the Irish Literary Society. Other prominent members were Tomás Ó Flannghaile and the journalist, W. P. Ryan (who is credited with having introduced Ó Conaire to the organization). Donnchadh Ó Súilleabháin, in an article in *An Glór* (5 February, 1944) says: 'When I joined in 1937 there were five branches operating. The High School, … Kensington School, Rotherhithe School, Highgate School and Forest Gate School. The following year, 1938, Barking School was added.' My translation. See Ryan, 1945: 162. See also Ó Súilleabháin (1989), Fahy (1902), and Ó Briain (1944).
5 Although Patrick Conroy / Pádraic Ó Conaire (he seems to have adopted this version of his name after he became involved in the League in London) would probably not have taught at all the locations across the city where the Gaelic League conducted Irish classes, Art Ó Briain, in his article in *The Capuchin Annual*, lists the numeous places where, between 1899 and 1902, Irish was taught: these included Bermondsey, Clapham, Chelsea, Dulwich, Peckham, Camberwell, Plumstead, Clerkenwell, Hoxton, The Borough, Deptford, Fulham, Hackney, Islington, Kensington, Limehouse,

Vauxhall in addition to the 'central' classes. In 1903 there were over 2,000 members in London and according to the 1904 Annual Review, there were now eighteen branches. The numbers began to drop following the outbreak of the war in 1914 and by 1917 there were only four schools remaining: see Ó Briain, 1944: 116–26.

6 First published in *An Claidheamh Soluis* in January 1907, having won first prize in the Oireachtas literary competition in 1906. This story subsequently appeared in Ó Conaire's first collection, *Nóra Mharcais Bhig agus Scéalta eile (Nóra Mharcais Bhig and other stories)*, published in 1909 by the Gaelic League.

7 *Deoraíocht* has been translated by Gearailt Mac Eoin as *Exile* (1994).

8 This and all subsequent quotations from 'Nóra Mharcais Bhig' are my own translations.

9 The full title of this essay, which won first prize in the Oireachtas Literary competition in 1908 was 'Early Irish literature and modern European literature compared in an attempt to establish which is the more appropriate model for emerging writers in Irish'. My translation.

10 My translation.

11 There is no suggestion in the story that the name carries (as might be expected) any oriental associations; instead, it seems to refer to 'Seán Buí' (literally 'yellow John', the Irish version of 'John Bull'). There is an interesting satirical cartoon by Robert Lynd, the London-based contemporary of Ó Conaire, in which he depicts a corpulent circus-owner under the heading 'John Bull's Famous Circus'. This appeared in the 21 March 1917 edition of *The Republic*, a separatist weekly paper founded and edited by Bulmer Hobson. The cartoon is reproduced in Hobson's (1968) *Ireland Yesterday and Tomorrow*. Tralee, Anvil Books: viii, facing 17.

12 30 July 1910. My translation.

13 September 1910. My translation.

14 My translation.

15 Ó Broin, 1984: 51. My translation. Declan Kiberd offered another interpretation, claiming that it was a Marxist novel, in his essay 'Pádraic Ó Conaire agus Cearta an Duine', *Pádraic Ó Conaire: Léachtaí Cuimhneacháin*. Eag. G. Denvir. Cló Chonamara, Indreabhán: 45–57.

16 William Carleton (1887) *Willie Reilly and his Dear Colleen Bawn*. Chicago, Belford, Clark and Co.

17 It can be assumed that this is a coded reference to seduction.

18 This story was first published in *An Claidheamh Soluis* in December 1909 and subsequently in the collection, *An Chéad Chloch (The First Stone)* (1914).

7

James Joyce's 'Londub'

Eleni Loukopoulou

James Joyce's interaction with London as a political and aesthetic force that shaped his work has a long and complex history. Although Joyce never lived in the city for anywhere near as long as his residence in Dublin (and later in Trieste, Zurich and Paris), the metropolis of the British Empire was the place where much of his work was published, especially during the formative period of his career. Throughout his life the city remained within Joyce's compass not simply as a site of publication, but as a place where he aspired to find 'a journalistic job' (Ellmann, 1983: 77) when he was a young man, as the city he moved to in April 1931 with the intention of living there permanently, and as the place where he married his long-term companion, Nora Barnacle in July of that year. By comparison, however, to the amount of research about the cities and geographies with which Joyce is associated, London is largely absent. Joycean scholarship has expanded the contextual spectrum of Joyce's peripatetic life and literary work to an impressive extent.[1] But, still, the focus tends mainly to serve the image of that well-worn binary opposition within Joycean studies – the European Joyce versus an Irish Joyce – and so, the role of London as a key literary context to his work has been sidestepped. Recently, a number of studies have stressed the need for a more nuanced attention to what Sean Latham has called 'the interlocking flows of social, historical and economic capital which structured the rise of modernism' (Latham, 2009: 150). Indeed, scholars such as John Nash have foregrounded new and dynamic contexts for literary modernism by paying attention to the cultural and political complexities of the relationship between Irish authors and English audiences and the varied networks of Irish modernism.[2]

However, the specificities of London's topographical, literary and geopolitical significance for Joyce's work remain underexplored. This chapter will discuss how London is inflected in Joyce's representations of Dublin and his life and literary trajectory. Close analysis of key extracts of his work will show how Joyce was in an often oppositional dialogue with representations of London in order to construct his own representations of Dublin in his texts. This exploration will shed new light on the ways that Joyce depicted London's actuality in his later work, and specifically how the toponyms of 'London' and 'Dublin' are present in the portmanteau word 'Londub' (*FW* 625.36) in *Finnegans Wake*.[3]

English town and Irish town

As soon as Joyce was paid for his first London publication, an article on Ibsen in the *Fortnightly Review* in April 1900, Joyce visited London. This visit offered Joyce the opportunity to represent its spaces through the local idiom. London was a site that formed one of his earliest literary epiphanies. This additional, but usually overlooked, dimension of Joyce's relationship with London merits further exploration especially in terms of his encounter with new linguistic idioms and familiarly strange places. When Joyce visited London for the first time in 1900 with his father, they apparently stayed in Kennington, a relatively under-privileged South London suburb. According to the biographers of Joyce's father, they chose the particular London quarter for its literary significance, in part because Joyce associated Kennington with William Blake and he wished to walk Blake's 'charter'd streets' (Wyse Jackson and Costello, 1997: 224). Taking into consideration Clare Hutton's work on the South London Irish literary and nationalist societies, the area may have had more specific Irish associations than the ones related to Joyce's literary aspirations.[4] During this visit, Joyce and his father visited relatives in the East End on Mile End Road, as well as various London music halls, 'the indigenous entertainment for Cockneys largely by Cockneys' (Matthews, 1938: 83). One product of Joyce's encounter with Cockney culture is the epiphany he composed after his visit to London, which referred to a Cockney allegation of incest in the Leslie family, with whom the Joyces became acquainted in Kennington:

> Eva Leslie – Yes, Maudie Leslie's my sister an'
>   Fred Leslie's my brother – yev
>   'eard of Fred Leslie?...(*musing*)...
>   O,' e's a whoite-arsed bugger... 'E's
>   awoy at present.......
>   (*later*)
>   I told you someun went with me
>   ten toimes one noight....That's
>   Fred – my own brother Fred....
>   (*musing*)... 'E is 'andsome...O I
>   *do* love Fred... (Joyce, 1991: 195)

This faithful transcription of a particular phonetic register was triggered by Joyce's encounter with a new linguistic idiom which he must have encountered for the first time in its authentic context. (London theatre groups would visit Dublin, as depicted in the *Dubliners* story 'Counterparts'). For Joyce, epiphanies were, among other things, the recordings of authentic linguistic moments that constituted the basic material for further use and elaboration in his writings. The cultural experience of the London music hall, another site of Cockney language, also left a great impression on Joyce. Back in Dublin, Joyce stated to Stanislaus: 'the music hall, not poetry, is a criticism of life' (Ellmann, 1983: 77). This statement sounds like a parody and critique of Yeats' contemporaneous declarations for art as 'a criticism of life', as F. S. L. Lyons explained in his cartography of the political and cultural forces competing in Joyce's Dublin. According to Lyons, the declaration reflects the limitations that the Gaelic Ireland movement imposed on artists due to their demands that the artistic work, written preferably in Irish, should aim at 'the restoration of a sense of separate Irish nationality' (Lyons, 1970: 17). Yeats reacted to such prescriptions by defending the right of the artist to 'express himself as he wished in English' (Lyons, 1970: 17). Joyce takes an even more different stance from them and finds authenticity in the language of the London music hall, which itself was a relatively recent and new formation, as Peter Ackroyd has explained:

> the literature of Cockney in the nineteenth century is for all practical purposes endless, but it found one specific focus in the language of the music hall … The routines of the 'halls' encouraged much elaboration and ingenuity, also, so that it can fairly be said that the standard of Cockney was set by the 1880s. (Ackroyd, 2000, 164–5)

On this first visit to London, Joyce would have heard the full Cockney context — the rapid, idiomatic interaction with other practitioners. Cockney's incorporation in the music hall made it a representative of the evolving and living language of the city's modernity and of imaginative linguistic experimentation. Traces of this early interest in the transcription of dialects and the demotic can be found in parts of *Ulysses*, where the polyphonic urban canvas of Dublin found a written record, and was even mingled with London's accents and idioms. But before I discuss this aspect of London's hovering presence in Joyce's later work, I would like to look at another aspect of Joyce's first encounter with the metropolis of the British Empire: its toponymic similarity to Dublin's.

Joyce was preoccupied with urban correspondences throughout his life and work. These two cities shared not only a similar atmosphere and interlinked institutional and political history but even the same toponymical and linguistic referential matrix within which the urban experience is lived and regulated. This applies also to numerous other Irish towns as is evident in nineteenth-century travel books. The illusion of spatial duality is recorded in the writings of the Irish-born folklorist T. C. Croker (1798–1854), who was one of the first to publish a collection of Irish folk tales and travelogues addressing an English and especially London readership. After extensive travelling in Ireland between 1812 and 1822, Croker published *Researches in the South of Ireland* in London in 1824 with the aim of introducing Ireland to English readers. His aim was to eliminate the negative bias against the Irish by praising the beauty of the landscape and the culture and ultimately to promote a spirit of reconciliation after the numerous rebellions and the 1800 Acts of Union (effective from 1801). His account of Limerick's topography is revelatory, especially for his reference to London:

> *Limerick is divided, like almost every town in Ireland, into English Town and Irish Town;* the former … has some well-built and handsome streets; the best houses are of red brick, much in the style of London, with areas and a flagged pavement, which makes the place more agreeable to the pedestrian than Cork. The old, or Irish Town … is picturesque, narrow and dirty. (my italics) (Croker, 1969: 49)

Alongside the targeted English readers, it is important to reflect on the potential impact this kind of description had on the Irish readers (either based in Ireland or immigrants in Britain) who could well have read Croker's accounts of Ireland. The measure of comparison of Irish towns was England and specifically London. Whenever Croker explains the historical significance of a sight or event he frames it in comparison with British history and specifically in relation to London's topographies. For instance, he explains the cultural and political significance of Limerick by informing the reader that it received the Royal charter and the right to elect a mayor earlier than London and Dublin (Croker, 1969: 39–40). When Crocker identifies such toponymical and historical conjunctions his aim is to flatter English readers, and probably with an underlying agenda of reconciliation.[5] Nonetheless, for Joyce, a nationalist, and writing after the Famine, this kind of geo-spatial conflation poses problems of representation. In *Ulysses*, and especially in the 'Wandering Rocks' episode, Joyce draws attention to the geopolitical superimposition of London upon Dublin when he notes the use of the name of London upon Dublin's map:

> Two old women fresh from their whiff of the briny trudged through
> Irishtown along London bridge road, one with a sanded tired umbrella, one
> with a midwife's bag in which eleven cockles rolled (*U* 10.818-20) (Joyce, 2002: 199)

The tone here is comic. The two lower class old women are depicted as trudging along 'London bridge road' carrying peculiar objects. Although most towns across England might have a 'London bridge' or a 'London Road' in their toponymic maps, once these street names are encountered within a colonial (or 'semi-colonial') context, such as Dublin's, and against local linguistic formations, then the paradoxical division of 'English' and 'Irish' town that Crocker observed, becomes even more forceful. This imposition of London over Ireland's and in Joyce's case over Dublin's map demonstrates the dominant assumption of the time: London was the imperial capital against which English and Irish readers would frame the historical development of Irish town planning, regulation and architecture.

It was not only the proliferation of identical toponymy in Joyce's Dublin that was striking but also the cultural flow from one capital to the other. For example, Dublin's Adelphi Theatre presented the same type of theatre productions as the one in London. These examples indicate a cultural and geopolitical superimposition enforced both on Dublin's topography and on Joyce's own generation while growing up in Dublin. Upon his first visit to London in 1900, as a young aspiring writer, and during his later frequent visits, especially during the 1920s, London's topographical and geopolitical significance became a constant of literary inspiration and even antagonism. One of the most stiking transformations of this urban duality into a textual network of powerful political allusions, is the portmanteau word of 'Londub' in *Finnegans Wake* discussed later in the chapter.

The strong interrelation between the spatial forms of cities and of the language that Joyce employed to render these urban spaces textually and poetically have preoccupied a number of critics and scholars. The toponymical correspondence has been summarized by Bernard McGinley:

> Dublin bore the imprint of the English city. There were familiar placenames such as Smithfield, Pimlico, Ely Place, Apothecaries Hall, Mecklenburgh Street, Holles Street, Essex Street, Belgrave Square, Constitution Hill, Mansion House, Sackville

Street, Waterloo Road, Fleet Street and Temple Bar, Grafton Street, Duke Street, Gloucester Road, Mount Street, Ranelagh, Henrietta Street, Little Britain, the Bridewell – and even London Bridge. Joyce knew that Dublin had never been fully an Irish city.[6]

McGinley's observation that Dublin 'had never been fully an Irish city' offers the groundwork for further explorations of the ways London is superimposed on Dublin's map. This overlapping of toponyms, sites, urban spaces and institutions would have deeply struck Joyce and his generation of Irish intellectuals upon visiting the capital during a period marked by divergent forms of Irish cultural nationalism.

This relationship becomes a paradox in Joyce's writings about Dublin, especially when London seems to hover over Dublin in Joyce's complex networks of textual allusions. Due to the geopolitical and literary interconnectedness and proximities between the two cities but also due to, as Lynne Innes has put it, Joyce's 'awareness of London as a centre of empire' (Innes, 2000: 151). While composing *Dubliners*, Joyce would frequently compare his writings with depictions of London, and was thus keeping up-to-date with contemporary or recent depictions of London in literature to detect the most suitable author of his liking. In September 1905 Joyce from Trieste wrote to his brother, Stanislaus, in Dublin:

> Will you read some English 'realists' I see mentioned in the papers and see what they are like — Gissing, Arthur Morrison and a man named Keary. I can read very little and am as dumb as a stockfish. But really I think that the two last stories I sent you are very good. (Joyce, 1966a: 111)

In the same letter, a few lines later, his comment on the paucity of literary representations of Dublin in comparison to a flood of writings about London shows his concerns at the time:

> When you remember that Dublin has been a capital for thousands of years, that it is the 'second' city of the British Empire, that it is nearly three times as big as Venice it seems strange that no artist has given it to the world. (Joyce, 1966a: 111)

In this statement Joyce foregrounds a persistent concern of his: a comparison between London and Dublin as the 'first' and the 'second' cities of the whole of the British Empire. That Joyce considers Dublin as the 'second' capital of the Empire might seem paradoxical considering that Glasgow or Manchester or even Calcutta were larger and even economically much stronger than Dublin.

In a subsequent letter to Stanislaus (10 January 1907), Joyce compares his approach and methods to depict Dublin in his short stories that would subsequently become *Dubliners* to Arthur Morrison's *Tales of Mean Streets*, set in London (1894). He then comments, 'I suppose after all there must be some merit in my writing' (Joyce, 1966a: 205). Much later he would refer to the book in *Finnegans Wake* as 'mean straits' (*FW* 539.22). As soon as Thomas Burke's *Limehouse Nights: Tales of Chinatown* was published in 1917, Joyce asked for a copy from its publisher Grant Richards (also publisher of *Dubliners*, 1914) (Gillespie, 1986: 60). In his 1920 letter to Frank Budgen, he describes the state of Bloom in the 'Ithaca' episode of *Ulysses* as a Cockney who 'romances about Ithaca (Oi, want teh gow beck teh the Mawl Enn Rowd, s'elp me!)' (Joyce, 1957: 152). As Louis Mink notes, the name of the road is present in the 'Anna Livia Plurabelle' section of *Finnegans Wake* in a transmuted form: 'wensum farmerette walking the pilend roads' (*FW* 200.19) (Mink, 1978: 407).

Although it is well known that Joyce's repertoire of literary readings ranged widely (from Russian and French to Irish authors) the above examples show that the London authors were of special interest for him due to the hierarchical superiority of the imperial metropolis in relation to Dublin, but also due to the wide-ranging literary depictions of London's cityscape. Such complex cultural, geo-historical and political transactions between London and Dublin have been encapsulated in the term 'Londublin' that Jay Clayton coined in 1995 to succinctly discuss Joyce's rendering of Dublin in *Ulysses* under the Dickensian influence:

> to a degree Joyce found distressing, nineteenth-century London was internal to Dublin, traceable in its monuments and street names, in the condition of its port and shipping industry, in its popular songs, and most important, in its language and culture. (Clayton, 1995: 340)

Through comparative analysis and historical contextualisation, Clayton discussed Dickens' pre-eminent influence and presence in Joyce's literary explorations. For instance, he compares aspects of the story 'The Parable of the Plums' (*U* 7.1057-58), in the finale of the 'Aeolus' episode of *Ulysses*, with Dickens' *Martin Chuzzlewit*. Clayton draws parallels between the way Dickens describes the Monument in London, 'a 202 foot pillar ... from which one could gain a view of the city ... [and Joyce's] tale of an outing to Nelson's Pillar' when two lower-class Dublin women are depicted to view Dublin from the top of the pillar (Clayton, 1995: 335). Indeed, Clayton's point is valuable. In his essay, 'The Centenary of Charles Dickens' (1912), Joyce compared Dickens's significance to that of Shakespeare's because both 'influenced the spoken language of the inhabitants of the British Empire' (Joyce, 2000: 186). Joyce also stressed that Dickens was 'the great Cockney' (Joyce, 2000: 182) and that 'the life of London is the breath of his nostrils' (Joyce, 2000: 184). In Joyce's schema, Dickens is identified with London's vernacular as he asserts that Dickens became a canonical writer thanks to his literary representations of London: 'It is certainly by his stories of the London of his own day that he must finally stand or fall' (Joyce, 2000: 184). Joyce's essay on Dickens reveals a deep admiration for his treatment of London, suggesting that he had found in Dickens a model and exemplar for his own treatment of Dublin. Is this though a case of a mere intertextual engagement?

Clayton convincingly demonstrates that Joyce's interest in Dickens is not merely stylistic, but mainly ideological. And this is manifested in 'The Centenary of Charles Dickens'. Joyce studies Dickens's literary techniques for means of depicting the minutiae of everyday city life, and at the same time deconstructs London's centrality as the centre of British imperialism:

> Joyce's Dublin rewrites Dickens's London in a way that reveals their fates as twinned historically. The famous particularity and immediacy of Joyce's city has

disguised until recently its links with a global imperial economy and a dominant
British culture.

…..

> By recording how individuals actually live in this 'second' city, Joyce undoes the
> priority of the 'capital city of the world'. The streets of Dublin may be inscribed by
> an imperial power, but they are also traversed by comical, irreverent, sometimes
> angry citizens, all of whom are capable of outlandish reinventions of their urban
> world. (Clayton, 1995: 339-40)

Joyce thus uses Dickens's London writings as a model to help him write about Dublin's
everydayness, while subverting Dickens's writings about the first capital of the British
Empire to write about Dublin, the second capital. Clayton's perceptive analysis of
Joyce's Dickensian Dublin opens up new lines of enquiry about the ways London as
a topographical model and as a city most prominent in nineteenth-century literary
urban explorations permeates Joyce's texts on many levels.

Taking into account that in April 1931 Joyce moved to London (with the intention
of becoming a permanent resident, a plan he had to abandon due to his daughter's
illness in autumn 1931), that it was in London that he was married to Nora in the same
year, and that during his stay in London he negotiated and signed an advantageous
contract with Faber and Faber for *Work in Progress* (the early name for *Finnegans
Wake*), the portmanteau word of 'Londub' acquires biographical resonances, since it
was composed in a retrospective mood much later, in 1938. In the rest of this chapter I
will explore the connection with London in the use of the portmanteau word 'Londub'
(*FW* 625.36) in the final monologue of Anna Livia Plurabelle before she dissolves into
the sea. My argument is that 'Londub''s structural development and allusions dialectically evoke the historical and geopolitical interconnectedness of two important
cities in Joyce's life: London and Dublin. A discussion of the multilayered formation
of 'Londub' will unpack the position of London as the 'other capital' in relation to
Dublin.

'Londub'

In the finale of *Finnegans Wake*, we hear Anna Livia Plurabelle's voice for the first
time (Hayman, 1977: vii) when she exclaims 'Soft morning, city!' (*FW* 619.20). ALP
is the personification of Dublin's Liffey with hundreds of other riverine tributaries of
the world fusing into it. On one level, ALP's monologue is an account of her story
with HCE.[7] She guides us through their flirting and courtship and when the narrative
reaches the point of their wedding the reader is given details about the location
of the ceremony: the 'wedding town' is named as 'Londub' (*FW* 625.35-6). Before
settling on this final, printed version of his neologism, Joyce expended a remarkable
amount of time and effort on the development of the word. For example, on the
fifth typescript of *Finnegans Wake* we read Joyce's handwritten addition: 'Turn again,
weddingturn, of Lundob!' (Joyce, 1977: 283). And after this elaboration, he further

changed this phrase to 'Turn agate, weddingtown! Laud, [~~man~~] men of Londub' (Joyce, 1977: 284). After Joyce's handwritten amendment, the phrase 'Turn agate, weddingtown! Laud, men of Londub' was mistakenly inserted in the galley proof: 'So side by side, turn agate, weddingtown, laud men of Londu.' During the corrections of the galleyproofs in November 1938, Joyce noticed the printing mistake and required that 'Londu' should be corrected to 'Londub' – an accidental confirmation of the strength of his belief in this word formation (Joyce, 1977: 325). Subsequently, the phrasing was consolidated as 'turn agate, wedding-town, laud men of Londub!' (*FW* 625.5–6).

The actual spelling of the word 'Londub' (as well as its capitalization) merit some attention. Roland McHugh suggests that 'Londub' relates primarily to Dublin (McHugh, 2006: 625) but the problem here is that 'Londub' is not an exact anagram for Dublin. The expert in geographical configurations in *Finnegans Wake*, Louis Mink considers 'Londub' to refer to London (Mink, 1978: 387). Why is it that the two authors of the most substantial reference books on *Finnegans Wake* offer such contradictory interpretations? Why, for that matter should this most Janus-faced of neologisms be made to refer to either / or of these options, when it can just as satisfyingly be read as summoning and conjoining both cities within the textual world of the novel? Joyce juxtaposes fragments from the beginning of the names of the cities of London and Dublin by splitting each word in half and then dialectically creating a portmanteau word using as components the first half of each word: 'Lon-Dub'. As is evident from one of Joyce's notebooks for *Finnegans Wake*, he used the short form 'Dub' for Dublin (Joyce, 2003a: 90), but the structure of the word 'Londub' presents difficulties if it is broken into the two cities London or Dublin. Joyce's linguistic and cultural explorations could be an entry point for reading 'Londub' as a completely new formation. The complexity lies in its new telling of history and the historicity of places, the telling of 'makeup things' and the showing of 'every simple storyplace we pass' (*FW* 625.5–6) that is, which ALP and her stranger (and we as readers) pass. Joyce has worked through a system of distortions and translations to produce 'Londub', evoking spatial images and associations. As Dirk Van Hulle notes, 'each portmanteau word in *Finnegans Wake* is usually the result of several successive distortions' and this process allows 'their meanings, associations, and resonances to interact, causing an energetic effect of simultaneity' (Van Hulle, 2008: 83). This effect however, does not serve merely textual purposes, nor is its main aim to further the reader's pleasure.

Joyce's textual explorations on the gradual formation of 'Londub' merit careful examination because the meaning or the images that this linguistic cluster projects, further complicate the understanding of the printed word 'Londub' as an exemplification of Joyce's reflection on history and geography. The two capital cities that had preoccupied Joyce since at least 1905 (when he ranked Dublin second only to London as regards cultural and geopolitical significance (Joyce, 1966a: 111)) are present in the phrase: 'turn agate, wedding-town, laud men of Londub!'. There may be a number of entry points to read the extract in which 'Londub' is located, but here I would like to focus on the ways that London is evoked. McHugh suggests that the word wedding-town refers to the 'pantomime' storyline about London's celebrated Lord Mayor Dick

Whittington, who decided to leave London as he was unsuccessful in his initial quest for success there (McHugh, 2006: 625–6). On his way out of the city, 'agate', near modern Archway, he was called back to London by the apparent message of London's Bow Bells: 'turn again'. Joyce alludes to this calling with the use of punctuation; an exclamation mark: 'First we turn by the vagurin here and then it's gooder. So side by side, turn agate, wedding-town, laud men of Londub!' (*FW* 625.34–36). The prompt 'turn' is repeated twice. First, ALP navigates her stranger and her reader through her geospatial transitions, and then this prompt is conflated with the London hero Dick Whittington. Joyce may have considered this prompt by London's Bow Bells as a standard London line. The significance of the prompt 'turn' in the composition of the formation 'wedding-town' and its association with Whittington is evident in the fact that in its first version, 'turn' is even part of the word wedding. It is 'weddingturn' (Joyce, 1977: 283). That Joyce assigned significance to this London myth is evident in a reference to Whittington's story in the essay on Charles Dickens. There he praised Dickens as a London author, and even paralleled Whittington's trajectory with that of Dickens':

> The church bells which rang over his dismal, squalid childhood, over his strug-
> gling youth, over his active and triumphant manhood, seem to have called him
> turn again whenever, with scrip and wallet in his hand, he intended to leave the
> city and to have bidden him turn again, like another Whittington, promising
> him (and the promise was to be amply fulfilled) a threefold greatness. (Joyce,
> 2000: 184)

Despite the references to London and its pantomime mayor, ALP refers to London as a place through which she and her 'strangerous' pass during the telling of her story, but where they do not stay as she will soon dissolve into the Irish Sea. Indeed, Emer Nolan has described this event as a 'powerful and local instance of a universal recurrence, as all the rivers of the world debouch finally into a specific and generic Irish Sea' (Nolan, 2007: 180). In this transitory stage, though, ALP shows her 'strangerous' 'every simple storyplace' (*FW* 625.5–6) they pass and tells the story of numerous London-Dublin cultural and geo-historical configurations.

The word 'laud' (preceding 'Londub') is a further example of the ways in which such conjunctures are foregrounded by Joyce. It can be read in a number of ways but emphasis should be placed on London's dominance, in its power relations with Dublin, and its geo-historical transactions with Dublin. If we look at the syntac-tical significance of the word in the final formation 'laud men of Londub', 'laud' is printed with a lower-case first letter, which may be understood syntactically as a verb prompting praise. In an earlier revision of the phrase in the fifth typescript, Joyce spelt 'Laud' with a capital L: 'Turn agate, weddingtown! Laud, [man] men of Londub' (Joyce, 1977: 284) and in this form it inevitably evokes William Laud (1573–1645), Bishop of London (1628–33), Archbishop of Canterbury (1633–45) and during the same period, Chancellor of the University of Dublin. If the word Laud in the phrase 'Laud, [man] men of Londub' does indeed refer to William Laud a possible reason may be the fact that ecclesiastical Dublin used to be under the direct power of Canterbury. Indeed, 'there developed a strong link between Dublin and Canterbury, and 12th-century bishops [in Ireland] were usually monks from the Canterbury province'[8] (Cannon, 2009: 217). While political power over Dublin was administered from London, it was the case that ecclesiastic power emanated from Canterbury, and that Archbishop Laud had been in ecclesiastic control of all three cities. Finally, the word Laud could also recall the name of King Lud, of Celtic origin,

> who is supposed to have reigned in the century of the Roman invasion. He laid out the city's streets and rebuilt its walls. Upon his death he was buried beside the gate which bore his name, [Ludgate] and the city became known as *Kaerlud* or *Kaerlundein*, 'Lud's City'. (Ackroyd, 2001: 11)

London's Celtic founder, or re-builder, Lud, might have been an intriguing figure for Joyce, who had grown up in a city that was designed according to models of British city planning and a great number of its numerous districts, squares and streets were designed by 'major architects from London' (Harvey, 1949: 79) and named after places in London. Earlier in the novel, Lud is present in the formation 'Lludd hillmythey' (*FW* 331.09) which evokes 'Lud's Town, Ludgate Hill' (Mink, 1978: 109). Ludgate Hill is possibly indicated in the beginning of the following page in the formation 'Ludegude' (*FW* 626.06) which echoes Ludgate, the gate beside which Lud was buried in London. Similarly, at the beginning of *Finnegans Wake*, HCE, ALP's husband, is buried under Dublin: his head lies on the side of Howth Hill and his toes on the side of Magazine Mount in Phoenix Park (*FW* 7.29–32).

The figure of Lud as the founder of London accords with many of the themes in the 'Haveth Childers Everywhere' section of *Finnegans Wake* where HCE, awoken now, prides himself on being a founder of cities and conqueror and husband of the riverine figure ALP. To write this section during 1929–30, Joyce used the *Encyclopædia Britannica* as a key source, and together with his assistants, they made notes about numerous world capitals, including London. Additionally, Joyce drew on his own visits to and residence in London, and the text refers to aspects of the city that are Irish-related. Extensive notes from the entry on London in the *Encyclopædia Britannica* can be found in the *Finnegans Wake* notebook VI.B.29. We read 'wapping' and 'old stairs' (Joyce, 2003b: 202c and 202d) in reference to the area of Wapping, also mentioned in *FW* 533.17 as 'those whapping oldsteirs'. In 'Haveth Childers Everywhere' there are allusions to institutions of philanthropy and to London's East End. For example, the line 'Stepney's shipchild…waif of his bosun' (*FW* 578.36–579.01) alludes to the reformer, Thomas John Barnardo, a Dubliner, who founded 'Dr Barnardo's Homes' for the reclamation of waif children' in 1871 in South Causeway, Stepney.[9] In notebook VI.B.29 we find details about the river Thames (Joyce, 2003b: 118), St. Pancras Station, and then Poplar. There is an impressive selection of information about areas from South London and the East End, typically populated by Irish emigrants to London: Shoreditch, Bethnal Green, Lambeth, Lewisham, the River Lea, Blackheath and Woolwich, Aldgate (and the main street there, the Minories), and Elephant and Castle (Joyce, 2003b: 118–122). Peter Linebaugh has meticulously researched the cultural and social movements in London that would lead to the substantial role of Irish immigrants in the formation of an active proletariat. As Linebaugh has noted, after the suppression of the Irish language by the Penal Code in eighteenth-century Ireland, 'in hard times it migrated to England and thrived in the boozing kens of London. In the metropolis, it became a language of supplication' (Linebaugh, 2003: 290). Linebaugh's point highlights the two-way transaction between the centre and the periphery. London functioned as a matrix of cultural and political forces in which even Irish as a language mixed with and was in turn shaped by London's various dialects.

References to London life, though, are interwoven in a text ostensibly 'about' Dublin that is also in textual conversation with numerous other cities. Jean-Michel Rabaté notes that during 1929–30 Joyce was keen to produce pairs of incongruent city-spaces such as 'Bulafests' and 'Corkcuttas' (*FW* 541.16–17): 'Dublin is always compared and paired with other cities; cities tend to be coupled, thus New York goes with Kyoto (*FW*, 534.2), Budapest with Belfast, Cork with Calcutta (541.16), Bucharest with Berlin (540.21), London with Buenos Aires (540.34–35)' (Rabaté, 2001: 192). Rabaté considers that in this way 'the city becomes a way of reading the world, a series of dynamic intertranslations' (Rabaté, 2001: 192). As Rabaté explains, the effect of coupling cities is important in 'Haveth Childers Everywhere' because 'geography is not inanimate, but caught up in a spiral of love and carnal desire: we never forget that HCE uses the recitation of cities so as to praise his wife and sing their love' (Rabaté, 2001: 184): hence, the conjoining of London and Dublin in the finale of *Finnegans Wake* takes on a heightened resonance in the love-story that the novel proclaims. But what kind of 'love-story' does the freshly coined signifier, 'Londub', exemplify? I want to argue that through the conflation of the names of London and Dublin the focus is on a recourse, a re-examination of a long-standing cultural and geo-historical negotiation between the two cities. It is through portmanteau words such as 'Londub', as well as the use of London's toponyms throughout *Finnegans Wake*, that Joyce explores interactions between London and Dublin on various levels. His interest in the history of the cities that played a key role in his life: Dublin, where he grew up and tackled textually in his writings, and London, a centre of political, and economic power, and a publishing centre. Simultaneously, Joyce's interest in the two cities has a transformative impetus: to reinvent the present drawing on the past.

Luke Gibbons' point about Joyce's 'complex and unsettling' vision of history and of the past as a 'destabilizing rather than a conservative force' is relevant here (Gibbons, 1991: 6). I would similarly argue that through centripetal and centrifugal processes portmanteau words such as 'Londub' deterritorialize texts and contexts. They set apart long-lasting territorial and textual connections and reconfigure them. While *Finnegans Wake* may be constructed through a vast number of references to numerous cities, and to London's cartography, all these are interwoven in a story about Dublin, its river and mountain, and geo-history.

In the finale of *Finnegans Wake* the idea of negotiation becomes a prevalent force. And this is intensified if the context of composition of this extract is considered in relation to the 1938 Anglo-Irish Agreement that 'marked the culmination of a remarkably successful guerrilla diplomatic campaign to revise the [1921] Treaty out of existence' (Lee, 1989: 214). The Agreement was negotiated over four months in London with the Irish Prime Minister Éamon de Valera heading the Irish delegates, and dealing face-to-face with the British Prime Minister Neville Chamberlain. As Joseph Lee explains, de Valera 'sought *rapprochement*' because of the imminence of the war, 'with the danger of Ireland becoming embroiled as long as Britain held the Treaty ports of Berehaven, Cobh and Lough Swilly' which were retained in 1921 (Lee, 1989: 211–12). Following the ratification of Bunreacht na hÉireann / the Irish Constitution in 1937 (articles Two and Three of which claimed sovereignty over the entire island of Ireland) de Valera's negotiations in London in 1938 were aimed mainly at resolving pressing issues such as partition, the ports and economic collaboration. As Lee notes, 'on the British side, Neville Chamberlain was also consumed with anxiety about the danger of imminent conflict. He was determined to secure a friendly Ireland at his back' (Lee, 1989: 212). Although the issue of partition was not resolved, Lee argues that the Anglo-Irish Agreement

> represented in domestic politics, no less than in international relations, a deserved triumph for de Valera. ... The agreement terminated the economic war, granting some preferential treatment to British industrial exports to Ireland in return for the elimination of the special restrictions on Irish agricultural imports to Britain. ... Above all, Britain returned the ports. ... The British gain was largely psychological. London was now satisfied that Ireland would not be used as a base, insofar as de Valera could ensure that, for hostile operations against the United Kingdom in the event of war (Lee, 1989: 214).

Given that the negotiations were widely covered in the press, as Chamberlain himself had ensured 'that the ports agreement got a positive reception in the British media' (Ferriter, 2007: 127), such developments would have no doubt attracted Joyce's attention. During these lengthy diplomatic exchanges in London, an Irish Prime Minister and his delegation were treated as serious players to be considered at the table of negotiations: this, in itself, was a remarkable event. The parallel development of the textual and the contextual is evident in a likely reference to de Valera's negotiations and efforts in London in 1938: 'And we'd be married till delth to uspart. And though dev do espart. O mine! Only, no, now it's me who's got to give. As duv herself div' (*FW* 626.31–3). The words and phrases 'dev', 'now it's me who's got to give', 'duv', 'div' echo both a process of give and take and de Valera's universal nickname, Dev, the Taoiseach who was negotiating unprecedented new relations between London and Dublin.

Conclusion

The portmanteau word 'Londub', coined in 1938 after the 1936 publication of *Ulysses* by The Bodley Head in London and after the 1938 Anglo-Irish Agreement, represents the culmination of Joyce's long-standing preoccupation with the cultural and historical developments in the relationship between the 'first' and the 'second' cities of the British Empire (up to 1922). During Joyce's lifetime, Dublin became the 'first' city of a new state. 'Londub' stands for the dialectical role of London's position in the Joycean *oeuvre* on three levels: biographical, historical/contextual, and compositional. In biographical terms, Joyce married Nora in London in 1931, at a moment of his life when he had decided to re-launch his London career and life. As this chapter has shown, the long and intertwining histories of the two cities preoccupied Joyce at least since 1900; this is also evident in the ways he recorded diverse aspects of London's topography in *Finnegans Wake*.

Jay Clayton's insightful formation of 'Londublin' as exemplary of the negotiations of power and textual interactions between London and Dublin in *Ulysses* has been pitched against 'Londub', a word formation produced by Joyce himself and monumentalized in *Finnegans Wake*. 'Londub' subverts the concept of London as the 'capital city of the world' as Dickens described it. As Clayton has shown, Joyce used textual material from Dickens's writings on London to promulgate Dublin as a location at the forefront of twentieth-century literature. Joyce's tendency to rewrite texts into his own work goes beyond issues of intertextuality. 'Londub' exemplifies Joyce's famous skill to weave into his writings commentaries about the particular historical conditions underlying the production and publication of his work. The portmanteau word 'Londub' is a new concept, a spatial technicality that Joyce created in the fifth revision of ALP's monologue in November 1938. The new state of affairs between London and Dublin brought about by the Anglo-Irish Agreement offered Joyce the textual and historical conditions to produce a portmanteau word that would express a dialogue and a correspondence undertaken in equal terms. In a way, the cycle that started with the foundation of the Free State (1922) ended with the 1938 Anglo-Irish Agreement, and as a recording of this particular cycle *Finnegans Wake* can be considered as 'the literary form of the Free State in its deceptive originality, its contrariness, its uncertainty of decision (or decision of uncertainty)' (Nash, 2006: 160). The State's political fluctuations up to November 1938 are transcribed in the peculiar linguistic formations of Joyce's final novel. As an aspiring writer in London's publishing world, Joyce complained and indirectly declared his ambitions when he declared in 1905 that 'no artist has given it [Dublin] to the world' (Joyce, 1966a: 111). This is extravagantly realized in *Finnegans Wake*. Joyce's own publishing success in London's literary market with the lifting of the ban and commercial availability of *Ulysses* in 1936 and publication of *Finnegans Wake* in 1939 put his writings about Dublin on the map of London's and by extension the British Empire's literary industry. The authorial and territorial inferiority he discerned when in 1905 he called Dublin 'the second city of the British Empire' (Ellmann, 1983: 208n) in relation to London's predominance is revised in 1938 into a more equitable imagined relationship in the textual and contextual formation of 'Londub'.

Notes

1 See, for instance, Seamus Deane (1990) 'Joyce the Irishman', *The Cambridge Companion to James Joyce*. Derek Attridge (ed.). Cambridge, Cambridge University Press: 31–53; John McCourt (2000) *The Years of Bloom: James Joyce in Trieste 1904–1920*. Dublin: The Lilliput Press; and Jean-Michel Rabate (2009) 'Paris', *James Joyce in Context*. John McCourt (ed.). Cambridge, Cambridge University Press: 216–27.

2 See, for example, John Nash (2006), *James Joyce and the Act of Reception: Reading, Ireland, Modernism*. Cambridge, Cambridge University Press. See also David Ayers

(2007) 'Review of Tim Armstrong, *Modernism: A Cultural History*', *James Joyce Quarterly*. 44 (4): 844–8. On Joyce's textual handling of Irish and British historical transactions see Seamus Deane (1986) ' "Masked with Mathew Arnold's Face": Joyce and Liberalism', *James Joyce: The Centennial Symposium*. M. Beja, P. Herring, M. Harmon, D. Norris (eds). Urbana and Chicago, University of Illinois Press: 9–20. See also Andrew Gibson (2002) *Joyce's Revenge: History, Politics and Aesthetics in Ulysses*. Oxford, Oxford University Press.

3   James Joyce (1992) *Finnegans Wake*. London, Penguin. I will cite it in the chapter as *FW* followed by page and line number.

4   Clare Hutton (2006) 'Joyce, the Library Episode, and the Institutions of Revivalism,' *Joyce, Ireland, Britain*. Andrew Gibson and Len Platt (eds). Gainesville; F. L. : University Press of Florida: 122–138.

5   Joyce may well have read works by T. C. Croker (1798-1854). According to Luca Crispi's recent work, Joyce had noted Croker's name in his 1902 notebook. Crispi, Luca (2009) 'A Commentary on James Joyce's National Library of Ireland 'Early Commonplace Book': 1903–1912 (MS 36,639/02/A)', *Genetic Joyce Studies* 9. <http://www.antwerpjamesjoycecenter.com/GJS9/GJS9_LCrispi.htm>

6   Bernard McGinley, 'Charter'd Streets: Joyce's London and Londoners,' paper delivered to XVII International James Joyce Symposium, Goldsmiths College, London, 2000.

7   See Charles Altieri (1988), ' "Finnegans Wake" as Modernist Historiography,' *NOVEL: A Forum on Fiction*. 21 (2/3): 238–50. Also, Vicki Mahaffey (1993) ' "Minxing Marrage and Making Loof": Anti-Oedipal Reading', *James Joyce Quarterly*. 30 (2): 219–37.

8   John Cannon (ed.) (2009) *A Dictionary of British History*. Oxford, Oxford University Press.

9   According to Mink (499) and McHugh (578–9), the reference is to Barnardo's.

Architectural London: Elizabeth Bowen in Regent's Park

Allan Hepburn

Elizabeth Bowen thought of London in terms of architecture, especially houses. For her, buildings can elaborate virtues such as civility, independence of thought, and responsibility towards others. London, as a centre of metropolitan modernism, diminishes these virtues because of its magnitude; in the crowded metropolis, the competing demands of inhabitants cannot be reduced to a single set of civic principles or behaviours. Furthermore, in Bowen's mind, a fictional London, 'pieced together out of Dickens, E. F. Benson, E. Nesbit, Galsworthy, Conan Doyle and of course Compton Mackenzie' (Bowen, 1986: 86), exists alongside, or nestled within, architectural London. In 'Coming to London', she claims that the city loomed like a physical obstacle to understanding: 'it was like a hand too near my eyes' (Bowen, 1986: 85). As a composite of buildings and stories, it blocked every other view. In *The Death of the Heart, The Demon Lover and Other Stories*, and various essays about London, Bowen casts architecture in terms of neighbourhoods, urban planning, and British heritage.

Bowen almost always thought of metropolitan London in relation to rural Ireland. Such a bifurcated view is hardly surprising given the fact that, as well as living in a nineteenth-century terrace house on Regent's Park from 1935 until 1952, she owned a Georgian country house in County Cork from 1930 until 1959. In *Pictures and Conversations*, the autobiography that she was working on when she died in 1973, she admits that, 'possibly, it was England that made me a novelist' (Bowen, 1975: 23). She does not mean this statement in a straightforward way: England cannot lay sole claim to the making of her style or subject matter. Rather, her coming to England makes her see discrepancies between the English environment and her Irish heredity. About her arrival in England she writes:

> from now on there was to be (as for any immigrant) a cleft between my heredity and my environment – the former remaining, in my case, the more powerful. Submerged, the mythology of this 'other' land could be felt at work in the ways, manners and views of its people, round me. (Bowen, 1975: 23)

Conscious of her place within a lineage of Anglo-Irish writers – she lists Goldsmith, Sheridan, Wilde, Yeats, Shaw, and Beckett – Bowen also remembers her Anglo-Irish ancestors, 'none of whom had resided anywhere but in Ireland for some centuries, and some of whom may never have been in England at all' (Bowen, 1975: 23). Bowen's rootedness in Ireland sharpens her sense of estrangement in England. She uses her estrangement to advantage, namely, like Sheridan, to 'swoop down on the English' (Bowen, 2010: 239).

In novels and short stories, Bowen deals with the national and colonial legacies that persist between England and Ireland. Characters move back and forth between the two countries, much as Bowen did herself. In *The Heat of the Day*, Stella Rodney travels from London to a country house in Ireland during the Second World War; she finds the rural, unelectrified darkness of Mount Morris more complete than any blackout in wartime London. In *A World of Love*, Antonia, shifting between winters in London and summers on her dilapidated country estate in Ireland, carries an aura of decadence and dislocation wherever she goes. This splicing together of scenes in London and scenes in Irish settings is a commonplace in Bowen's fiction. In the central section of *The House in Paris*, Karen Michaelis, who lives 'in one of the tall, cream houses in Chester Terrace, Regent's Park' (Bowen, 2002: 68), invites herself for a fortnight's visit with her Aunt Violet and Uncle Bill Bent in Rushbrook, County Cork. Their country house having 'been burnt in the troubles' (Bowen, 2002: 74), the Bents choose to stay on in Ireland in a suburban villa rather than live in England; Violet's relatives think this decision 'insecure and pointless, as though she had chosen to settle on a raft' (Bowen, 2002: 75). Views of Ireland, contrasted as they are between those who live there and those who live in England, are incommensurate, nor can they ever be made to join up. The 'ambivalence as to all things English, a blend of impatience and evasiveness, a reluctance to be pinned to a relationship' (Bowen, 1986: 86) that Bowen felt as an Anglo-Irish writer, emerges in her consciousness of Ireland as the periphery to any narrative about London.

Coming to London in *The Death of the Heart*

Bowen understands London primarily in terms of its neighbourhoods: Trevor Square in *Friends and Relations*, St. John's Wood in *To the North*, Regent's Park in *The Death of the Heart*. Although London might contain 'a plethora of cities jostling for precedence within the same ever-expanding and unstable space' (Freeman, 2007: 15), Bowen fixes her attention on drawing-rooms in middle-class and aristocratic houses. On 31 July 1935, she wrote to Virginia Woolf that she had been looking at houses in the capital after years of living in Old Headington, near Oxford. Bowen's husband, Alan Cameron, had taken up an appointment as Secretary to the Central Council of London Broadcasting at the BBC, a position that he kept until 1945. Having a taste for well-proportioned, classical buildings, Bowen set her sights on 2 Clarence Terrace, Regent's Park: 'The reason to take it is that it is, in a bare plain way, very lovely with green reflections inside from the trees such as I have only seen otherwise in a country house' (Bowen, 1986: 211). The blending of outside with inside – the reflections of trees on interior walls – creates a rural effect that defies, or subdues, the bustle of surrounding

London. The virtue of a house, to Bowen's mind, is its connection to its environment: outdoors and indoors communicate with each other. Her idea of a beautiful house, as she told three interviewers on the BBC in 1959, involved rooms with 'repeating shape, the idea of reflection in from trees' (Bowen, 2010: 331). In *Bowen's Court*, the book that she wrote about the history of her family and their Irish property in County Cork, she praises the play of outdoor and indoor weather in similar terms: 'Indoors, the rooms with these big windows not only reflect the changes of weather but seem to contain the weather itself' (Bowen, 1999: 22). Bowen understood that her temperament, on the whole, was more rural than urban. She preferred a '[h]ouse in the country; enough but not too much garden. Friends within reach but not on one's doorstep. House should be, ideally, eighteenth-century: not too large. Countryside should be quiet and remote as possible' (Bowen, 2010: 232).

Clarence Terrace, designed by John Nash and built in 1827, met many of Bowen's criteria for a countrified house in the city. In 'Regent's Park and St. John's Wood', Bowen summarizes Nash's intentions to build 'twenty-six villas (in the Italian sense), each artfully set in the landscape of grass, water and trees' (Bowen, 2008: 101). Nash anticipated twentieth-century urban planning by imagining houses surrounded by green space and by thinking of city design on a monumental scale. Bowen found the right balance of urban and rural elements in Nash's design for Regent's Park; the lake and trees nearby satisfied her need for the bucolic. The terrace houses, set back from the outer ring of Regent's Park, achieve a sense of polite retirement, in which neighbourliness does not interfere with intimacy: 'Self-sufficiency, but not isolation, seems to me to be the ideal' (Bowen, 2010: 232). Civility and restraint combine within the long regular façades of the Regent's Park terrace houses. As John Summerson explains, Nash used a

> scenic method of façade-design. Two immense palaces and several small attendant villas are suggested by the Park front of York Terrace, but the whole range of building is in reality a set of forty-nine houses of almost identical accommodation. (Summerson, 1935: 188)

The façade creates a visual deception: unity of architectural effect is created by subduing parts to the whole.

Architecture exemplifies political convictions and their afterlife. The terrace houses around Regent's Park, built in the 1820s, are not just quite eighteenth century, but they do exemplify Georgian values: stability, unity, grandeur, and colonial expansion. Clarence Terrace might have appealed to Bowen because of its resemblance, however indirect, to Bowen's Court. Italian villas inspired the terrace houses around Regent's Park, just as they inspired the architecture of her house in Ireland that was, in the words of its last owner, 'a high bare Italianate house' (Bowen, 1999: 21). Throughout *Bowen's Court*, Bowen describes her inherited country house according to its Georgian symmetries and Italian plasterwork friezes: the house, she says, is 'severely classical and, outside and inside, is very bare' (Bowen, 1999: 23). A walled property, Bowen's Court flourished in its country isolation: 'it has no castle and belongs to no neighbourhood, being much lonelier in its situation than any other big house in the country round' (Bowen, 1999: 20). Similarly, the houses on Clarence Terrace orient themselves towards Regent's Park, so that while neighbours exist, they live in direct visual relation to the park and indirect next-door-neighbour relation to each other. In this regard, the green park around Bowen's Court that keeps neighbours at a distance is replicated, with modifications for urban location, to the dignified terrace houses around Regent's Park. Bowen's habit of contrasting English and Irish architecture implies that modernism does not occur 'only within the teeming, colonized spaces of the eccentric city' (DiBattista, 2007: 231). To import country values of civility and neighbourliness into London, or to find those values embodied in a terrace house on Regent's Park, is to keep in mind that no metropolis exists apart from its peripheries.

Despite the formal regularity of its frontage, the back of Bowen's Court was incomplete: 'It was intended to form a complete square, but the north-east corner is missing' (Bowen, 1999: 21). Bowen means that the house as a structure was never finished, but she also conveys the awareness that a country house, passed along from one generation to the next, never can be brought to completion – every generation adds to it, in one direction or another. In 'The Big House', an essay published in 1940, Bowen wonders about the younger generations who have taken on the burden of maintaining Irish country houses:

> The young cannot afford to be stupid – they expect the houses they keep alive to inherit, in a changed world and under changed conditions, the good life for which they were first built. The good in the new can add to, not destroy, the good in the old. (Bowen, 1986: 30)

In Bowen's formulation, houses, not people, inherit. The specific 'good' of Irish country houses – if 'good' means ideals to be lived up to – is handed down from eighteenth-century Europeans who were committed to what is 'humanistic, classic and disciplined' (Bowen, 1986: 27). Houses, having inherited these qualities, instill them in their inhabitants. In *The Heat of the Day*, Roderick Rodney inherits an Irish country house from a remote relative, Cousin Francis. In his will Cousin Francis stipulates that Roderick 'may care in his own way to carry on the old tradition' (Bowen, 2002a: 95). Roderick puzzles over this legal phrasing that might imply either that he should care in his own way, or that he should carry on the old tradition in his own way. Regardless of the interpretation, he is obliged by the terms of the will to continue the traditions imposed by the house itself. As a custodian of property, Roderick should add to, not destroy, the good in the old. In this sense, Mount Morris, like Bowen's Court, remains a work in progress, even as it is a repository of accumulated history.

Houses embody their histories; they have a politics and a purpose. Speaking of Bowen's Court, Bowen claims that 'all thought starts in feeling, and all thought is dominated by the symbolism of the dream. Bowen's Court is no more than itself. But it is a 1775 house, boldly letting in light and exultantly serious' (Bowen, 1999: 161–2). Anglo-Irish power imbues Bowen's Court; its Georgian solidity bespeaks its political immovability and colonial intentions in Ireland. In a similar vein, John Nash's original conception for Clarence Terrace was a grandiose adaptation of Greek elements to urban London. He envisioned 'a large central block joined to side-wings by Ionic colonnades and decorated with caryatids and sarcophagi above the cornice. The design as executed is a drastic simplification of this' (Summerson, 1935: 190).

Nash's regal conception of Regent's Park, with a pair of circular roads and a crowning Valhalla, never actually came to fruition:

> The Park as we know it is simply a tree-planted public open space with houses on three sides. As Nash imagined it, it was very different: a private garden city for an aristocracy, shut in with a belt of terraces, dominated by the great double circus, and crowned by the outline of the Valhalla. That was a great design, of which the Regent's Park of to-day is only a fragment. (Summerson, 1935: 175)

In 'Regent's Park and St. John's Wood', Bowen remembered this passage and quoted it more or less accurately, without attributing it to Summerson: 'The new Regent Street, cut through from south to north, was to terminate in something newer still: "a private garden city for the aristocracy"' (Bowen, 2008: 101). Bowen was particularly taken by Summerson's description of Regent's Park as an enclave and, in line with his characterization, in 'Regent's Park and St. John's Wood' she exaggerates what she sees as the defensive aspect of the private garden city:

> Of the great gated enclosure to be called Regent's Park, the terraces, with their theatrical palace-like painted façades, facing in on the green, were to be, as it were, palisades – and, about the terraces' dun brick backs, turned upon all the rest of London, there is still something daunting and palisade-looking. (Bowen, 2008:101)

In *The Death of the Heart*, 'the city outside the park' (Bowen, 2000: 3) has an identity distinct from the park itself: it exists, as if inimically, beyond the palisade. The neighbourhood that turns its back on the city ceases to be neighbourly and the inhabitants begin to think of themselves, to their detriment, as a breed apart. In *The House in Paris*, with its claustrophobic interiors, and in *The Death of the Heart*, in which Anna Quayne reigns over her chilly drawing-room and Thomas Quayne retreats to his study, architecture twists feelings. Whatever the original virtues of architectural spaces, those who inhabit these spaces adapt them to their own personalities.

In this regard, the terrace houses around Regent's Park create strained, even histrionic, behaviours. *The Death of the Heart* is dominated by the trope of theatricality. Eddie, not alone in his histrionics, is called 'a little actor' (Bowen, 2000: 153). He does clever imitations of Anna making moues and of a society lady coming to tea. Even Matchett, the stolid servant at Windsor Terrace, does a 'faultless impersonation' of a housemaid (Bowen, 2000: 164). Portia resembles 'one of those children in an Elizabethan play who are led on, led off, hardly speak and are known to be bound for some tragic fate which will be told in a line' (Bowen, 2000: 390). Sincerity is at a premium in the novel. Irene, who acts on her passions more than is good for her, knows 'that nine out of ten things you do direct from the heart are the wrong thing' (Bowen, 2000: 68). She ought to act more, not less, for her passionate sincerity leads her into trouble. Architecture in Regent's Park reinforces theatricality. According to Summerson, John Nash was a man 'to whom human relationships were more important for their multiplicity and variety than for their intrinsic value' (Summerson, 1935: 180). The theatricality inherent in Nash's architecture replicates his delight in 'multiplicity and variety' – passing sensation and dazzling effect rather than any constancy of the human heart. In *Georgian London*, a book that Bowen reviewed for *The Tatler*, Summerson describes the 'extravagant scenic character' of stucco terrace houses in Regent's Park: 'They are dream palaces, full of grandiose, romantic ideas such as an architect might scribble in a holiday sketch-book' (Summerson, 1946: 165). Summerson concludes that the houses, however magnificent they appear, are, in fact, a 'sham' (Summerson, 1946: 165).

Bowen also thought that the Regency terrace houses, for all their dignity, conveyed flashiness without depth. In *The Death of the Heart*, the house at 2 Windsor Terrace strikes Thomas Quayne as 'empty, stagey, E-shaped, with frigid pillars cut out on black shadow: a façade with no back' (Bowen, 2000: 53). The house that has a façade but no back is a house where dissimulation thrives. In 'Britain in Autumn', Bowen echoes this description of the terrace houses: 'Round three sides of the Park stand cream-coloured Regency terraces of pillared theatrical beauty, built by Nash. ... The terrace is E-shaped, set back behind a garden' (Bowen, 2008: 52). Between novel and essay, she repeats the adjective, 'E-shaped', as if the terrace were a linguistic cipher to be decoded. The houses are 'stagey' and 'theatrical'. Such architectural theatricality cannot create authentic civic virtues. The houses might be beautiful, but the goal that such beauty serves is doubtful. When she revised 'Britain in Autumn' for publication as 'London, 1940', Bowen emphasized the solitude of the terrace houses after some of them had been wholly or partly demolished during the Blitz:

> At nights, at my end of my terrace, I feel as though I were sleeping in one corner of a deserted palace. I had always placed this Park among the most civilized scenes on earth; the Nash pillars look as brittle as sugar (Bowen, 1986: 24)

Even while the terrace houses embody artificiality, they stand for the conviction that civility is a public good. The prospect of demolition brings to the fore the value of theatricality as an aspect of civilization vested in architecture.

Bowen and her husband Alan Cameron occupied 2 Clarence Terrace in autumn 1935, but even before that date Bowen inhabited the house in her thoughts. She wrote to Virginia Woolf on 26 August 1935:

> I am so glad you think the Regent's Park house is a good plan. Though the lease is not signed yet, I am living in it in imagination already: I hope this is not what used to be called tempting providence. I do think it would be nice to live by that lake. (Bowen, 1986: 214)

Interiors inspired Bowen. As a young girl, she accompanied her mother on house visits on the southern coast of England: 'They became connoisseurs of villas, adept at extracting keys from house agents and then getting rid of the agent. And of each rented villa in which they lived, each fantasy home, they made a "pavilion of love"' (Glendinning, 2005: 28). In *The Death of the Heart*, Portia and Eddie creep into an uninhabited boarding house at Seale-on-Sea: 'There is nothing like exploring an empty house' (Bowen, 2000: 255) explains the narrator, although this illicit visit reinforces Portia's sense that no house can be a home for her. All the interior spaces in the novel have a hollowness about them. Even the Karachi Hotel, created by knocking together two large houses in Kensington, cannot disguise the 'extensive vacuity' of its interior (Bowen, 2000: 374).

As a young woman, Bowen had ambitions to be an architect (Bowen, 2010: 232 and 330). Shortly after she moved into Clarence Terrace in autumn 1935, Bowen wrote to Isaiah Berlin, 'I'd like you to see this house, which is nice though I still feel rather like a cat in a strange yard' (Isaiah Berlin Archives MS 245). Nonetheless, the house became a hub for literary London in the late 1930s; Stephen Spender, Rosamond Lehmann, T. S. Eliot, William Plomer, Virginia Woolf and others came to tea or dinner. As many of her friends noticed, Bowen adapted the house to her fictional purposes. Charles Ritchie writes that *The Death of the Heart* provides 'an exact description of her house and of her husband. The position of the sofa in the drawing-room, the electric fire in his "study" are all described exactly as they are' (Bowen and Ritchie, 2008: 25). When Elizabeth Bowen and Alan Cameron left 2 Clarence Terrace in 1952, Louis MacNeice moved in after T. S. Eliot recommended him as a suitable tenant.

The ostensible subject of *The Death of the Heart* is the betrayal of adolescent affection, but one of the less obvious subjects of the novel is London itself. Characters funnel into the metropolis, then shunt back out again. A host of minor characters revolves through the city. The Peppinghams, up from the country, lunch with Anna. Denis, cousin to Anna, goes to Turkey and leaves his flat to Eddie. Matchett, formerly a servant to Thomas' mother, 'had come on to 2 Windsor Terrace with the furniture that had always been her charge' (Bowen, 2000: 25). As a destination or as a place to live, London regulates lives. Three times a year, Anna sends Mrs. Heccomb, her former governess, a day-ticket to come up to London so that they can talk over Anna's various worries. Major Brutt thinks that opportunity might strike him in the metropolis. Eddie follows a similar intuition. Sent down from Oxford after causing a minor scandal, Eddie mooches off friends in London, including Anna and a gullible couple called the Monkshoods. He writes a satirical novel and gains a position in Thomas' advertising agency through Anna's intercession. When Eddie ventures to Seale-on-Sea for the weekend, he can think only about posting a letter to London and keeping up various emotional tangles in his absence. '"London"', he claims, '"seems beautifully far away"' (Bowen, 2000: 243), but it is not so far that he can forget about it. He cuts his weekend short and returns to the metropolis.

In *The Death of the Heart*, London mainly filters through Portia's perceptions. For the most part, Anna and Thomas leave Portia alone to wander about the city. In fact, Thomas chides himself for letting '"a girl of that age run round London alone"' (Bowen, 2000: 394). The novel roughly charts Portia's movements through the metropolis. On one occasion, Eddie and Portia visit the zoo in Regent's Park, then have tea at Madame Tussaud's. On another occasion, Portia and St. Quentin, having met by chance, amble along Wigmore Street, through Mandeville Place, and down Marylebone High Street. On an excursion arranged by her schoolmistress, Portia looks at a model of London burning and the teacher warns the schoolgirls that they must do their best 'to prevent a future war' (Bowen, 2000: 148). In another of her passionate confrontations with Eddie, this one the last, Portia meets him in Covent Garden. As against her 'home life (her new home life) with its puzzles' (Bowen, 2000: 72), where dissimulation stands guard, the streets of London allow for chance encounters and exploration. Part of the exhilaration of living in London is its unexpectedness. At Seale-on-Sea, Portia thinks about architectural collapse as an abiding terror in the city: 'That terror of buildings falling that one loses in London returned to Portia' (Bowen, 2000: 170). Growing accustomed to this terror does not mean that the buildings are any less imposing; rather, in London, Portia learns to live with that terror induced by buildings. The density of the city shelters and consoles her in a way that domestic interiors, especially the interiors of Windsor Terrace, cannot.

In *The Culture of Cities*, published in the same year as *The Death of the Heart*, Lewis Mumford argues that

> The story of every city can be read through a succession of deposits: the sedimentary strata of history. While certain forms and phases of development are successive in time, they become, through the very agency of the civic process, cumulative in space. The point of maximum accumulation, the focus of past achievements and present activities, is the metropolis. (Mumford, 1938: 223)

Whereas a 'city', Mumford implies in this definition, has an archaeology of diachronic stories, the 'metropolis' treats these stories as synchronic and ongoing. These stories, circulating at the same time, overlap and break in on each other. Because of these multiple vectors operating within urban space, the metropolis exceeds any single citizen's comprehension. London certainly exceeds Portia's imagining of it, and certainly no one in London does anything that she can predict. Moreover, she has no opportunity to share her own story, including the death of her mother and her burgeoning love affair with Eddie. She is given no occasion to express her feelings, which isolates her further.

In *The Death of the Heart*, London inhibits thinking and feeling for everyone. Anna reproves Mrs. Peppingham for expressing an opinion: "'That is the worst of London: one never thinks'" (Bowen, 2000: 339). Although the statement pertains to Anna's will not to breach decorum and offer a personal opinion, she shifts the blame to London. If one does not think in London, one frets and feels. By enforcing social relations in which appearances take priority over integrity, London creates loneliness and isolation. No one feels this urban anomie more acutely than Portia does. As she tells Eddie, "'When I first came to London, I was the only person in the world'" (Bowen, 2000: 136). She means that she had no one in whom she could confide. She also means that London provides opportunities to fall in love, as Portia does with Eddie. Although Thomas believes that '[i]t was only fair, it was only proper … that Portia should come to London' (Bowen, 2000: 47), Portia understands that the Quaynes do not especially want her there or anywhere. She confides to her diary, 'they wished I was not here' (Bowen, 2000: 145). Anna forbids authentic feelings, in herself and others. 'In fact, something edited life in the Quaynes' house' (Bowen, 2000: 221), the narrator claims. In 'edited life', feelings that ought to be there, or were once there, have been deleted. For Portia, 'family feeling' (Bowen, 2000: 245) has been edited out of Windsor Terrace, and it cannot be recovered.

In her essays and novels, Bowen had a great deal to say about houses as habitats. For her, the house functions as a training ground where residents learn such civic virtues as privacy, sharing, independence 'without dissidence', and originality (Bowen, 2010: 171–2). Instead of offering a sense of home, Windsor Terrace is merely a decorated interior. Anna, playfully striking at Thomas's head, orders him to "'have some ideas about home —'" (Bowen, 2000: 314), but she breaks off the sentence because an idea of home is the last thing that the Quaynes can manage. 'The Idea of the Home', as Bowen argued in a speech of that title, implies that whatever 'goes on within four walls has a continuous and creative effect, whether good or bad, on the individual inner being' (Bowen, 2010: 162). She makes a special plea for adolescents, who require physical space for psychological growth: 'Can psychological living-space be achieved when physical living-space is restricted?' (Bowen, 2010: 170). Portia does not know how to take up space within Windsor Terrace. Her presence there, which is supposed to last only for a year, remains spectral. With a shade of menace, the narrator in *The Death of the Heart* forecasts her fate: 'In the home of today there is no place for the miss: she has got to sink or swim' (Bowen, 2000: 49). After reading Portia's diary on the sly, Anna is determined that Portia sink once and for all. Portia, on the other hand, has no idea why she is 'tacitly watched' (Bowen, 2000: 176) by Anna and her friends. The distortion that runs through all feelings in the novel is not even understood by Portia as a distortion. In this regard, London is to her a composite of half-lit intentions and covert hostilities.

The allegiance that develops between Major Brutt and Portia is based on their both being displaced to London, as well as their both being despised by Anna. Neither of them masters the metropolis and its social intricacies. In effect, they belong nowhere. Major Brutt, who has had postings abroad – Anna vaguely remembers that he had 'the management of a quite large estate' in Malay (Bowen, 2000: 339) – is forever out of step with the times. The narrator, given to occasional interruptions and voice-overs that fix characters within contexts, defines Brutt's relation to London in erotic terms:

> He was the man from back somewhere, out of touch with London, dying to go on somewhere after a show. He would be glad to go on almost anywhere. But London, these nights, has a provincial meanness bright lights only expose. After dark, she is like a governess gone to the bad, in a Woolworth tiara, tarted up all wrong. But a glamour she may have had lives on in exiles' imaginations. Major Brutt was the sort of man who, like a ghost with no beat, hesitates round the West End about midnight – not wanting to buy a girl, not wanting to drink alone, not wanting to go back to Kensington, hoping something may happen. It grows less likely to happen – sooner or later he must be getting back. If he misses the last tube, he will have to run to a taxi; the taxi lightens his pocket and torments him, smelling of someone else's woman's scent. Like an empty room with no blinds his imagination gapes on the scene, and reflects what was never there. If this is to be all, he may as well catch the last tube. He may touch the hotel porter for a drink in the lounge – lights half out, empty, with all the old women gone to bed. There is vice now, but you cannot be simply naughty. (Bowen, 2000: 53–4)

The sudden turn to 'you' in this conjectural passage rings with reproach. Major Brutt might deliver this reproach to himself – he chastises himself in the second person – but it might just as easily be a taunt made by the narrator, given to moments of acerbity, to Major Brutt. The nature of the 'vice' that afflicts Brutt remains murky; it might be drinking alone or entertaining lascivious thoughts about women. Whatever the vice, it fails to measure up to the imaginary pleasures that London – an allegorical tart in a cheap tiara – has on offer. Paradoxically, this passage intrudes on the narrative while Major Brutt sips a glass of whiskey at Clarence Terrace; instead of passing his evening desperately combing the West End for an encounter, he is comfortably ensconced with an old acquaintance. If the narrative sketches a trajectory of failure and missed opportunities, a trajectory that on other, less sociable evenings Major Brutt might already have followed – or that he will in the future follow – he manages to catch hold of glamour on this particular evening with the Quaynes. In general, London taunts Major Brutt with imagined pleasures. Prim and seedy at the same time, London, the governess gone bad, allows nothing to be fulfilled, certainly not Major Brutt's vague sexual longings.

London exacts purpose from people, at least as far as Portia can tell: 'She had watched life, since she came to London, with a sort of despair – motivated and busy always, always progressing: even people pausing on bridges seemed to pause with a purpose; no bird seemed to pursue a quite aimless flight' (Bowen, 2000: 72). The mention of couples pausing on bridges recalls the opening scene of the novel, in which Anna and St. Quentin pause, purposefully, on a bridge in Regent's Park to discuss Portia's diary. Anna quotes the first line of the diary: ' "So I am with them, in London" ' (Bowen, 2000: 9). St. Quentin comments on the style of the sentence, with its thoughtfully placed comma. Yet he does not comment on the substance of the sentence, brought into relief by the stylish comma, namely that Portia has an awestruck sense of London and no other place. The sentence repeats with variations throughout the novel. 'I am not there' (Bowen, 2000: 179), thinks Portia about Windsor Terrace when she is at Seale-on-Sea. 'I am back here, in London. They won't be back till tomorrow' (Bowen, 2000: 297), she writes upon her return. The variations on this sentence turn on Portia's sense of being in or out of London. Between the first and third iteration, Portia emphasizes her separation from Thomas and Anna. Whereas she is 'with them, in London' in the first iteration, she is back in London without them in the last. To be in London is not, at least for Portia, a guarantee of being wanted there. The sentences, however varied, indicate that any trip to London is a return. When Anna gives a version of this sentence – ' "Well, here we are back" ' (Bowen, 2000: 314) – she states the obvious and takes for granted that London is the place where everyone ultimately ends up.

If London is a destination, it is not a happy destination. People gather there because they have no other place to go. Portia, like 'a refugee' (Bowen, 2000: 385), comes to the metropolis because her father makes her over to Thomas, her half-brother, in the belief that she would otherwise miss something essential: ' "normal, cheerful family life" ' (Bowen, 2000: 13). In the original draft of *The Death of the Heart*, the nineteen-year-old protagonist and her family are 'Irish refugees' who arrived in London sometime in the 1920s (HRC 1.4). Family feeling does not take root between Portia and the Quaynes. *The Death of the Heart* therefore offers speculations on the kind of homes that Londoners do create. The narrator, interrupting the narrative with a series of observations on the difference between homes and habits, notes that feeling, which is directed outwards from the individual as an expression without destination, is not the same as sentiment, which develops between people as a natural expression of love: 'It is not our exalted feelings, it is our sentiments that build the necessary home. The need to attach ourselves makes wandering people strike roots in a day: wherever we unconsciously feel, we live' (Bowen, 2000: 180). The narrator remains sceptical of such transitory feelings, for wandering people – among whom an indistinct 'we' figures – will feel anywhere and therefore strike roots that are factitious.

Portia feels at ease outdoors:

> She enjoyed being in the streets – unguarded smiles from strangers, the permitted frown of someone walking alone, lovers' looks, as though they had solved something, and the unsolitary air with which the old or the wretched seemed to carry sorrow made her feel people that at least knew each other, if they did not yet know her, if she did not yet know them. (Bowen, 2000: 72–3)

The inscrutable lives of Anna and Thomas Quayne never yield to Portia's pondering; by contrast, Londoners in the street have the capacity for being known. Portia, nonetheless, remains outside the affective life of these anonymous Londoners. She does not know them, nor they her. When she runs away from Windsor Terrace to Major Brutt's hotel in Kensington, she does so in search of a refuge or habitat that feels more like a home than Thomas and Anna's house with its strained atmosphere. 'In this airy vivacious house, all mirrors and polish', confides the narrator about the Quaynes' residence, 'there was no place where shadows lodged, no point where feeling could thicken. The rooms were set for strangers' intimacy, or else for exhausted solitary retreat' (Bowen, 2000: 50). Portia tells Brutt in a roundabout fashion that her coming to London was an inevitability but an unhappy one: '"I see now that my father wanted me to belong somewhere, because he did not: that was why they have had to have me in London. I hope he does not know that it has turned out like this"' (Bowen, 2000: 383).

Wartime London and after

The Second World War radically altered Bowen's idea of London. In an autobiographical sketch that she wrote for publicity purposes in 1948 and revised in 1952, she identifies herself as one of the stalwart civilians who stayed on during the Blitz:

> I would not have missed being in London throughout the war for anything: it was the most interesting period of my life. It was interesting to see the quiet old English capital converted into a high-pressure cosmopolitan city' (HRC 1.5).

While working as an ARP warden, Bowen continued to write short stories, principally those collected in the volume *The Demon Lover and Other Stories*. Being a Londoner in wartime meant fighting the people's war: 'the only interruption [to writing] being the necessity to clean up my house from time to time, when it had been blasted' (HRC 1.5). In Bowen's conception of national belonging, civic obligations go hand-in-hand with personal responsibilities. It is a duty to write, just as it is a duty to serve as a warden and to clean up one's bomb-damaged house. In fact, twice during the war – in 1940 and 1944 – bombs landed on Bowen's house in Clarence Terrace. The house was reconstructed, but houses in adjacent terraces, utterly flattened, could not be salvaged. In 'Regent's Park and St. John's Wood', Bowen wonders about the fate of urban property after the war:

> Ominously, lines of bomb-damaged villas are being left to rot, trees of their gardens growing in at their windows; someone is waiting, greedy, for their ideal sites. Over these little cadavers it is impossible not to shed a tear – they were so smiling, gay, neat, compact, warm; so much what so many people want, above all, today. (Bowen, 2008: 105)

She fears real-estate developers will tear down villas and put up hulking, brick mansion blocks out of keeping with the 'romantic privacy' of St. John's Wood and the 'august showiness' (Bowen, 2008: 104) of Regent's Park. Like many people in London at the end of the war, Bowen conjectured that bomb-shattered areas would serve private interests, not the public good. In terms of architecture and urban planning, the reconstruction of London in the postwar period was an opportunity to rethink social goals.

At the same time as she thinks about the future, Bowen is alert to the steep costs of holding onto architectural heritage. In 'Britain in Autumn', she mentions the bombing of St. Paul's Cathedral, which miraculously survived fire-bombing in the City on the night of 30 December 1940, but she does so with an unexpected shift in perspective: 'We feel strongly about these men, who saved St. Paul's Cathedral. We feel far less strongly about St. Paul's' (Bowen, 2008: 75). Bowen writes down the importance of architecture in 'Britain in Autumn' in order to write up the heroic contribution of civilians fighting the war. Lives are worth more than buildings. But Bowen, like many who wrote about blitzed houses, thought of buildings as surrogates for people. Villas are 'little cadavers' (Bowen, 2008: 105). Buildings where people shelter 'strained with battened-down human life' (Bowen, 1945: 213). In one of his wartime letters, Louis MacNeice describes Virginia Woolf's house, split open by bombs, as 'disembowelled' (MacNeice,1990: 102). Bowen's fiction evokes wartime history through architecture and human bodies. In *The Heat of the Day*, bombs gash buildings and reduce them to rubble: 'The first generation of ruins, cleaned up, shored up, began to weather – in daylight they took their places as a norm of the scene' (Bowen, 2002: 100). On the morning after bombardments shake London, Stella Rodney shouts down from her flat to a neighbour to ask which parts of the city have been damaged during the night. The novel gives information about casualties, both human and architectural. Louie Lewis' parents are 'wiped out during the Battle of Britain' (Bowen, 2002: 13), along with their retirement home by the sea; of the house nothing remains but 'thin air' (Bowen, 2002: 372). Short stories such as 'Oh, Madam ...' and 'In the Square' concern bombed London houses, their interiors sliced through and their storeys hanging in mid-air, and the inhabitants who do not know how long their buildings will stand.

When *The Demon Lover* was published in the United States in 1945 – renamed *Ivy Gripped the Steps and Other Stories* for the American audience – Bowen supplied a preface in which she fashions herself as a documentarian of bombed London architecture. She wishes that the stories in the volume contained 'more "straight" pictures of the British wartime scene. Such pictures could have been interesting: they are interesting in much of the brilliant reportage that exists' (Bowen, 1945: xii). If she documents the ravages of war, she does so without directly representing bombard-ments or firestorms. By the same token, she argues:

> I do not feel I 'invented' anything written here. It seems to me that during the war in England the overcharged subconsciousness of everybody overflowed and merged. It is because the general subconsciousness saturates these stories that they have an authority nothing to do with me. (Bowen, 1945: viii)

Neither conscious nor unconscious, this wartime 'subconsciousness' extends from one person to the next in a web of responsibility. In the strained circumstances, people act without thinking, and spontaneous subconscious response is to be praised. The stories in *The Demon Lover* are not '"straight" pictures' of wartime because they aim to capture feeling rather than fact. Nonetheless, many of the stories in the volume are haunted by locations outside of bombardment. 'Sunday Afternoon', for example, takes place at an Irish house, but remoteness from the Blitz does not prevent awareness of destruction in London. Henry, who works in London, has been bombed out: '"I lost my flat, and everything in my flat"' (Bowen, 1945: 21). He tries to dissuade Maria from going to London to participate in the war effort. In this sense, Bowen documents the war by inference, not direct pictures.

The stories in *The Demon Lover* represent London as spectral. Houses, as well as people, are immaterial. 'The violent destruction of solid things, the explosion of the illusion that prestige, power and permanence attach to bulk and weight, left all of us, equally, heady and disembodied', writes Bowen in the preface to these stories: 'Walls went down; and we felt, if not knew, each other' (Bowen, 1945: viii–ix). The sudden disappearance of protecting walls exposes feelings as much as interiors. In *The Death of the Heart* the walls and doors in Windsor Terrace barricade lives from prying eyes, but the blasting apart of buildings in 'The Demon Lover' leaves no opportunity for concealment. Characters, unhoused, wander about London. In 'Mysterious Kôr', lovers have no place to go. In 'In the Square', couples are thought to use empty houses to consummate their fugitive passions. No one lives anywhere permanently. In 'In the Square', Magdela claims that the house where she lives '"seems to belong to everyone now"' (Bowen, 1945: 8). In wartime, all property, being in the service of the state, is communal property. The people who live with Magdela are always poised to push off. Gina, for instance, feels 'it was time to clear out of this house' (Bowen, 1945: 11), but she cannot decide when and how to leave. No proprietary sense of housing and houses remains.

Certain writers saw the wartime demolition of buildings as an opportunity for rebuilding the city along modern principles. In Louis MacNeice's opinion, 'some of the more pretentious commercial architecture is aesthetically improved by bombing' (MacNeice, 1990: 102). He agreed with Ritchie Calder, who called the Blitz 'the biggest slum-clearance scheme in British history' (MacNeice, 1990: 127). Levelled buildings in London gave impetus to urban planning schemes with a focus on improved housing and more green spaces. *The Beveridge Rep*ort (1942), the bestselling government report that outlined a system for postwar social security and compensation, sought to remedy 'the Squalor which arises mainly through haphazard distribution of industry and population' (Beveridge, 1942: 170). Crowded housing in the poorest parts of London needed social intervention. *The Beveridge Report* coincided with the pressing need to figure out what to do with urban populations dislocated by the war. As Bowen understood, blitzed areas were ripe for property speculation by developers. The Utthwatt Commission, set up to investigate the problem of speculation, reported in *Compensation and Betterment* (1942) that 'the rights of development in all land outside built up areas should be vested in the state immediately, and that within the towns and cities, authorities should have wider and simpler power to purchase areas as a whole' (Calder, 1969: 534). If the state controlled property, it could develop land for the good of all. Conservatives opposed the Utthwatt recommendations, and the report, consequently, was shelved.

Nevertheless, postwar reconstruction was inseparable from the larger aims of social equity and development, particularly urban planning that would benefit the whole population. As J. A. Yelling explains, 'the most popular form of town planning lay in the improvement of housing conditions. Beveridge called for a "revolution in housing standards" as a means of reducing "the greatest inequality between different sectors of the community"' (Yelling, 2000: 490). These aims had a direct impact on London redevelopment. In two plans for London, *County of London Plan* (1943) and *Greater London Plan* (1944), Patrick Abercrombie focused on 'hierarchical interclass cooperation through the promotion of revitalized and collective civic life' (Hornsey, 2010: 14). He wanted to move over a million people from slums to eight planned suburban communities outside the green belt around London (Hornsey, 2010: 40). Abercrombie moved towards this concept of planned life in London by casting the metropolis as 'a network of local neighbourhoods', each with its own municipal buildings and local centres (Hornsey, 2010: 14).

This conception of urban planning coincides with Bowen's idea of the rural city, in which the neighbourhood takes precedence over the metropolis. Her essay on 'Regent's Park and St. John's Wood' bears out the conviction that local allegiances create a sense of urban belonging. 'Regent's Park and St. John's Wood' was commissioned for *Flower of Cities: A Book of London* (1949). This collection features 22 essays about commerce, law, architecture, museums, the BBC, and specific neighbourhoods in London. William Sansom contributes thoughts on Soho; Leonard Woolf writes about the glories of Bloomsbury; Stevie Smith invokes the rich complexity of life in suburbs; and John Betjeman sketches out the 'personalities' of the city's great railway stations. In its organization, the volume conveys the impression that London is a network of neighbourhoods sustained by urban infrastructures such as the radio, the railway and underground, and the port. In part a historical account of London – the title derives from William Dunbar's invocation, 'London, thou art the flower of cities all' – the essays reinforce an idea of the city as historically layered, multiple, and therefore metropolitan. In postwar reconstruction, the past needs to be acknowledged even as change inevitably occurs. 'The wall between the living and the living became less solid as the wall between the living and the dead thinned', writes Bowen in *The Heat of the Day* (Bowen, 2002: 100). Bowen's architectural metaphor of the thinning wall figures the mingling of past and present, as well as the architectural losses and rebuilding in London. In the metropolis most of all, the thinning wall instigates new concepts of neighbourhood and urbanism.

If nations write their legacies in buildings, the disappearance of buildings during the war foretold a transformation not just in British housing but in national identity itself. At the end of the war, Bowen wondered if the architectural legacies of London would be or could be restored. In *The Death of the Heart*, architecture around Regent's Park creates littleness of behaviour, but Bowen does not challenge the fundamental meaning of Georgian buildings. By comparison, in *The Demon Lover and Other Stories* and *The Heat of the Day*, she expresses scepticism about carrying on tradition, in the sense of keeping up houses and the values that they represented. Among other patterns, the war interrupted lineage and the transmission of property. In 'Ivy Gripped the Steps', a house in the coastal town of Southstone passes from one owner to the next, without any sense of continuity: 'the property passed to an heir who could not be found – to somebody not heard of since Singapore fell or not yet reported anything more than "missing" after a raid on London or a battle abroad. Legal hold-ups dotted the worldwide mess ...' (Bowen, 1945: 142). The sentence, ending in ellipses, ties the fate of the house to the unresolved fate of the owner. It is possible that no one is left to inherit this seaside property. Perhaps no one cares to inherit it. The tradition that Bowen values – 'The good in the new can add to, not destroy, the good in the old' (Bowen, 1986: 30) – may not be viable after a war that reconfigured the nature of the 'good' and to whom that 'good' applied. Buildings having been destroyed, there were no physical structures where the good and the new could enhance the old.

During the war, Bowen imagined her house in County Cork as 'the picture of peace' (Bowen, 1999: 457). The picture, although illusory, sustained her through the conflict: 'War made me that image out of a house built of anxious history' (Bowen, 1999: 457). Shortly after Bowen left London in 1952 to move permanently, as she thought, to Bowen's Court, her husband died. For seven years, she struggled to meet the rising costs of upkeep, but in 1959 she sold the house to a local farmer who tore the whole building down. 'It was a clean end,' writes Bowen, adding, 'Bowen's Court never lived to be a ruin' (Bowen, 1999: 459). Throughout much of her life, architecture consoled Bowen; houses were places of refuge for her imagination. After the demolition of Bowen's Court, her consolations became light, space, and memory, rather than buildings. *The Heat of the Day* was the last of her novels to be set, principally, in London.

Note

Archival material in the Elizabeth Bowen Collection at the Harry Ransom Humanities Research Center at the University of Texas, Austin is cited by box and file number.

9

'To be Tired of this is to Tire of Life': Louis MacNeice's London

Simon Workman

Louis MacNeice was a consummate poet of the metropolis, and while he wrote some remarkable poems set in rural locales (especially coastal and archipelagic settings), the predominant locus of his poetry was the city. He stands alongside Eliot, Auden and Larkin in terms of how powerfully his verse redirected the aesthetics of twentieth-century poetry towards the urban. As Edna Longley has astutely observed, 'MacNeice has not yet received his due for making urban landscapes part of the regular fabric of poetry' (Longley, 1988: 46). It is important to stress, too, that MacNeice not only helped to make inner-city environments an habitual source and site of inspiration for poets, but that his verse was key to the absorption into the poetic lexicon of the relatively new and often discomfiting landscape of *sub*-urbia as it emerged and expanded through his lifetime. He was one of the first poets to consistently write of this relatively uncharted territory – between the heart of a conurbation and its rural surrounds – and make of it high art.[1] That is not to suggest, however, that MacNeice idealized urban living, for the poet was often deeply conflicted in his response to city life, finding it by turns enlivening, hostile, debilitating, and heartening. In the poem 'Birmingham', for example, MacNeice bewails the dehumanizing effects of the daily grind on the majority of urbanites, noting how, to the west of the city:

> the factory chimneys on sullen sentry will all night wait
> To call, in the harsh morning, sleep-stupid faces through the daily gate.
>
> (MacNeice, 2007: 23)

However, when a city, particularly London, was under threat from war or when MacNeice linked it to Love, it often transformed into a vividly sensuous or sumptuously melancholic landscape – a place which could become everywhere 'littered with remembered kisses' (MacNeice, 2007: 107).

MacNeice's first encounter with London, as a young boy making his way to boarding school in England, foregrounds the poet's lifelong fascination with the exhilarating rhythms of the city and its visceral delights:

> Waking up on the night train from Stranraer to Euston, I said to myself 'I am in England' but could not believe it. There was nothing to prove we were in England;

it was night same as anywhere else … we might be in Ireland. But London was more convincing. It was a cab which smelt and a roar of houses and grime, grime, and the yelps of boys selling chocolate and never in the world had there been so much so quickly. (MacNeice, 1965: 63)

In contrast to the death-shadowed, religion-heavy, claustrophobia of his childhood home in small-town Carrickfergus, London seems something rather exotic, something other – a joyously brazen mix of grime, chocolate and glamour; an electrifying, heady blend of strange odours and endless rows of towering houses. What is also of interest in this passage is MacNeice's sense of London as a symbol and touchstone of the 'real' England. It hints at a tendency in MacNeice's later life to view London as the sole barometer of the social and economic state of England (and even Britain) while partially ignoring other regions. However, in his early career as a lecturer, in Birmingham, during the 1930s, MacNeice's political consciousness was not so dependent on the lens of London. During this period he became especially attuned to the social realities and cultural contexts of a range of English city dwellers. Indeed, as Derek Mahon argues: 'If Dublin could be reconstructed from the pages of *Ulysses*, as Joyce claimed, the pre-war urban England of rainy tramlines, Corner Houses, Bisto Kids and Guinness Is Good For You could probably be roughly simulated from a reading of [Graham] Greene and MacNeice' (Mahon, 1974: 115). MacNeice's time as a lecturer in Birmingham, particularly after his wife Mary left him, had important effects on his writing as it brought him into closer contact with less rarefied sections of English society, thereby broadening, enriching and democratizing his outlook and his aesthetic. However, despite the brilliance of many of MacNeice's poems set in Birmingham, it is the poet's London poems that shine brightest. Commenting on the poet's decision to move there to lecture at Bedford College in 1936, Anthony Cronin observes: 'in a very natural way dictated by his upbringing and background, he decamped to London; and no-one surely can deny that he wrote most of his best poetry while in that place and about that place' (Cronin, 1982: 201).

The poetic work which both Cronin and Mahon identify as the very best of MacNeice's London poetry is, of course, his masterpiece *Autumn Journal* (1939). This long poem offers a vivid collage of snapshots documenting the changing atmosphere and topography of London as it gears up for war. The poem also provides a sense of the changing feelings and attitudes of a community of Londoners under increasing threat. Above all, *Autumn Journal* achieves a remarkable inclusivity and breadth of perspective and these features are linked to MacNeice's conception of what a poet should be at this time. For MacNeice, poetry should seek to include the whole array of life as experienced by the community within which it is written. His prescription for the prospective poet, in his critical study *Modern Poetry* (1938), reveals a man of eclectic interests who is yet an ordinary man writing of ordinary things:

I would have a poet able-bodied, fond of talking, a reader of the newspapers, capable of pity and laughter, informed in economics, appreciative of women, involved in personal relationships, actively interested in politics, susceptible to physical impressions. (MacNeice, 1938: 23)

Autumn Journal puts this manifesto into practice and functions as a type of artistic apotheosis of MacNeice's writing from the period. As Edna Longley observes: 'all the currents of MacNeice's writing during the 1930s flow into *Autumn Journal* and find a new dynamic there: lyrics, eclogues, prose, the Audenesque play *Out of the Picture*, images, strategies ... His entire creative kaleidoscope breaks up and reforms' (Longley, 1988: 56). Describing the poem to T. S. Eliot in a letter in November 1939, MacNeice states that:

> It is written in sections averaging about 80 lines in length. This division gives it a *dramatic* quality, as different parts of myself (e.g. the anarchist, the defeatist, the sensual man, the philosopher, the would-be good citizen) can be given their say in turn. It contains rapportage, metaphysics, ethics, lyrical emotion, autobiography, nightmare ... The writing is direct; anyone could understand it. I think this is my best work to date; it is both panorama and a confession of faith. (Quoted in Stallworthy, 1995: 232)

The sheer range of modes and tones MacNeice deftly integrates into the poem gives it an extemporaneous, fluid quality which generates a surprising momentum in a relatively long verse narrative. London is very much at the heart of the poem and functions almost as a living character. Vast wide-angled shots of the cityscape blend with intimate portraits of city-dwellers and street scenes (in a manner which may owe something to the pioneering work of the GPO Film Unit in the mid–1930s.) The reader is exposed to a varied cast of characters and voices, a rich collection of sounds, images, textures and smells as MacNeice constructs a vivid and sensuous portrait of the city:

> A smell of French bread in Charlotte Street, a rustle
>   Of leaves in Regent's Park
> And suddenly from the Zoo I hear a sea-lion
>   Confidently bark.
> And so to my flat with the trees outside the window
>   And the dahlia shapes of the lights on Primrose Hill ...

(MacNeice, 2007: 110)

The material and materiality of the city are made palpable to the reader in a dense farrago of impressions of London at different times, in varied weathers, and through changing moods. MacNeice describes how, in October, rain comes 'whipping around the ankles/ In waves of white at night' flooding 'the raw clay trenches' meaning '(the parks of London/ Are a nasty sight)'(MacNeice, 2007: 120). While later in the poem MacNeice looks over North London to see:

> ... the November sun at nine o'clock
> Gild the fusty brickwork of rows on rows of houses
>   Like animals asleep and breathing smoke ...

(MacNeice, 2007: 141)

The poem begins in late August with MacNeice travelling to London by train from sleepy Hampshire, which seems strangely and gravely insulated from the imminent change ahead:

And I am in the train too now and summer is going
     South as I go north
Bound for the dead leaves falling, the burning bonfire,
     The dying that brings forth
The harder life, revealing the trees' girders,
     The frost that kills the germs of *laissez-faire*;
West Meon, Tisted, Farnham, Woking, Weybridge,
     Then London's packed and stale and pregnant air.

                                        (MacNeice, 2007: 102)

The simple litany of suburban stations reveals the magnitude of London's environs; there are quiet multitudes orbiting its centre that must also face the 'harder life' in which reality will be stripped back to its bare branches. As the train reaches London's centre there is a moment of compression as though all outworn modes of thought are collapsing inwards towards an uncertain end. Throughout the poem the city itself seems to bristle with a forbidding future as the casual, quotidian, ephemeral life of its citizens becomes darkened by an encroaching sense of inexorable tragedy. The usual distractions of city life can no longer occlude the threat of war:

Something out of the usual, a Pimm's Number One, a Picon –
     But did you see
The latest? You mean whether Cobb bust the record
     Or do you mean the Australians have lost their last by ten
Wickets or do you mean the autumn fashions –
     No, we don't mean anything like that again.
No, what we mean is Hodza, Henlein, Hitler,
     The Maginot Line ...

                                        (MacNeice, 2007: 109)

Nothing, apparently, can permanently prevent the 'heavy panic that cramps the lungs and presses / the collar down the spine'(MacNeice, 2007: 109). Objects within the cityscape are persistently converted into metaphors shadowing unnerving historical and political forces at play. In Piccadilly Circus, for example, the glowing 'electric signs' are described as 'crude as Fate'. While in a nearby Corner House, 'carpet-sweepers' seem to 'advance between the tables after crumbs ... like a tank battalion/ In answer to the drums' (MacNeice, 2007: 110). Further out in suburban London:

     ... [a] black
Scarecrow holds a fort of grimy heads of cabbage
     Besieged by grimy birds
Like a hack politician fighting the winged aggressor
     With yesterday's magic coat of ragged words.

                                        (MacNeice, 2007: 144)

Autumn Journal is not only attuned to the seasonal and meteorological shifts in the city but is also animated by London's rapidly changing terrain and what it implies:

... Hitler yells on the wireless,
   The night is damp and still
And I hear dull blows on wood outside my window;
   They are cutting down the trees on Primrose Hill.
The wood is white like the roast flesh of chicken,
   Each tree falling like a closing fan ...

(MacNeice, 2007: 115)

MacNeice writes later, with gallows humour typical of Londoners at this time, that Primrose Hill is:

No longer one of the sights of London but maybe
We shall have fireworks here by this day week.

(MacNeice, 2007: 114)

MacNeice is particularly attuned to the visual transformation of the city but he also gives special attention to the aural world of the metropolis and the sounds that seem to augur war and catastrophe. In the course of the narrative, distant voices, broadcasts, songs, mutterings on the street, the echoes of mechanical machinery as well as natural and animal noises all intermingle to create a dissonant and haunting soundscape reflecting the sense of moral discord and political indeterminacy of the period. In section V, sounds infringe upon the peace, auguring nightmares close at hand:

Nothing remains but rock at this hour, this zero
   Hour of the day.
Or that is how it seems to me as I listen
   To a hooter call at six
And then a woodpigeon calls and stops but the wind continues
   Playing its dirge in the trees, playing its tricks,
And now the dairy cart comes clopping slowly –
   Milk at the doors –

   ...

And now the woodpigeon starts again denying
   The values of the town
And a car having crossed the hill accelerates, changes
   Up, having just changed down.
And a train begins to chug and I wonder what the morning
   Paper will say,
And decide to go quickly to sleep for the morning already
   Is with us, the day is to-day.

(MacNeice, 2007: 111)

The acoustical perception displayed by MacNeice in *Autumn Journal* bears comparison to Virginia Woolf's *Between the Acts* (1941) which is also set on the eve of war conveying the sense of imminent threat. As Melba Cuddy-Keane makes clear, like

MacNeice, Woolf is highly alert to the variety of sounds which seem to emerge from all directions playing upon the imagination:

> As if the microphone had been set up in a village on a day in June in 1939, *Between the Acts* records a multiplicity of disparate, varying, and often contradictory voices, diffused through time and space yet sounding together. The literal chorus of medieval pilgrims, weaving in and out of the trees at the back of the stage, weaves into itself the words of the play, fragments of choric conversation in the audience, the great yearning bellows of the cows, the scratching and trillings of the gramophone ... simple single notes played on a piano, feet crunching on the gravel, the 'ding dong' of the cracked old church bell, the scrunch of automobile wheels, the hush of silence in an empty room. ... The voice of a clergyman, 'summing up', is broken up by the sounds of leaves rustling ... As in 'Kew Gardens', human, natural, and mechanical sounds are enfolded in each other. (Cuddy-Keane, 2000: 93)

The complex multi-layered soundscapes which Woolf describes in *Between the Acts* are also present in *Autumn Journal* although related more to urban than rural society. Both MacNeice and Woolf are possessed of a particularly keen auditory imagination and both writers allow the rich aural world that they are depicting to infuse their mode of representation. As in *Between the Acts,* there is a sense in certain sections of *Autumn Journal* that sounds are being presented in an almost unrestrained manner, as though the poem is merely echoing the aural textures of the world of the author. Indeed, the poem's fluidity of form is often intrinsically linked to the frenetic beat and tempo of urban life as the traffic and trains and shoppers and pigeons all commingle in a crazed ballet. The poetic structure may also have been inflected by the music and rhythms of the city's pubs and smoky dance halls, particularly the impulsive swing and whirl of Jazz. Indeed, the critic Katy Evans-Bush suggests that 'Jazz's sensibility of improvisation, looseness of syntax and beat, are everywhere in the poem. Written at speed as events unfolded ... *Autumn Journal* is, in large part, a riff' (Katy Evans-Bush, 2007).

The profound sensitivity to the aural as displayed in *Autumn Journal* meant that MacNeice was particularly suited to writing for radio when he began working for the BBC in 1941. MacNeice's decision to join the BBC was by no means a straightforward affair for the poet, for not only did it mean actively committing to the British cause during the war, but it also meant using his literary skills for propaganda work. The war created a crisis of conscience for MacNeice testing many of his allegiances, not least among which was his complex relationship to Ireland (now neutral), which he had struggled to clarify in poems such as *Autumn Journal* and 'Valediction'. However, despite some early indecision before the war began, it seems clear now that MacNeice was, in the final analysis, committed to the Allied cause and to the propagandist programmes he was requested to write and produce for the BBC. Indeed, he was to write later that during the war he wrote 'propaganda features, which ... I thought necessary and which I did as well – and that also means as truthfully as I could' (quoted in Whitehead, 1989: 111).

The first series that MacNeice worked on for the BBC was aimed at the United States of America, and according to Barbara Coulton the poet had 'made his interest in such propaganda clear in his original application to the BBC' (Coulton, 1980: 42). The series was called *The Stones Cry Out* and took as its theme old buildings in London symbolizing traditional values and Anglo-American heritage under threat of bombardment. Even before his formal appointment by the BBC, MacNeice had already written one script for this series called 'Dr Johnson Takes It' (5 May 1941)[2] relating a dramatized visit to the damaged house in London's Gough Square, where Johnson produced *A Dictionary of the English Language*. The programme uses the figure of the heroic lexicographer as a personification of English tenacity and by implication a celebration of the language uniting the English and American peoples. In another programme written as a freelance, called 'Cook's Tour of the London Subways' (25 March 1941), MacNeice had again shown his skill in writing for a North American audience. This 15-minute playlet follows a young man who encounters a Mrs. Van Winkle Brown who has not been in London since 1930. The young man takes her on a tour of Underground stations converted to air-raid shelters. Mrs. Van Winkle Brown and the thousands of Americans listening in are then introduced to a series of voices of Londoners – suffering but stoic, and ready to resist and overcome. 'Cook's Tour' was also MacNeice's first published radio work, having been shortened and adapted for *The Listener* a month after its broadcast, and appropriately set alongside sketches reminiscent of Henry Moore's haunting paintings of sleeping Londoners in the Underground.

Undoubtedly, MacNeice's best script for the series was 'Westminster Abbey' which was originally broadcast on 27 May 1941 for the Overseas Service, and then again on 7 September 1941 for Home Service consumption. The date is significant as it was the first anniversary of the beginning of the Blitz. From the outset, the announcer sets a solemn tone that stresses the Abbey's function as a shrine of Englishness:

> The building is a beautiful church but it is something much more than that. It is the repository of English history and an acknowledged national symbol. The history contained in its walls and the nation of which it is a symbol still remain alive after a year of devastation. (MacNeice, 1941: 1)

The script is 45 minutes long and focuses on the hit taken by the Abbey during an air-raid on May 1941. The thrust of the piece is similar to MacNeice's previous scripts – it reinforces the shared history between the American and English people while also emphasizing the spirit and resolve of the English men and women who are represented in a range of voices from different classes. What is most interesting about the programme is the way in which MacNeice controls the aural elements of the script. MacNeice utilizes the whole range of his sound palette here, deftly interweaving voices and skilfully incorporating a range of sound effects, hymns and chants into the programme, establishing a dynamic rhythm to the narrative. Yet MacNeice also exploits another acoustic effect that is uniquely powerful on radio – silence. After the announcer's first paragraph we are brought into the world of Westminster Abbey and asked to dwell on its captivating soundscape:

| LIGHT VOICE: | You are listening to a choir singing in Westminster Abbey. |
| WOMAN'S VOICE: | Voices floating among pointed arches. |

DARK VOICE:	In a forest of fretted stone.
WOMAN'S VOICE:	And now you are listening to the Abbey itself,
DARK VOICE:	Now you are listening to silence,
	(Pause)
LIGHT VOICE:	We will take you into this silence.

(MacNeice, 1941: 3)

Given that MacNeice is attempting to foreground certain abstract or immaterial qualities linked to the Abbey – its history, its tradition and the atmosphere of solemn serenity within its walls – the decision to draw the listener into noiseless 'dead air' is effective. As the radio critic Andrew Crissel makes clear, silence, if used correctly, can add an extra dimension to a radio programme: 'Because radio silence is total (unlike film and theatrical silences, which are visually filled) it can be a potent stimulus to the listener, providing a gap in the noise for his imagination to work' (Crissel, 1994: 53). In 'Westminster Abbey', the silence provides a pause in the action so that the listener can begin to conceptualize the Abbey in his or her mind's eye; while at the same time it mimics the mysterious and dignified aura of the building with its soundless, pregnant air. There is perhaps another reason why MacNeice may have sought to foreground silence and dwell on its properties, one closely related to the changing aural climate of London which was now under frequent German bombardment. In radio, as in life, the meaning of silence is defined by the context in which it exists – the silence at a memorial for example is different to the silence before a concert soloist begins to play. In a war-torn city, silence usually has an entirely different meaning to silence in peace-time and for a city under regular nightly bombardment one would assume that a cessation of the constant thud of bombs would be a relief. However, the following broadcast by Edward Murrow, from London on 13 September 1940, reveals that silence, far from functioning as a redemptive pause in the action, could actually have an insidiously destructive effect on morale:

> This is London at three-thirty in the morning. This has been what might be called a 'routine night' – air-raid alarm at about nine o'clock and intermittent bombing ever since. ... The aircraft barrage has been fierce but sometimes there have been periods of twenty minutes when London has been silent. Then the big red buses would start up and move on till the guns started working again. That silence is almost hard to bear. One becomes accustomed to rattling windows and the distant sound of bombs, and then there comes a silence than can be felt. You know the sound will return. You wait and then it starts again. That waiting is bad. It gives you a chance to imagine things. (Murrow, 1968: 57)

In another raid nine days later Murrow again reveals how disturbing the silence could be, yet his view now is more nuanced:

> I'm standing again tonight on a rooftop looking out over London, feeling rather large and lonesome. In the course of the last fifteen or twenty minutes there has been considerable action up there, but at the moment there's an ominous silence hanging over London. But at the same time a silence that has a great deal of dignity. (Murrow, 1968: 59)

Silence, then, could be an elevating force invoking, perhaps, the quiet stoicism of the people, connected by a common burden and resisting without fuss; yet it could also be a terrible pause for reflection, a palpable void in which the isolated mind is buffeted by imaginary thoughts of mutilation, total destruction, and mass death. In 'Westminster Abbey', MacNeice shows his sensitivity to the heightened significance of silence in war-time London and his script suggests an attempt to recode such silences in positive terms:

DARK VOICE:	The words of the poets are written on the silence. On the silence of the solitary mind; on the silence of the empty church. Listen to the silence of the aisles.
	(Pause)
	The Abbey is afloat on the night of London … with all these dead aboard her – a crew or cargo of bones. But echoes of a past life cannot be completely destroyed. The past continues to live and the silence is ready to talk.
WOMAN'S VOICE:	Echoes in the poet's corner – echoes of rhythmical language.

(MacNeice, 1941: 6)

The striking image of the Abbey as a ship afloat in the darkness of London suggests that the values it symbolizes will persevere, echoing into the darkness, and resonating with those minds that are alive to understand them. The Abbey is stirringly imagined here as a moveable feast for the inner ear, an echo-chamber for the auditory imagination.

As well as reinforcing notions of Englishness and English values rooted deep in race memory, 'Westminster Abbey' also turns its attentions to the German bombers which have come close to destroying the building:

WOMAN'S VOICE:	On September 7th last year a horde of shadows flew over London.
DARK VOICE:	Ghosts of an evil past, prophets of an evil future.
LIGHT VOICE:	Dark-winged shadows flitting across the roofs, shadows of destroying birds.
DARK VOICE:	Shadows of the Crooked Cross.
WOMAN'S VOICE:	The eagles with yellow eyes flew in from over the Channel. They hovered over the dome of St. Pauls … and over the towers of the Abbey …

(MacNeice, 1941: 7)

The vocabulary is highly evocative: MacNeice has reconceptualized the bombers as spectral birds in thrall to the crooked cross – *der Hakencreuz* – the swastika, which stands in opposition to the cross we would imagine in St. Pauls or the Abbey. MacNeice also draws a contrast between the silence of the Abbey and the terrible sounds of the German planes roving overhead:

WOMAN'S VOICE:	Listen; what is that?
	(*Drum roll representing planes*)
PLEBEIAN VOICE:	What do you think?
LIGHT VOICE:	Who is on the watch tonight?
PLEBEIAN VOICE:	Tom, Dick, Harry; Robinson and Brown.
PREACHER:	We made a prayer unto our God and set a watch against
	Them, day and night, because of them.
	(*Drum roll louder*)
PLEBEIAN VOICE:	Waiting by the hydrants; waiting with sandbags and
	Hydrant pumps.
LIGHT VOICE:	Some on the triforium level. Some on the roof level
	(*A. A. Gunfire*)
PREACHER:	Let them be as chaff before the wind and let the
	Angel of the Lord chase them.
DARK VOICE:	Heinkels and Junkers – a tangle of metal.
PREACHER:	They return at evening and make a noise like a dog
	and go round about the city.
	(*Noise of bombs*)

(MacNeice, 1941: 8)

MacNeice attempts to recreate on air the sounds of the bombardment while also building the atmosphere of panic that the bombing creates. In the poem 'The Trolls' written at the same time as 'Westminster Abbey', MacNeice again seeks to reflect the aural experience of the German attacks:

In the misty night humming to themselves like morons
They ramble and rumble over roof tops, stumble and
    shamble from pile to pillar
In clodhopping boots that crunch the stars.

(MacNeice, 2007: 217)

As Edna Longley notes: 'The sound and fury of the Blitz give MacNeice's onomato-poeia grim licence' (Longley, 1988: 87); yet as in 'Westminster Abbey', MacNeice counters the terror and destruction of warfare through an emphasis on 'incarnate value' and the power of human expression to transcend the ravages of existence:

Halfwit demons who rape and slobber, who assume
That when we are killed no more will be heard of us –
Silence of men and troll's triumph.
A wrong – in the end – assumption.
Barging and lunging out of the clouds, a daft
Descent of no-good gods, they think to
Be rid for ever of the voice of men but they happen
To be trying what even trolls
Can never accomplish, they happen
To be – for all their kudos –

Wrong, wrong in the end.

(MacNeice, 2007: 219)

In a sense radio itself serves as a metaphor for the poem's message – despite the destruction of cities and the death of thousands, the 'voice of men' transmits across the ether, sounding in homes around the country and reverberating in the 'solitary mind' of the listeners.

'The Trolls' can be grouped with MacNeice's 'Brother Fire' and 'Troll's Courtship' to form a series of three poems which attempt to represent the terrifying destructive power of the Blitz. However, while 'The Trolls' had drawn primarily on the auditory dimensions of the Blitz, the other two poems give greater focus to the visual effects of the bombing. All three poems can be compared with a series of prose accounts for the American journal *Common Sense* in which MacNeice had described in graphic detail the fires that raged through London after a bombardment. In a remarkable description of a raid on 10 May 1941, viewed from the dome of St. Paul's Cathedral, MacNeice zones in on the rich spectrum of colour within the voracious conflagration that has engulfed parts of the city:

> When the day came up and the planes had gone, London was burning still; you could stand on top of the dome and warm your hands at it. I had never before realized the infinite variety of fire – subtleties never attained by any Impressionist painter. These fires were a wedding of power with a feminine sensuous beauty. A glowering crimson power mottled with black; a yellow liquid power – a kind of virgin birth which is sheer destruction; a cracking, a hissing, and an underground growling. But up above were the softest clouds of smoke – soft as marabou – purple and umber and pink and orange which spread out and shaded off to blue. Looking at these fires from above I got them in perspective. When the fire takes over a new building, first of all it is the building that is on fire, but later it is the fire that is the solid object, the building is just a gimcrack screen that the fire has folded around itself. (MacNeice, 1990: 133–4)

MacNeice's remarkable concentration on the minutiae of tint and movement reflects the aesthetic appeal of this vast, catastrophic spectacle. The flames seem to exert a hypnotic power over the poet as he becomes enamoured by the terrible beauty of the 'birth which is sheer destruction'. That is not to say that MacNeice was not aware of the grim human tragedy that was occurring all around him, but rather to underline the ambivalence of the poet's response to the disaster. While the destructive pandemonium of the Blitz could devastate communities, it could also bring a clarification or heightening of perspective. Indeed, MacNeice comments after one raid that: 'There is, in some quarters, an understandable swing back to religion but the revival or religion (with its ordinary connotations) is something I neither expect nor desire. What *is* being forced upon people is a revival of the religious sense' (MacNeice, 1990: 133–4).

In the poem 'Brother Fire', this sense is brought to the fore and as Terence Brown observes, MacNeice 'addresses, with Franciscan humility, the principle of negation at work in the fire looting the city, reckoning it a force of purgation and spiritual renewal: "Which gluttony of his for us was Lenten fare"'(Brown, 2010: 150). The fire is personified as a primitive, mythical being rabidly consuming human life, yet is also seen as a physical manifestation of more guarded unconscious desires:

> O delicate walker, babbler, dialectician Fire,
> O enemy and image of ourselves,
> Did we not on those mornings after the All Clear,
> When you were looting shops in elemental joy
> And singing as you swarmed up city block and spire,
> Echo your thoughts in ours? 'Destroy! Destroy!'

(MacNeice, 2007: 217)

As in 'The Trolls' and 'Troll's Courtship', MacNeice seeks to allegorize the elemental (sometimes regenerative) energies of fire and destruction as they rove mercilessly through the city; yet he also posits a belief in the value of life as it becomes heightened in the face of death, which now acts as 'a stimulus, a necessary horizon'(MacNeice, 1990: 142). These poems of the Blitz demonstrate how MacNeice's experience of wartime London led him to abjure the more journalistic mode used in earlier poetry, such as *Autumn Journal*, and to experiment in a more condensed, parabolic form of verse in which real and unreal, private and public, conscious and unconscious are powerfully fused together.

While the early war years of the Blitz had brought misery and anxiety, they had also been met with a certain bravado and joviality. In the final year of the war, when V1 and V2 rockets were falling with devastating unpredictability, the citizens of the city had reached a point of exhaustion. Even peace could do little to alleviate the weariness of the city's inhabitants who had suffered five years of bombing and death. Reality seemed to pale as it became clear that the vigour and bravura of London had all but collapsed. The atmosphere became rather cheerless and oppressive as commodities were rationed and the city struggled to recover from the devastation. The author C. B. Purdom described the post-war city as 'dulled by such extensive drabness, monotony, ignorance and wretchedness that one is overcome by distress' (quoted in Ackroyd, 2000: 753). MacNeice registers the bleak mood of the city in his sonnet 'Aftermath', in which the poet bewails the collapse of the fragile, promising proto-community which seemed to be taking root in the war years. The more relaxed social conditions of wartime London were gradually tightened and redefined; and as Peter Ackroyd notes, in post-war London, 'the chummy egalitarianism of enforced contact between the classes were phenomena strictly of the past' (Ackroyd, 2000: 753). This was a particularly bitter pill to swallow for MacNeice, who writes ruefully in 'Aftermath' that 'What was so large and one / Is now a pack of dog's-eared chances' as society again became stratified, disparate and distinct: 'the bandaging dark which bound / This town together is loosed' (MacNeice, 2017: 255). The use of the verb 'loosed' may be an intended echo of Yeats's 'The Second Coming' in which a new, apocalyptic era is, chillingly, 'loosed' upon the world. There is a similar sense of paradox in Yeats's description of the 'mere anarchy' which destabilizes society and MacNeice's depiction of the 'bandaging dark' which holds the community of Londoners together. In both poems, there is also a pained awareness that a new and disturbing epoch is emerging in which the oneness, unity and perhaps political aspirations of the previous era cannot hold.

MacNeice's scepticism about the socio-economic fabric of post-war London was only to harden as time went by, and later in his life the city became a symbol of the cultural vacuity and historical amnesia which seemed to characterize post-war English life. In the poem 'New Jerusalem' written in 1962, for example, MacNeice adopts a voice of simpering irony, advising:

Bulldoze all memories and sanctuaries: our birthright
Means a new city, vertical, impersonal,
Whose horoscope claimed a straight resurrection
Should Stimulant stand in conjunction with Sleeping Pill.

As for the citizens, what with their cabinets
Of faces and voices, their bags of music,
Their walls of thin ice dividing greyness,
With numbers and mirrors they defy mortality.

(MacNeice, 2007: 592)

The reborn city is one of compulsive, illusory distractions born out of a society more firmly tethered to a rampant consumer culture. Now, there is no time for 'quiet and self-communing' or space to 'ponder the simple unanswerable questions' as MacNeice had done over 20 years ago in 'London Rain' (1939) in which the sound of rain on the city streets inspires the poet to an imagined journey across the roof-tops of London as religious, moral and metaphysical questions are considered. Now, the city's joyless and featureless new buildings, replete with straight lines and hard edges, seem disconnected from London's populace creating an atmosphere of bland, dreary conformity. They stand as a material reflection of a culture of mass production in which individuality, idiosyncrasy and community are increasingly under threat. As Brown notes, MacNeice found this culture increasingly depressing and was 'assailed by a sense of meaning, vitality, being drained from things as they proliferate in endless repetitive availability which is the motor of modern commerce' (Brown, 1998: 164). In 'New Jerusalem' London seems to function as an index of English culture and society and it is significant that the sensuous vibrancy of London in *Autumn Journal* stands in stark contrast to MacNeice's later portraits of the metropolis in which narrators and characters are overwhelmed by an alienating cityscape.

In several of these later poems set in London (including 'Charon', 'The Taxis', 'Sunday in the Park') the personae often find themselves in a surreal, Ballardian world of strange voices, figures, sounds, and inexplicable happenings. The poetic narratives seem to replay private nightmares and public histories in miniature, with London used as a sinister setting or shifting backdrop. MacNeice's past life in London, particularly of the war years, has become part of the poet's private mythology; a rich seam of memory exerting an ambiguous, ghostly power over future perspectives. The cityscape becomes a dark stage on which existential and autobiographical questions can be played out. This is particularly clear in the memorable poem 'Charon' (1962), that compresses Man's voyage through life into the frame of a single (and extremely singular) trip on a London bus. However, as in other poems such as 'The Taxis' and 'Figure of Eight', the journey rapidly descends into nightmare territory interweaving the quotidian with the terrifyingly absurd. In the poem's opening, the passengers are warned by a watchful conductor to hold on to a 'dissolving map', suggesting not only a physical action but also a more oblique act of memory or imagination. As the bus sets off, the narrator tells us:

> We moved through London,
> We could see the pigeons through the glass but failed
> To hear their rumours of wars, we could see
> The lost dog barking but never knew
> That his bark was as shrill as a cock crowing,
> We just jogged on, at each request
> Stop there was a crowd of aggressively vacant
> Faces, we just jogged on[.]

(MacNeice, 2007: 592)

The rumours of wars, the images of pigeons, and the shrill cock-crow all invoke the London of *Autumn Journal* and the war poems. However, the final sections of the poem make it clear just 'how bleak MacNeice's vision of ordinary life had become, and how much more sophisticated his craft' (Marsack, 1982: 149). Having arrived at the foggy banks of the Thames, the bus finally stops and the conductor instructs those on it to 'Take the ferry' (593). The passengers are then dramatically confronted by the eponymous 'Charon', who in Greek mythology traditionally demanded an obol for passage across the River Styx. MacNeice's Charon, who speaks in terse, compact prose, is particularly unsettling because he is entirely passionless in contrast to the bristling, flashing-eyed Charon of the *Inferno*:

> He looked at us coldly
> And his eyes were dead and his hands on the oar
> Were black with obols and varicose veins
> Marbled his calves and he said to us coldly:
> If you want to die you will have to pay for it.

(MacNeice, 2007: 593)

In this suddenly chthonic realm the blackness of the ferryman's hands disconcertingly reveals that he was also the bus conductor of the poem's opening, thus producing an unsettling sense of circularity and entrapment. 'Charon' is a far cry from the more journalistic approach MacNeice had deployed in *Autumn Journal* and derives much of its power from the poet's particular blend of ancient and modern, exemplified in the unnerving conflation of nightmare logic and real-world commerce revealed in the ferryman's final dictum. The poem bears the influence of Eliot in terms of how time seems to melt as mythic landscapes meld into historical moments in the confusion of modernity. However, MacNeice also draws on older forms of parable writing by authors such as Bunyan and Herbert, in terms of the double-level approach to the narrative. The passengers are modern-day pilgrims moving unwittingly towards the afterlife in an obliquely allegorical cityscape, shot through with images that seem to seethe with ominous import. MacNeice's darkling vision of London in the poem is both expansive in the sense that the cityscape becomes universalized as part of a spiritual narrative, and contractive in the way that it draws the reader into nightmare scenes specifically related to the poet's private memory of public events.

MacNeice's final word on London is contained in one of his last poems, 'Goodbye to London', which was written just under a year before the poet's death in 1963. The poem derives its seven-stanza form and its refrain from Dunbar's poem 'In Honour of the City of London', which famously declares: 'London thou art the flour of cities all' (quoted in Longley, 1995: 464–5) However, MacNeice's poem tends towards irony and solemnity where Dunbar's is unambiguously celebratory. The poem succinctly telescopes MacNeice's diverse impressions of London as the verse moves through the arc of his life in the metropolis. He describes how, as a child, the city was 'an ocean of drums and tumbrils', a mixture of 'horsepiss and petrol', while during his 'peering teens' it was a 'kaleidoscope / Of wine and ice, of eyes and emeralds' (MacNeice, 2007: 608). Later, MacNeice remembers it as 'a place to live in and love in' and that he 'jockeyed her fogs and quoted Johnson: / To be tired of this is to tire of life' (MacNeice, 2007: 608). The fourth stanza returns to MacNeice's wartime experience of the city and the tone of the poem darkens from here:

> Then came the headshrinking war, the city
> Closed in too, the people were fewer
> But closer too, we were back in the womb.
>> Nevertheless let the petals fall
>> Fast from the flower of cities all.
>
> From which reborn into anticlimax
> We endured much litter and apathy hoping
> The phoenix would rise, for so they had promised.
>> Nevertheless, let the petals fall
>> Fast from the flower of cities all.

(MacNeice, 2007: 609)

London is no longer the richly variegated, exhilarating cityscape of his youth and young manhood, but rather a bland, alienating urban sprawl – a tiring, uninspiring disappointment. If, for a time, MacNeice was a spokesman for London, articulating the hopes and fears of a community under threat, he was also its elegist, remembering happenings now lost in time. In the final stanza both roles coalesce as the poet laments both the city that was and never was:

> And nobody rose, only some meaningless
> Buildings and the people once more were strangers
> At home with no one, sibling or friend.
>> Which is why now the petals fall
>> Fast from the flower of cities all.

By the end of his life MacNeice had read London and its community from all manner of perspectives and charted its progress through numerous contexts. On radio and in his prose he had helped to construct the myth or emblem of London valiantly facing death in an unassuming, understated manner. In his poetry he had envisioned and reinvented the cityscape as variously haunting, exuberant, surreal, heartbreaking, utopian and dystopic. He was London's good citizen and its prophet of doom, and had been its awed visitor and its wearied resident. It is unsurprising, then, that Derek Mahon could imagine MacNeice as 'the voice / Of London, speaking of lost illusions' in his uncollected poem of 1995, titled 'MacNeice's London' (quoted in McDonald, 2003: 59). The irony of this position – an Irish poet as the voice of the English capital – has been emphasized by MacNeice's critics in recent years.[3] What deserves equal emphasis, however, is how fully MacNeice embraced the community of Londoners with whom he suffered during the war. As Robyn Marsack argues: 'MacNeice found in the atmosphere of threatened London exactly that sense of community whose passing from more primitive regions he had regretted' (Marsack, 1982: 69). One might add that London may also have temporarily alleviated the regret (and bitterness) MacNeice had felt at his early isolation within his community in his childhood home in Ireland. This perhaps explains why MacNeice's artistic interactions with London seem to invert the poetic principles of another Irish poet of the time, Patrick Kavanagh, who had championed a parochial form of verse which was, according to Antoinette Quinn, 'anti-metropolitan or, rather, indifferent to the metropolis' (Quinn, 1996: xxiii). The 'Kavanaghesque paradigm', as one critic has termed it, states that the parochial writer is authentic because rooted in a local community or 'parish', while the provincial writer is less vital because an outsider to an intimately known communal consciousness. Yet MacNeice's writing seems to achieve a remarkable authenticity and élan when regarding London; and it might be said that if Kavanagh ignored the metropolis by writing of the parish, MacNeice found the parish by writing of the metropolis. For it was as a Londoner (particularly during the war) that the poet felt a stronger sense of belonging and rootedness than perhaps at any other time in his life. The war years dissolved many of the barriers of nationality, religion and class which had prevented MacNeice from ever feeling fully integrated into a community, and it is perhaps for this reason that the poet felt such a profound sense of disappointment, of 'lost illusions', when the war came to an end. Yet even in his last years, when he had tired of the city and, perhaps, tired of life, London remained a potent source of inspiration. As MacNeice makes clear in 'Goodbye to London', even departure from the city will not immunize him from its effects, for it has irrevocably reshaped the contours of his poetic imagination; seen through the kaleidoscope of memory, London's past lives and landscapes remain such stuff as poems are made on:

> Having left the great mean city, I make
> Shift to pretend I am finally quit of her
> Though that cannot be so long as I work.
>   Nevertheless let the petals fall
>   Fast from the flower of cities all.

(MacNeice, 2007: 608)

Notes

1 See, for example, the following MacNeice poems: 'Birmingham', 'Spring Voices', 'Sunday Morning', Section III of *Autumn Journal*, 'Jigsaws', 'The Park' 'Windowscape'.

2 All unpublished scripts referred to in the essay can be accessed on microfiche (as well as some hard copy) at the BBC Written Archives Centre, Peppard Road, Caversham Park, Reading, RG4 8TZ, UK. All page numbers cited are from the original script. Recordings of MacNeice's programmes can be accessed at the Sound Archive in The British Library, St. Pancras, 96 Euston Road, London, NW1 2DB.

3 See Peter McDonald (2003) 'Louis MacNeice: irony and responsibility', *The Cambridge Companion to Contemporary Irish Poetry*. Matthew Campbell (ed.). Cambridge, Cambridge University Press: 55–75.

Bibliography

'A. E.' (1930) 'Foreword', *Collected Poems of Katharine Tynan*. London, Macmillan, vii–xiii.

Ackroyd, P. (2001) *London: the Biography*. London, Vintage.

Adams, H. (1995) *The Book of Yeats's Vision*. Ann Arbor, University of Michigan Press.

Altieri, C. (1988) '*Finnegans Wake* as Modernist Historiography'. *NOVEL: A Forum on Fiction*, 21 (2/3): 238–50.

Anon. (1884) 'Katharine Tynan's Poems', *The Irish Monthly*, 12 (138), pp. 618–624.

Anon. (1885) 'Miss Tynan's "Louise de la Valliére", &c', *The Irish Monthly*, 13 (145): 377–382.

Anon. (1885) 'New Books', *The Irish Monthly*, 13 (144): 331–334.

Anon. (1896) 'Notes on New Books', *The Irish Monthly*, 24 (273): 167–168.

Anon. (1902) 'Review of *Mrs Warren's Profession*', *The Times*. 7 January: 12.

Anon. (1908) 'New Books', *The Guardian*. 15 May 1908: 5.

Anon. (1926) 'Mrs Warren's Profession', Programme. Strand Theatre London.

Anon. (1969) 'Back to Methuselah', Programme. National Theatre, London.

Anon. (1970) 'Mrs Warren's Profession', Programme, National Theatre, London.

Arata, S. (1996) *Fictions of Loss in the Victorian Fin de Siècle: Identity and Empire*. Cambridge: Cambridge University Press.

Ayers, D. (2007) 'Review of Tim Armstrong's *Modernism: A Cultural History*', *James Joyce Quarterly*. 44 (4): 844–8.

Beveridge, W. (1942) *Social Insurance and Allied Services*. New York, Macmillan.

Bowen, E. (1935) 'Letter to Isaiah Berlin'. Bodleian Library, Oxford University. Isaiah Berlin Archives, MS 245.

—(1936) 'Anna'. Harry Ransom Humanities Research Center, University of Texas, Austin. Elizabeth Bowen Collection, Box 1, file 4.

—(1945) *Ivy Gripped the Steps and Other Stories*. New York: Knopf.

—(1952) 'Autobiographical Sketch'. Harry Ransom Humanities Research Center, University of Texas, Austin. Elizabeth Bowen Collection, Box 1, file 5.

—(1975) *Pictures and Conversations*. New York: Knopf.

—(1986) *The Mulberry Tree: Writings of Elizabeth Bowen*. Hermione Lee (ed.). New York: Harcourt Brace Jovanovich.

—(1999) *Bowen's Court and Seven Winters*. London, Vintage.

—(2000) *The Death of the Heart*. New York, Anchor.

—(2002a) *The Heat of the Day*. New York, Anchor.

—(2002b) *The House in Paris*. New York, Anchor.

—(2008) *People, Places, Things: Essays by Elizabeth Bowen*. Allan Hepburn (ed.). Edinburgh: Edinburgh University Press.

—(2010) *Listening In: Broadcasts, Speeches, and Interviews by Elizabeth Bowen*. Allan Hepburn (ed.). Edinburgh, Edinburgh University Press.

Bowen, E. and Ritchie, C. (2008) *Love's Civil War: Letters and Diaries 1941–1973*. Victoria Glendinning with Judith Robertson (eds.). Toronto, McClelland and Stewart.

Boyd, E. (1923) *Ireland's Literary Renaissance*. London, Grant Richards.

Brooker, P. (1988) *Bertolt Brecht: Dialectics, Poetry, Politics*. Beckenham, Croom Helm.

Brown, S. J. (1935) 'The Question of Irish Nationality', *Studies: An Irish Quarterly Review*. 63 (475), 432–44.

Brown, T. (1998) 'MacNeice and the Puritan Tradition', *Louis MacNeice and His Influence*. Kathleen Devine and Alan J. Peacock (eds.). Gerrards Cross: Colin Smythe: 22–33.

—(2010) 'Louis MacNeice and the Second World War', *The Literature of Ireland: Culture and Criticism*. Cambridge, Cambridge University Press: 142–55.

Brown, T. E. (1912) 'To the Editor of the *Scots Observer*', undated, reprinted in Stuart Mason, S. (1912) *Oscar Wilde: Art and Morality*. London, Frank Palmer.

Burne-Jones, G. (ed.) (1904) *Memoirs of Edward Burne-Jones*. 4 vols. London, Macmillan.

Calder, A. (1969) *The People's War: Britain 1939–45*. London, Jonathan Cape.

Cannon, J. (ed.) (2009) *A Dictionary of British History*. Oxford: Oxford University Press.

Carleton, W. (1887) *Willie Reilly and his Dear Colleen Bawn*. Chicago, Belford, Clark and Co.

Chesterton, G. K. and Paine, R. (2006) *The Autobiography of G. K. Chesterton*. San Francisco, Ignatius Press.

Clayton, J. (1995) 'Londublin: Dicken'ss London in Joyce's Dublin', *Novel: A Forum on Fiction*, 28 (3): 327–42.

Conolly, L. W. (2004) '*Mrs Warren's Profession* and the Lord Chamberlain', *Shaw: The Annual of Bernard Shaw Studies*. (24): 46–95.

Coulton, B. (1980) *Louis MacNeice in the BBC*. London, Faber and Faber.

Craft, C. (2005) 'Come See About Me: Enchantment of the Double in *The Picture of Dorian Gray*', *Representations*. 91: 109–36.

Crisell, A. (1994) *Understanding Radio*. London, Routledge.

Crispi, L. (2009) 'A Commentary on James Joyce's National Library of Ireland 'Early Commonplace Book': 1903–1912 (MS 36,639/02/A)', *Genetic Joyce Studies* 9. <http://www.antwerpjamesjoycecenter.com/GJS9/GJS9_LCrispi.htm>

Croker, T. C. (1969) *Researches in the South of Ireland: Illustrative of the Scenery, Architectural Remains and the Manners and Superstitions of the Peasantry, with an Appendix Containing a Private Narrative of the Rebellion of 1798*. Reprint of the 1824 ed., With a New Introduction by Kevin Danaher. New York, Barnes and Noble.

Cronin, A. (1982) 'Louis MacNeice: London and Lost Irishness', *Heritage Now: Irish Literature in the English Language*. Dingle, Brandon: 197–202.

Cuddy-Keane, M. (2000) 'Virginia Woolf, Sound Technologies, and the New Aurality', *Virginia Woolf in the Age of Mechanical Reproduction*. Pamela L. Caughie (ed.). London, Garland: 81–95.

Daly, D. (1974) *The Young Douglas Hyde: The Dawn of the Irish Revolution and Renaissance 1874–1893*. Totowa, Rowman and Littlefield.

Daly, N. (1999) 'The Colonial Roots of Dracula', *That Other World: The Supernatural and Fantastic in Irish Literature*. Bruce Stewart (ed.). Gerrards Cross, Colin Smythe: 40–51.

De Bhaldraithe, T. (Eag.) (1982) *Pádraic Ó Conaire: Clocha ar a Charn*. Baile Átha Cliath, An Clóchomhar Teo.

Deane, S. (1986) ' "Masked with Mathew Arnold's face": Joyce and Liberalism', *James Joyce: The Centennial Symposium*. Morris Beja (ed.). Urbana, University of Illinois Press: 9–20.

—(1990) 'Joyce the Irishman', *The Cambridge Companion to James Joyce*. Derek Attridge (ed.). Cambridge, Cambridge University Press: 31–53.

—(1997) *Strange Country: Modernity and Nationhood in Irish Writing Since 1790*. Oxford, Oxford University Press.

DiBattista, M. (2007) 'Elizabeth Bowen's Troubled Modernism', *Modernism and Colonialism: British and Irish Literature, 1899-1939*. Richard Began and Michael Valdez Moses (eds.). Durham, Duke University Press: 226-45.

Ellmann, R. (1954) *The Identity of W. B. Yeats*. London, Macmillan.

—(1983) *James Joyce*. Oxford, Oxford University Press.

—(1983), *James Joyce* (new and revised edn). Oxford, Oxford University Press.

—(1987, 2nd edn) *Yeats: The Man and the Masks*. Harmondsworth, Penguin.

Empson, W. (1982) 'Yeats and Byzantium', *Grand Street*. 1 (4): 67-85.

Evans-Bush, K. (2007) '"The Tawdry Halo of the Idle Martyr": MacNeice's "Autumn Journal"', *Contemporary Poetry*, <http://www.cprw.com/Bush/macneice.htm>

Fabian Society London (1885-1887) 'Minute Books 23 December-21 January': 1.

Fahy, F. A. (1902) 'The Gaelic League in London', *An Gaodhal / The Gael*. (January): 1-7.

Ferriter, D. (2007) *Judging Dev: A Reassessment of the Life and Legacy of Eamon de Valera*. Dublin, Royal Irish Academy.

Fitzgerald, David (1989) 'A Curious Middle Place: the Irish in Britain, 1871-1921', *The Irish in Britain, 1815-1939*. Roger Swift and Sheridan Gilley (eds.). New York, Barnes and Noble.

Forman, H. B. (1897) *The Books of William Morris*. London, Hollings.

Foster, R. F. (1997) *W. B. Yeats: A Life. Vol. 1: The Apprentice Mage 1865-1914*. Oxford, Oxford University Press.

—(2003) *W. B. Yeats: A Life. Vol. II: The Arch-Poet 1915-1939*. Oxford, Oxford University Press.

Freeman, N. (2007) *Conceiving the City: London, Literature, and Art, 1870-1914*. Oxford, Oxford University Press.

Gahan, P. (2010) 'Bernard Shaw and the Irish Literary Tradition', *Shaw: The Annual of Bernard Shaw Studies*. 30: 1-26.

Gibbons, L. (1991) 'Montage, Modernism and the City', *The Irish Review*. 10: 1-6.

Gibson, A. (2002) *Joyce's Revenge: History, Politics and Aesthetics in Ulysses*. Oxford, Oxford University Press.

—(2006) *James Joyce*. London, Reaktion Books.

Gillespie, M. P. (ed.) (1986) *James Joyce's Trieste Library: A Catalogue of Materials at the Harry Ransom Humanities Research Center, University of Texas at Austin*, with the assistance of Eric Bradford Stocker. Austin, The Harry Ransom Humanities Research Center.

Glendinning, V. (2005) *Elizabeth Bowen: A Biography*. New York, Anchor.

Glover, D. (1996) *Vampire Mummies and Liberals: Bram Stoker and the Politics of Popular Fiction*. Durham, Duke University Press.

Greenslade, W. (1994) *Degeneration, Culture and the Novel, 1880-1940*. Cambridge, Cambridge University Press.

Hamilton, R. H. (1980) 'Bernard Shaw's Reflections on Being a City Councilman', *Public Administration Review*. 40 (4): 317-20.

Harvey, J. (1949) *Dublin: A Study in Environment*. London, B. T. Batsford.

Hayman, D. (1977) 'Preface', Finnegans Wake: Book IV: A Facsimile of Drafts, Typescripts, and Proofs, *The James Joyce Archive*, vol. 35, M. Groden (general editor), arranged by D. Rose with the assistance of J. O'Hanlon. New York, Garland Publishing: vii-xi.

Hayman, R. (1983) *Brecht: A Biography*. London, Weidenfeld and Nicholson.

Hobson, B. (1968) *Ireland Yesterday and Tomorrow.* Tralee, Anvil Books.

Holroyd, M. (1988) *Bernard Shaw. Vol. 1, 1856-1898: The Search for Love.* London, Chatto and Windus.

Hornsey, R. (2010) *The Spiv and the Architect: Unruly Life in Postwar London.* Minneapolis, University of Minnesota Press.

Hunt, A. (1989) 'Review of *Mrs Warren's Profession*', *The Guardian.* 25 February: 66.

Hutton, C. (2006) 'Joyce, the Library Episode, and the Institutions of Revivalism', *Joyce, Ireland, Britain.* Andrew Gibson and Len Platt (eds.). Gainesville; University Press of Florida: 122-138.

Hyde, D. (1986) *Language, Lore and Lyrics.* Breandan O Conaire (ed.). Blackrock, Irish Academic Press.

Innes, C. L. (1993) *Woman and Nation in Irish Literature and Society: 1880-1935*, Athens, University of Georgia Press.

—(2000) 'Modernism, Ireland and Empire: Yeats, Joyce and their Implied Audiences', *Modernism and Empire: Writing and British Coloniality, 1890-1940.* Howard J. Booth and Nigel Rigby (eds.). Manchester and New York, Manchester University Press: 137-55.

Jeffares, A. N. (1977) *Yeats: The Critical Heritage.* London, Routledge.

Joyce, J. (1930) *Anna Livia Plurabelle, Fragment of "Work in Progress." Criterion Miscellany* — No. 15. London, Faber and Faber.

—(1957) *Letters of James Joyce. Vol. 1.* Stuart Gilbert (ed.). New York, Viking.

—(1966a) *Letters of James Joyce Letters. Vol. 2.* Richard Ellmann (ed.). New York, Viking.

—(1966b) *The Letters of James Joyce. Vol. 3.* Richard Ellmann (ed.). New York, Viking.

—(1977) '*Finnegans Wake*: Book IV: A Facsimile of Drafts, Typescripts, and Proofs,' *The James Joyce Archive*, Vol. 35, Michael Groden (general editor), arranged by Danis Rose with the assistance of John O'Hanlon. New York, Garland Publishing.

—(1991) *Poems and Shorter Writings.* Richard Ellmann, A. Walton Litz, and John Whittier-Ferguson (eds.). London, Faber and Faber.

—(1992) *Finnegans Wake.* With an introduction by Seamus Deane. London, Penguin.

—(2000a) *Dubliners.* Harmondsworth, Penguin.

—(2000b) *Occasional, Critical, and Political Writing.* Edited with an Introduction and Notes by Kevin Barry, Translations from the Italian by Conor Deane. Oxford: Oxford World's Classics.

—(2002) *Ulysses*, Hans Walter Gabler (ed.) with Wolfhard Steppe and Claus Melchior. London, The Bodley Head.

—(2003a) *The Finnegans Wake Notebooks at Buffalo. Notebook VI.B.1.* Vincent Deane, Daniel Ferrer, Geert Lernout (eds.); Introduction: G. Lernout; Bibliographic Description: Luca Crispi. Turnhout: Brepols Publishers.

Joyce, P. W. (1909) *Old Irish Folk Music and Songs.* London and New York, Longman, Green and Co.

Joyce, S. (2002) 'Sexual Politics and the Aesthetics of Crime: Oscar Wilde in the Nineties', *ELH.* 69 (1): 501-23.

Kiberd, D. (1983) 'Pádraic Ó Conaire agus Cearta an Duine', *Pádraic Ó Conaire: Léachtaí Cuimhneacháin.* Eag. G. Denvir. Indreabhán, Cló Chonamara.

—(1991) 'The London Exiles: Wilde and Shaw', *The Field Day Anthology of Irish Writing, Vol. III.* Derry, Field Day Publications: 372-6.

—(1996) 'Oscar Wilde - The Artist as Irishman', *Inventing Ireland: The Literature of the Modern Nation.* London, Vintage: 33-50.

Latham, S. (2009) 'Twenty-first-century Critical Contexts', *James Joyce in Context*. John
     McCourt (ed.). Cambridge, Cambridge University Press: 148–59.
Le Fanu, J. S. (2008) 'Carmilla', *In A Glass Darkly*. Oxford, Oxford University Press.
Lee, J. J. (1989) *Ireland, 1912-1985: Politics and Society*. Cambridge, Cambridge
     University Press.
Lewis, L. and Smith, H. J. (1936) *Oscar Wilde Discovers America: 1882*. New York,
     Harcourt, Brace and Company.
Linebaugh, P. (2003) *The London Hanged: Crime and Civil Society in the Eighteenth
     Century*. London, Verso.
Loeber, R. and Stouthamer-Loeber, M. (2005) 'Literary Absentees: Irish Women Authors
     in Nineteenth-Century England', *The Irish Novel in the Nineteenth Century*. Jacqueline
     Belanger (ed.). Dublin, Four Courts Press: 67–186.
Longenbach, J. (1991) *Stone Cottage: Pound, Yeats and Modernism*. New York and Oxford,
     Oxford University Press.
Longley, E. (1988) *Louis MacNeice: A Study*. London, Faber and Faber.
Lyons, F. S. L. (1970) 'James Joyce's Dublin', *Twentieth Century Studies*: 6–25.
MacDonald, P. (1999) 'A Poem for All Seasons: Yeats, Meaning, and the Publishing
     History of "The Lake Isle of Innisfree" in the 1890s', *Yearbook of English Studies*. 29:
     202–30.
MacNeice, L. (1938) *Modern Poetry*. Oxford, Oxford University Press.
—(1965) *The Strings Are False. An Unfinished Autobiography*. Eric Robertson Dodds (ed.).
     London: Faber and Faber.
—(1990) *Selected Prose of Louis MacNeice*. Alan Heuser (ed.). Oxford, Clarendon
     Press.
—(2007) *Collected Poems*. Peter McDonald (ed.). London, Faber and Faber.
Mahaffey, V. (1993) ' "Minxing Marrage and Making Loof": Anti-Oedipal Reading', *James
     Joyce Quarterly*. 30 (2): 219–37.
Mahon, D. (1974) 'MacNeice in England and Ireland', *Time Was Away: The World of Louis
     MacNeice*. Terence Brown and Alec Reid (eds.). Dublin, Dolmen.
Marez, C. (1997) 'The Other Addict: Reflections on Colonialism and Oscar Wilde's
     Opium Smoke Screen', *ELH*. 64 (1): 257–87.
Marsack, R. (1992) *The Cave of Making: the Poetry of Louis MacNeice*. Oxford, Clarendon
     Press.
Mason, S. (1912) *Oscar Wilde: Art and Morality*. London, Frank Palmer.
Matthews, W. (1938) *Cockney, Past and Present: A Short History of the Dialect of London*.
     London, George Routledge and Sons.
McCourt, J. (2000) *The Years of Bloom: James Joyce in Trieste, 1904-1920*. Dublin, The
     Lilliput Press.
McDonald, P. (2003) 'Louis MacNeice: Irony and Responsibility', *The Cambridge
     Companion to Contemporary Irish Poetry*. Matthew Campbell (ed.). Cambridge,
     Cambridge University Press: 55–75.
McGann, J. (1993) *Black Riders: The Visible Language of Modernism*. Princeton, Princeton
     University Press.
McGinley, B. (1996) *Joyce's Lives: Uses and Abuses of the Biografiend*. London, University
     of North London Press.
—(2000) 'Charter'd Streets: Joyce's London and Londoners', paper delivered at XVII
     International James Joyce Symposium, Goldsmiths College, London.
McHugh, R. (2006) *Annotations to Finnegans Wake* (3rd edition). Baltimore, The Johns
     Hopkins University Press.

—(ed.) (1953) *W. B. Yeats: Letters to Katharine Tynan*. Dublin, Clonmore and Reynolds.

McLaughlin, J. B. (1913) 'Katharine Tynan', *The Ampleforth Journal*, (18): 277–295.

McLaughlin, J. (2000) *Writing the Urban Jungle: Reading Empire in London from Doyle to Eliot*. Charlottesville and London, University of Virginia Press.

Merriman, V. (2010) 'Bernard Shaw in Contemporary Irish Studies: "Passé and Contemptible"?', *Shaw: The Annual of Bernard Shaw Studies*. 30: 216–35.

Mills Harper, G. (1987) *The Making of Yeats's 'A Vision': A Study of the Automatic Script*. London, Macmillan.

—(ed.) (1992) *Yeats's Vision Papers*. London, Macmillan.

Mills Harper, M. (2006) *Wisdom of Two: The Spiritual and Literary Collaboration of George and W. B. Yeats*. Oxford, Oxford University Press.

Mink, L. O. (1978) *A Finnegans Wake Gazetteer*. Bloomington and London, Indiana University Press.

Moore, M. (1998) *The Selected Letters of Marianne Moore*. Bonnie Costello, Celeste Goodridge, and Cristanne Miller (eds). London, Faber and Faber.

Morash, C. (1995) ' "Ever Under Some Unnatural Condition": Bram Stoker and the Colonial Fantastic', *Literature and the Supernatural*. Brian Cosgrove (ed.). Dublin, Columba Press: 95–118.

Morris, W. (1868–70) *The Earthly Paradise*. 4 vols. London, F. S. Ellis.

—(1891) *News From Nowhere*. London, Reeves and Turner.

—(1896–7) *The Earthly Paradise*. Hammersmith, Kelmscott Press.

—(1910–15) *The Collected Works of William Morris*. 24 vols. London, Longmans.

—(1984–96) *The Collected Letters of William Morris*. 3 vols. Norman Kelvin (ed.). Princeton, Princeton University Press.

Mumford, L. (1938) *The Culture of Cities*. London, Secker and Warburg.

Murray, P. (2005) *From the Shadow of Dracula: A Life of Bram Stoker*. London, Pimlico.

Murrow, E. R. (1968) *In Search of Light: the Broadcasts of Edward R. Murrow, 1938–1961*. Edward Bliss (ed.). London, MacMillan.

Myers, F. W. H. (1885) 'Automatic Writing', *Proceedings of the Society for Psychical Research*. 3: 1–63.

Nash, J. (2006) *James Joyce and the Act of Reception: Reading, Ireland, Modernism*. Cambridge, Cambridge University Press.

Ní Chnáimhín, Á. (1947) *Pádraic Ó Conaire*. Baile Átha Cliath: Oifig an tSoláthair.

Nolan, E. (2007) *Catholic Emancipations: Irish Fiction from Thomas Moore to James Joyce*. Syracuse, Syracuse University Press.

Ó Briain, A. (1944) 'Gaedhil thar Sáile', *The Capuchin Annual*. 116–26.

Ó Broin, T. (1984) *Saoirse Anama Ui Chonaire*. Galway, Officina Typographica.

Ó Conaire, P. (1909) *Nóra Mharcais Bhig agus Scéalta Eile*. Baile Átha Cliath, Conradh na Gaeilge.

—(1910) *Deoraíocht*. Baile Átha Cliath, Conradh na Gaeilge.

—(1914) *An Chéad Chloch*. Baile Átha Cliath, Conradh na Gaeilge.

—(1973) *Deoraíocht*. Baile Átha Cliath, Cló Talbot.

—(1989) *Bairbre Rua agus Drámaí Eile*. Eag. P. Ó Siadhail. Indreabhán, Cló Iar-Chonnachta.

—(1994) *Exile (Deoraíocht)*. Trans. G. Mac Eoin. Indreabhán, Cló Iar-Chonnachta.

—(2007, 2nd ed.) *An Chéad Chloch*. Eag. P. Riggs. Cork, Mercier Press.

Ó Donghaile, D. (2011) *Blasted Literature: Victorian Political Fiction and the Shock of Modernism*. Edinburgh, Edinburgh University Press.

Ó Súilleabháin, D. (1944) 'Conradh na Gaeilge Londain', *An Glór*. 5 (2): 1.

—(1989) *Conradh na Gaeilge i Londain: 1894–1917*. Baile Átha Cliath, Conradh na Gaeilge.

O'Mahony, N. T. (1931) 'Katharine Tynan's Girlhood', *The Irish Monthly*. 59 (696): 358–63.

Otis, L. (1999) *Membranes: Metaphors of Invasion in Nineteenth-Century Literature, Science and Politics*. Baltimore, The Johns Hopkins University Press.

Parkinson, T. and Brannen, A. (eds.) (1994) *Michael Robartes and the Dancer: Manuscript Materials. By W.B. Yeats*. Ithaca and London, Cornell University Press.

Pater, W. (1891) 'A Novel by Oscar Wilde' (originally published in *The Bookman*), reprinted in Mason, S. (1912) *Oscar Wilde: Art and Morality*. London, Frank Palmer: 188–95.

Peters, J. G. (1999) 'Style and Art in Wilde's *The Picture of Dorian Gray*: Form as Content', *Victorian Review*. 25 (1): 1–13.

Peterson, W. S. (1991) *The Kelmscott Press: A History of William Morris's Typographical Adventure*. Berkeley, University of California Press.

Pick, D. (1989) *Faces of Degeneration: A European Disorder, c.1848–c.1918*. Cambridge, Cambridge University Press.

Quail, J. (1978) *The Slow Burning Fuse: The Lost History of the British Anarchists*. London, Flamingo.

Quinn, A. (1996) 'Patrick Kavanagh: Poetry and Independence', *Patrick Kavanagh: Selected Poems*. Antoinette Quinn (ed.). London, Penguin: ix–xl.

Rabaté, J.-M. (2001) *James Joyce and The Politics of Egoism*. Cambridge, Cambridge University Press.

—(2009) 'Paris', *James Joyce in Context*. John McCourt (ed.). Cambridge, Cambridge University Press: 216–27.

Riggs, P. (1994) *Pádraic Ó Conaire: Deoraí*. Baile Átha Cliath, An Clóchomhar.

Riquelme, J.-P. (2000) 'Oscar Wilde's Aesthetic Gothic: Walter Pater, Dark Enlightenment, and *The Picture of Dorian Gray*', *Modern Fiction Studies*. 46 (3): 609–31.

Russell, M. (1896) 'Notes on New Books', *The Irish Monthly*. 24 (273): 167–8.

Ryan, M. (1945) *Fenian Memories*. Dublin, M. H. Gill.

Ryan, W. P. (1894 [1970]) *The Irish Literary Revival*. New York, Lemma.

Shaw, G. B. (1884) *A Manifesto – Fabian Tract 2*. London, Fabian Society.

—(1885) *To Provident Landlords and Capitalists: a Suggestion and a Warning – Fabian Tract 3*. London, Fabian Society.

—(1890) *What Socialism Is – Fabian Tract 13*. London, Fabian Society.

—(1892) *Vote! Vote!! Vote!!! Fabian Tract 43*. London, Fabian Society.

—(1898) 'Letter to the Editor', *The Daily Chronicle*. 30 April.

—(1900) *Women as Councillors – Fabian Tract 93*. London, Fabian Society.

—(1901) *Socialism for Millionaires – Fabian Tract 107*. London, Fabian Society.

—(1924) 'Mr Shaw Hits Back', *The Evening Standard*. 15 September.

—(1965) *Bernard Shaw Collected Letters 1874–1897*. Dan H. Laurence (ed.). London, Max Rienhardt.

—(1970a) 'Author's Apology', *Bernard Shaw's Collected Plays*. London, The Bodley Head: 253.

—(1970b) *Bernard Shaw Collected Plays with their Prefaces. Vol 1*. London, The Bodley Head.

Short, M. (1980) *Holst: The Man and His Music*. Oxford, Oxford University Press, 1990.

Stallworthy, J. (1995) *Louis MacNeice*. London, Faber and Faber.

Summerson, J. (1935) *John Nash: Architect to King George IV*. London, George Allen and Unwin.

—(1946) *Georgian London*. New York, Charles Scribner's Sons.

Swift, Roger (2002) *Irish Migrants in Britain, 1815–1914*. Cork: Cork University Press.

Tamen, M. (1998) '"Phenomenology of the Ghost": Revision in Literary History', *New Literary History*. 29 (2): 295–304.

Thoreau, H. D. (1980) *Walden*. London, The Folio Society.

Tidcock, M. (2002) *The Doves Press*. London, British Library.

Tynan, K. (1896a) 'The Wares of Autolycus: Plumbers and Electricians', *Pall Mall Gazette*. 9835: 4.

—(1896b) 'The Wares of Autolycus: Reflections', *Pall Mall Gazette*. 9731: 10.

—(1898) *The Wind in the Trees: A Book of Country Verse*. London, Grant Richards.

—(1899a) *She Walks in Beauty*. London, Smith, Elder and Co.

—(1899b) *The Dear Irish Girl*. London, Smith, Elder and Co.

—(1905) *Innocencies: A Book of Verse*. London, A. H. Bullen.

—(1906) *The Adventures of Alicia*. London, F. V. White.

—(1908a) *Peeps at Many Lands: Ireland*. London, Smith, Elder and Co.

—(1908b) *The House of the Crickets*. London, Smith, Elder and Co.

—(1912) *Heart O'Gold or The Little Princess: A Story for Girls*. London, Blackie and Son.

—(1913) *Twenty-Five Years: Reminiscences*. New York, Devin-Adair.

—(1914) *Irish Poems*. London, Sidgwick and Jackson.

—(1916) *The Middle Years*. London, Constable.

—(1919a) 'A Strayed Poet', *The Bookman*. May: 78–9.

—(1919b) *The Years of the Shadow*. London, Constable.

—(1922) *The Wandering Years*. London, Constable.

—(1924) *Memories*. London, Eveleigh Nash and Grayson.

—(1930) *Collected Poems*. London, Macmillan.

Van Hulle, D. (2008) *Manuscript Genetics: Joyce's Know-How, Beckett's Nohow*. Gainesville, University Press of Florida.

Webb, S. (1889a) *Facts for Londoners – Fabian Tract 8*. London, Fabian Society.

—(1889b) *Figures for Londoners – Fabian Tract 10*. London, Fabian Society.

Webb, T. (2010) 'London', *W. B. Yeats in Context*. David Holdeman and Ben Levitas (eds). Cambridge, Cambridge University Press: 80–8.

White, J. (2008) *London in the Nineteenth Century: A Human Awful Wonder of God*. London, Vintage.

Whitehead, K. (1989) *The Third Programme: A Literary History*. Oxford, Clarendon Press.

Wilde, O. (1889) 'Mr. Froude's Blue Book', *The Pall Mall Gazette*. Saturday 13 April: 3.

—(1909) 'Lecture to Art Students', *Collected Works*. Robert Baldwin Ross (ed.). Boston, The Wyman-Fogg Co.: 311–21.

—(1972) 'Irish Poets and Poetry of the Nineteenth Century', Robert Pepper (ed.). San Francisco, Book Club of America.

—(2000) *The Picture of Dorian Gray*. Harmondsworth, Penguin.

—(2003) 'Lord Arthur Saville's Crime', *The Complete Works of Oscar Wilde*. London, Harper Collins: 160–84.

Wills, C. (2011) 'Justified Ghosts', *Times Literary Supplement*. 5646 (15 June): 3–5.

Wyse Jackson, J. and Costello, P. (1997) *John Stanislaus Joyce. The Voluminous Life and Genius of James Joyce's Father*. London, Fourth Estate.

Yeats, W. B. (1889) *The Wanderings of Oisin and Other Poems*. London, Kegan Paul, Trench.

—(1891) *John Sherman and Dhoya*. London, T. Fisher Unwin.

—(1893) *The Celtic Twilight: Men and Women, Dhouls and Fairies*. London, Lawrence and Bullen.

—(1895) 'Irish National Literature', *Bookman*. 9 (48): 167–70.

—(1939) *The Collected Poems of W. B. Yeats*. London, Macmillan.

—(1959) *Explorations*. London, Macmillan.

—(1962) *A Vision*. (1937 version). London, Macmillan.

—(1970) *Uncollected Prose by W. B. Yeats. Vol.1*. John P. Frayne (ed.). London, Macmillan.

—(1975) 'Away', *Uncollected Prose by W. B. Yeats*. John P. Frayne and Colton Johnson (eds.) (first published in *Fortnightly Review*, April 1902: 267–82). London, Macmillan.

—(1986) *The Collected Letters of W. B. Yeats, Vol. 1, 1865–1895*. Eric Domville and John Kelly (eds.). Oxford, Oxford University Press.

—(1989) *Yeats's Poems*. A. Norman Jeffares (ed.). London, Macmillan.

—(1990) 'Easter, 1916' and 'The Second Coming', *W. B. Yeats: The Poems*. Daniel Albright (ed.). London, J. M. Dent.

—(1999) *Autobiographies*. William H. O'Donnell and Douglas N. Archibald (eds.). New York, Scribner.

—(2000) *Later Articles and Reviews. Uncollected Articles, Reviews, and Radio Broadcasts Written After 1900*. Colton Johnson (ed.). New York, Scribner.

Yeats, W. B. and Johnson, L. (1908) *Poetry and Ireland: Essays by W. B. Yeats and Lionel Johnson*. Dundrum, Cuala Press.

Yelling, J. A. (2000) 'Land, Property and Planning', *The Cambridge Urban History of Britain. Vol. 3*. Martin Daunton (ed.). Cambridge, Cambridge University Press: 467–93.

Index